THREE
VIEWS
ON CHRISTIANITY AND SCIENCE

Books in the Counterpoints Series

Church Life

Evaluating the Church Growth Movement

Exploring the Worship Spectrum

Remarriage after Divorce in Today's Church

Understanding Four Views on Baptism

Understanding Four Views on the Lord's Supper

Who Runs the Church?

Bible and Theology

Are Miraculous Gifts for Today?

Do Christians, Muslims, and Jews Worship the Same God?: Four Views

Five Views on Apologetics

Five Views on Biblical Inerrancy

Five Views on Law and Gospel

Five Views on Sanctification

Five Views on the Church and Politics

Five Views on the Extent of the Atonement

Four Views on Christian Spirituality

Four Views on Christianity and Philosophy

Four Views on Creation, Evolution, and Intelligent Design

Four Views on Divine Providence

Four Views on Eternal Security

Four Views on Hell

Four Views on Moving Beyond the Bible to Theology

Four Views on Salvation in a Pluralistic World

Four Views on the Apostle Paul

Four Views on the Book of Revelation

Four Views on the Church's Mission

Four Views on the Historical Adam

Four Views on the Role of Works at the Final Judgment

Four Views on the Spectrum of Evangelicalism

Genesis: History, Fiction, or Neither?

How Jewish Is Christianity?

Show Them No Mercy

Three Views on Creation and Evolution

Three Views on Eastern Orthodoxy and Evangelicalism

Three Views on the Millennium and Beyond

Three Views on the New Testament Use of the Old Testament

Three Views on the Rapture

Two Views on Homosexuality, the Bible, and the Church

Two Views on the Doctrine of the Trinity

Two Views on Women in Ministry

THREE VIEWS ON CHRISTIANITY AND SCIENCE

Michael Ruse

Alister E. McGrath

Bruce L. Gordon

Paul Copan and Christopher L. Reese, general editors
Stanley N. Gundry, series editor

ZONDERVAN ACADEMIC

Three Views on Christianity and Science
Copyright © 2021 by Paul Copan, Bruce L. Gordon, Alister E. McGrath, Christopher L. Reese, and Michael Ruse

Requests for information should be addressed to:
Zondervan, *3900 Sparks Dr. SE, Grand Rapids, Michigan 49546*

Zondervan titles may be purchased in bulk for educational, business, fundraising, or sales promotional use. For information, please email SpecialMarkets@Zondervan.com.

ISBN 978-0-310-59854-1 (softcover)

ISBN 978-0-310-12036-0 (audio)

ISBN 978-0-310-59855-8 (ebook)

Cover design: Tammy Johnson
Cover photo: © ESB Professional / Shutterstock

Printed in the United States of America

20 21 22 23 24 25 26 27 28 29 30 /LSC/ 15 14 13 12 11 10 9 8 7 6 5 4 3 2 1

CONTENTS

Contributors 7
Introduction by Christopher L. Reese. 9

1. **INDEPENDENCE VIEW** 19
   MICHAEL RUSE

                        Responses
   ALISTER MCGRATH 47
   BRUCE GORDON 58

   Rejoinder 70

2. **DIALOGUE VIEW** 77
   ALISTER MCGRATH

                        Responses
   MICHAEL RUSE 104
   BRUCE GORDON 115

   Rejoinder 127

3. **CONSTRAINED INTEGRATION VIEW** 133
   BRUCE GORDON

                        Responses
   MICHAEL RUSE 164
   ALISTER MCGRATH 176

   Rejoinder 187

Conclusion by Paul Copan 197
General Index 209

CONTRIBUTORS

Michael Ruse is a former Lucyle T. Werkmeister Professor of Philosophy at Florida State University and professor emeritus at the University of Guelph in Canada.

Alister E. McGrath (DPhil, DD, DLitt, University of Oxford) is the Andreas Idreos Professor of Science and Religion, University of Oxford, director of the Ian Ramsey Centre for Science and Religion, and Gresham Professor of Divinity.

Bruce L. Gordon (PhD, Northwestern University) is Associate Professor of the History and Philosophy of Science at Houston Baptist University and a senior fellow of the Center for Science and Culture at Discovery Institute.

INTRODUCTION

CHRISTOPHER L. REESE

Writing in the first quarter of the twentieth century, British mathematician and philosopher Alfred North Whitehead warned, "When we consider what religion is for mankind, and what science is, it is no exaggeration to say that the future course of history depends upon . . . the relation between them."[1] Whitehead recognized that religion and science were two juggernauts of human experience whose warfare could threaten human harmony and flourishing. Scripture is clear that God is the author of both creation (Gen. 1:1) and Scripture (2 Tim. 3:16–17), and that creation reveals God's glory (Ps. 19:1–6). Moreover, in Genesis 1, in the garden, God instructed Adam and Eve to "be fruitful and increase in number; fill the earth and subdue it" (v. 28).[2] This "cultural mandate," as it is sometimes called, would require human beings "to draw out, work with, and benefit from [creation's] inherent potentialities as God's representatives on earth."[3] To do this effectively requires carefully observing and studying creation, which is one of the chief aims of science. Thus Christians, of all people, should be invested in the systematic study of the world as stewards of creation who see God's glory reflected in it.

On a very practical level, a lack of understanding of science can also harm our witness to the world. Augustine recognized this even in the

---

1. Alfred North Whitehead, *Science and the Modern World* (Cambridge: Cambridge University Press, 1926), 224.
2. In our view, Adam and Eve existed, and the interactions between them and God described in Genesis are historical. For defenses, see John C. Collins, "A Historical Adam: Old-Earth Creation View," in *Four Views on the Historical Adam*, eds. Matthew Barrett, Ardel B. Caneday, and Stanley N. Gundry, Zondervan Counterpoints Series (Grand Rapids: Zondervan, 2013); Hans Madueme and Michael Reeves, eds., *Adam, the Fall, and Original Sin: Theological, Biblical, and Scientific Perspectives* (Grand Rapids: Baker Academic, 2014).
3. Naomi Noguchi Reese, "Cultural Mandate," in *Dictionary of Christianity and Science: The Definitive Reference for the Intersection of Christian Faith and Contemporary Science*, ed. Paul Copan et al. (Grand Rapids: Zondervan, 2017), 149.

fifth century and lamented the possible outcome when Christians didn't know basic facts about the natural world.

> Now, it is a disgraceful and dangerous thing for an infidel to hear a Christian, presumably giving the meaning of Holy Scripture, talking nonsense on these topics; and we should take all means to prevent such an embarrassing situation, in which people show up vast ignorance in a Christian and laugh it to scorn. The shame is not so much that an ignorant individual is derided, but that people outside the household of the faith think our sacred writers held such opinions, and, to the great loss of those for whose salvation we toil, the writers of our Scripture are criticized and rejected as unlearned men. If they find a Christian mistaken in a field which they themselves know well and hear him maintaining his foolish opinions about our books, how are they going to believe those books in matters concerning the resurrection of the dead, the hope of eternal life, and the kingdom of heaven, when they think their pages are full of falsehoods on facts which they themselves have learnt from experience and the light of reason?[4]

Surveys show that there is a growing group of adults who no longer identify with a religious group—the so-called nones—and the vast majority of these were raised as a member of a particular religion, indicating that they walked away from the faith they grew up with. A recent Pew Research survey found that about "half of current religious 'nones' who were raised in a religion (49%) indicate that a lack of belief led them to move away from religion. This includes many respondents who mention 'science' as the reason they do not believe in religious teachings, including one who said 'I'm a scientist now, and I don't believe in miracles.'"[5] If we hope to be credible witnesses for the gospel in our day, we need to ensure that we don't make basic mistakes

---

4. St. Augustine, *St. Augustine: The Literal Meaning of Genesis*, eds. Johannes Quasten, Walter J. Burghardt, and Thomas Comerford Lawler, trans. John Hammond Taylor, 41st ed., vol. 1, Ancient Christian Writers (New York: Paulist, 1982), 42–43.

5. Michael Lipka, "Why Some Americans Left Religion Behind," Pew Research Center, August 24, 2016, https://www.pewresearch.org/fact-tank/2016/08/24/why-americas-nones-left-religion-behind/.

when it comes to science, and we need to think through how science relates to Scripture and core Christian beliefs. We can help our children and young adults do the same so that they don't run into unnecessary obstacles when attempting to reconcile their Christian beliefs with what they learn about science in school, from the media, or online. Of course, not everything labeled as "science" should be automatically accepted as authoritative, and there is always a considerable difference between empirical facts and how those facts should be interpreted.

Along with facts about science, Christians also need to learn to engage in civil discussions on these topics with one another and with nonbelievers. Few topics can get heated more quickly than issues related to science and Christianity. In an online Christian worldview forum I founded several years ago, we found it necessary to ban discussions of several science-related topics because they almost always devolved into name-calling arguments. On topics related to science, we should be guided by the maxim of seventeenth-century Lutheran theologian Rupertus Meldenius: "In essentials, unity; in non-essentials, liberty; in all things, charity." Throughout church history, orthodox Christians have routinely disagreed on matters pertaining to science and Christianity, and the same is true today. Even among evangelical scholars who share a high view of Scripture, disagreements are common. Most science-and-Christianity questions are not matters of theological primacy (such as God's trinitarian nature or Christ's substitutionary atonement), but are third- or fourth-rank issues.[6] Theologian and pastor Gavin Ortlund makes a wise observation concerning the interpretation of Genesis 1: "We can happily coexist within the church amid differences on this issue. Our unity in the gospel is not at stake. Instead, we should put more focus on the aspects of the doctrine of creation that Christians have classically emphasized and that are distinctive to a broadly Judeo-Christian worldview, such as creation ex nihilo, the historicity of the fall, and the fact that human beings are made in God's image. These are better hills to die on."[7]

---

6. Gavin Ortlund suggests a four-part taxonomy for evaluating the relative importance of Christian doctrines. He defines third-and fourth-rank issues as follows: "Third-rank doctrines are important to Christian theology, but not enough to justify separation or division. Fourth-rank doctrines are unimportant to our gospel witness and ministry collaboration." Gavin Ortlund, *Finding the Right Hills to Die on: The Case for Theological Triage* (Wheaton: Crossway, 2020), 143.

7. Ortlund, *Finding the Right Hills*, 143.

For all the preceding reasons, we believed it was important to produce the present volume. There are other multiple-viewpoint books on narrower topics in science and Christianity (such as creation and evolution, the historicity of Adam, and the early chapters of Genesis), but we thought it was important to explore the bigger picture and look at differing frameworks for relating Christianity and science as a whole. Whichever of these approaches one adopts carries implications for how one will think about individual issues. Our contributors present three different frameworks that represent the most common options Christians have adopted when it comes to relating science and Christianity. In the process they discuss a number of specific topics and, importantly, model a civil and friendly dialogue. This is even more significant given that one of our contributors, Michael Ruse, identifies as an agnostic. Readers will thus also benefit from seeing how two leading Christian scholars defend their approach to Christianity and science against skeptical objections.

Ways of Relating Christianity and Science

Before looking more closely at how Christianity and science relate, we should briefly define these terms as we are using them in the introduction and conclusion, as well as how our contributors understand them. By *Christianity*, we mean the essential teachings of the Christian faith derived from Scripture and affirmed by the great historical creeds of church history. Though we did not ask the contributors to formulate their definition of *Christianity*, this traditional definition seems implicit in the essays of all three contributors.[8] By *science* we mean, roughly, the attempted objective study of the natural world whose theories rationally connect to specific empirical phenomena and whose concepts and explanations do not (normally) depart from the natural realm.[9] Though, again, we did not request a definition of *science*, Alister McGrath and Michael Ruse would likely agree with this definition in the main, but object to the parenthetical "normally," since both believe scientists should practice

---

8. Michael Ruse has what seems at times *theological* reservations about some Christian doctrines—such as original sin—but doesn't deny that this and other teachings are representative of Christian orthodoxy. Both Alister McGrath and Bruce Gordon identify as evangelical Protestants, for whom this definition is likely uncontroversial.

9. This definition is adapted from the work of Del Ratzsch, *Science and Its Limits: Natural Sciences in Christian Perspective* (Downers Grove, IL: InterVarsity, 2000); see also his *Nature, Design, and Science: The Status of Design in Natural Science* (Albany: SUNY, 2001).

methodological naturalism (i.e., exclude supernatural explanations from their work). Bruce Gordon believes scientific descriptions *can* include supernatural explanations and, as an idealist, believes that the material world is phenomenological rather than substantial in nature.[10]

With those definitions in place, one of the most fruitful ways, in our view, of understanding the relationship between Christianity and science, in broad terms, is the *two-books metaphor*. This concept, which perhaps goes back as early as the church father Origen, understands knowledge of God as being available from two sources—the "book" of nature and the book of Scripture.[11] The book of nature—the natural world—is one key source of God's general revelation by which his existence and some of his attributes can be known, as mentioned earlier (Ps. 19:1–4; Rom. 1:18–20). The book of Scripture is God's special revelation, inspired by the Holy Spirit and recorded by human beings (2 Tim. 3:16–17; 2 Pet. 1:20–21). Since God is the author of both books, when rightly understood, they do not stand in conflict with each other. In this context, however, it is important to remember that our interpretations of each book are fallible and in most cases susceptible to revision. We must be cautious about equating our *interpretations* of Scripture with Scripture itself, and our interpretations of nature with nature as it truly is. Thus, when we encounter apparent contradictions between the books, we should strive to ensure that we are understanding and interpreting each accurately. In some cases we may need to revisit our understanding of Scripture, and in other cases we may need to verify that we're grasping facts about the natural world accurately and interpreting those facts properly.

However, given that science is largely practiced outside the church, additional considerations come into play regarding the relationship between science and Christianity. Pioneering science-and-religion scholar Ian Barbour famously proposed a four-part taxonomy for how the relationships between science and religion have been historically

---

10. Bruce explains, "Everything that happens in the world involves an occasion of direct divine action. . . . God is the sole efficient cause of every state of affairs in the universe not subject to the influence of creatures with libertarian freedom" (p. 155).

11. Robert C. Bishop, "Two Books Metaphor," in *Dictionary of Christianity and Science: The Definitive Reference for the Intersection of Christian Faith and Contemporary Science*, ed. Paul Copan et al. (Grand Rapids: Zondervan, 2017). Our discussion here reflects Bishop's observations.

understood, and we will utilize his categories here.[12] The positions of our three contributors also fall solidly into these camps, so we will take the opportunity shortly to introduce their respective viewpoints.

Conflict View

We should note, first, the one category that none of our contributors adopts, and which has the least evidential and historical support—the conflict view.[13] Unfortunately, this also happens to be the view most widely believed and promoted by popular culture today in the West. On this view, Christianity and science are locked in a never-ending battle in which only one can ultimately emerge victorious. The New Atheists, for example, constantly promote this idea in their numerous books and websites. Biologist P. Z. Myers's statement is illustrative of many others that could be cited: "Science and religion are two different ways of looking at the universe and changing the world, and I believe that you must set one aside to follow the other. . . . One is a method of analysis and experiment; the other is pretense and lies."[14]

Professional historians of science have demonstrated the falsity of the conflict view for the past forty years, but as one historian puts it, this is an idea "that wouldn't die." Instead, historians have recognized a *complex* relationship between science and religion that has played out over a period of centuries.[15] As historian of science David Lindberg

---

12. Ian G. Barbour, *When Science Meets Religion: Enemies, Strangers, or Partners?* (New York: HarperSanFrancisco, 2007). Where Barbour refers to religion, we will refer specifically to Christianity. A number of other typologies have been proposed for relating science and religion, but for our purposes Barbour's helpfully capture the main options. For other approaches, see Mikael Stenmark, "Ways of Relating Science and Religion," *The Cambridge Companion to Science and Religion*, ed. Peter Harrison (Cambridge: Cambridge University Press, 2016).

13. Michael holds an independence view but seems willing to shift to a conflict view if Christian claims are asserted to impinge on physical reality rather than remain in the realm of subjective opinion.

14. P. Z. Myers, *The Happy Atheist* (New York: Pantheon, 2013), 146, quoted in Ronald L. Numbers, "Revisiting the Battlefields of Science and Religion: The Warfare Thesis Today," in *Rethinking History, Science, and Religion: An Exploration of Conflict and the Complexity Principle*, ed. Bernard Lightman (Pittsburgh: University of Pittsburgh Press, 2019), 187. Though he formerly identified as a New Atheist, Myers later became disillusioned with the movement and disavowed it; see his blog post, "The Train Wreck That Was the New Atheism," Pharyngula, January 25, 2019, https://freethoughtblogs.com/pharyngula/2019/01 /25/the-train-wreck-that-was-the-new-atheism/.

15. Numbers, "Revisiting the Battlefields of Science and Religion: The Warfare Thesis Today," 183–85.

observes, "In those not infrequent cases where Christianity and science have attempted to occupy the same intellectual ground, the historical actors have generally preferred peace to warfare, compromise to confrontation, and have found means—through compromise, accommodation, clarification, reinterpretation, revision and the identification of outright error—of negotiating a state of peaceful coexistence."[16]

Further, a strong case can be made for a deep concord between Christianity and science because Christianity provides a worldview in which science can flourish, and a significant conflict between science and philosophical naturalism.[17] Given that God is the author of both Scripture and the natural world, the conflict view is not a live option for Christians.

Independence View

On the independence view, defended by Michael Ruse in this volume, Christianity and science cannot conflict because they represent two independent and autonomous fields. They ask different questions, employ different methods, and refer to different domains. As the late paleontologist Stephen J. Gould, who held this view (which he called "non-overlapping magisteria"), quipped, "To cite the old clichés, science gets the age of rocks, and religion the rock of ages; science studies how the heavens go, religion how to go to heaven."[18] While it's certainly true that the majority of work done by scientists is not relevant to Christian theology, Scripture makes claims about facts and events that impact the natural world. For example, if we possess immaterial souls, which Christians have traditionally understood as scriptural teaching, this should make a difference in how we understand our nature and how

---

16. David Lindberg, "Of War and Peace," *Science & Theology News* (March 2006): 33, quoted in John Hedley Brooke, "Science, Religion, and Historical Complexity," *Historically Speaking* 8, no. 5 (May/June 2007): 10–13.

17. For example, because we are made in God's image and designed by God to function in our physical environment, we can trust our senses to give us accurate information about the external world. Philosophical naturalism is the view that only physical entities exist. On this view, we have little confidence that the deliverances of reason can be trusted, since our faculties have been selected for their survival value rather than the ability to apprehend objective truth. See Alvin Plantinga, *Where the Conflict Really Lies: Science, Religion, and Naturalism* (New York: Oxford University Press, 2012).

18. Stephen Jay Gould, *Rocks of Ages: Science and Religion in the Fullness of Life* (New York: Ballantine, 2002), 6.

we interact with other human beings. It cannot be the case that we are both immaterial souls *and* chemical-biological machines. Also, if God designed our physical environment and biological life, we should expect to see some kind of empirical evidence for it.[19] Since this view drives a wedge between the book of nature and the book of Scripture, we believe this approach also fails to be a promising option for Christians.

Dialogue View

The dialogue view, presented in this volume by Alister McGrath, moves beyond the independence view to find points of contact between Christianity and science. As Pope John Paul II expressed, "Science can purify religion from error and superstition; religion can purify science from idolatry and false absolutes. Each can draw the other into a wider world, a world in which both can flourish" (p. 104). As Alister states, drawing on the two-books metaphor, his view aims to "set God's 'two books' alongside each other and allow them to enrich and inform their readers" (p. 127). Since this view values both Scripture and science and seeks to find fruitful connections between them, this is an approach Christians can embrace.

Integration View

The fourth and final view, integration, is championed here by Bruce Gordon (which he qualifies with the term "constrained"). Contrasting his view with Alister's, he writes, "Dialogue is nice, but it takes you only so far. Moving beyond milquetoast notions of mutually enriching conversations to a robust metaphysical *integration* of science and philosophical theology is necessary." On Bruce's view, science both points to God and requires God's existence to be carried out in a coherently rational way. Moreover, the naturalism underlying much modern science is both deficient as a worldview and as a basis for doing science. As philosopher Angus Menuge points out, one potential pitfall of this view is that theology will be too closely correlated with contemporary

---

19. In fact, we do see this evidence in the fine-tuning of the universe and in the non-material information necessary for life to function and grow in complexity. See Geraint F. Lewis and Luke A. Barnes, *A Fortunate Universe: Life in a Finely Tuned Cosmos* (Cambridge: Cambridge University Press, 2020); and Stephen C. Meyer, *Signature in the Cell: DNA and the Evidence for Intelligent Design* (New York: HarperOne, 2009).

scientific views that may turn out later to be wrong.[20] With that caveat, the strength of this view is that it seeks a unified approach to both God's Word and God's world.

The Shape of This Volume
Contributors

Before we briefly map out the content and format of this volume, we want to say more about our three contributors. Alister McGrath has doctorates in both biological sciences and theology and is the Andreas Idreos Professor of Science and Religion at the University of Oxford, director of the Ian Ramsey Centre for Science and Religion, and Gresham Professor of Divinity. He is the author of numerous books on the relationship between Christianity and science, including *Science & Religion: A New Introduction*, *The Dawkins Delusion? Atheist Fundamentalism and the Denial of the Divine*, and *The Territories of Human Reason: Science and Theology in an Age of Multiple Rationalities*.

Michael Ruse recently retired as the Lucyle T. Werkmeister Professor of Philosophy and director of the program in the history and philosophy of science at Florida State University. He is also professor emeritus at the University of Guelph in Canada and the author or editor of more than sixty books, including *Debating Design: From Darwin to DNA*, *On Faith and Science*, and *Can a Darwinian Be a Christian? The Relationship between Science and Religion*. His lifelong professional interest has been in the history and philosophy of biology, with special emphasis on evolutionary biology, and specifically the work and influence of Charles Darwin.

Bruce Gordon is associate professor of the history and philosophy of science at Houston Baptist University and a senior fellow of the Center for Science and Culture at Discovery Institute. He has authored numerous journal articles on the intersection of Christianity and science and edited or contributed to several books, including *The Nature of Nature: Examining the Role of Naturalism in Science*, *The Routledge Handbook of Idealism and Immaterialism*, *Problems in Epistemology and Metaphysics*,

---

20. Angus J. L. Menuge, "Science and Religion, Models of Relating," in *Dictionary of Christianity and Science: The Definitive Reference for the Intersection of Christian Faith and Contemporary Science*, ed. Paul Copan et al. (Grand Rapids: Zondervan, 2017), 608.

Two Dozen (or so) Arguments for God: The Plantinga Project, and *Christian Physicalism? Philosophical Theological Criticisms.*

Format and Content

As in other volumes in Zondervan's Counterpoints: Bible and Theology series, the contributors have written initial essays explaining and defending their frameworks for relating Christianity and science. The other contributors then responded to the opening essays, followed by a rejoinder from the original author. This format allows the reader to see the strengths and weaknesses of each viewpoint and decide for themselves which is the most compelling.

The contributors were asked to respond to two major questions in their initial essays, as well as a test case. The two questions were: "How do you view the relationship between Scripture and science?" and "In what ways does God act in the world?" (knowing, of course, that Michael would be skeptical that God, in fact, acts in the world). These two questions encompass a number of significant issues that are frequently discussed in works on Christianity and science, so we agreed that these should be answered while also welcoming other topics the contributors might wish to address.

The test case asked: "Can a scientific account alone, making reference only to natural laws and material entities, account for the appearance and nature of *Homo sapiens,* or does this also require reference to divine action? If it requires divine action, can this explanation be incorporated into a scientific account?" Most people are interested, naturally, in how both Christianity and science view the human person and whether or how these two perspectives should relate. This question also opened the door for the contributors to discuss their views of human origins—scientifically, theologically, and philosophically—and in particular how they evaluate methodological naturalism.

We general editors thank Alister, Michael, and Bruce for participating in this dialogue and hope the reader will benefit from this exchange involving three of the world's leading scholars on Christianity and science. Whatever your viewpoint, we hope it will be refined and that you will be inspired by the collegiality of this exchange.

CHAPTER ONE

INDEPENDENCE VIEW

MICHAEL RUSE

What is the relationship between Christianity and science? Before I give my answers to a number of pertinent questions, allow me to explain how I arrived at this conversation. I was raised (very intently) as a Quaker and lost my faith at about the age of twenty. Now at nearly four-score years, I am still a nonbeliever. I am not a New Atheist—or an old atheist for that matter. I am an agnostic. I truly don't know. By preference, I call myself a "skeptic," because often agnostics simply don't care. I do care very much; not so much because I am scared of what is going to happen—if I were a Christian, I would be a great deal more scared—but because asking questions is part of my nature. I am a professional philosopher![1]

---

1. For more years than I care to remember, I have been working on the ideas expressed in this essay, truthfully, from my loving and meaningful childhood in the Religious Society of Friends (Quakers). Thanks to my credentials as a Darwin scholar—*The Darwinian Revolution: Science Red in Tooth and Claw* (1979)—I was brought professionally into the science-religion relationship by my engagement in the fight against creationists, which I document in *But Is It Science? The Philosophical Question in the Creation/Evolution Controversy* (1988). Spurred by the encounter, I started to think seriously about my Darwinian take on philosophical issues, which can be found in *Taking Darwin Seriously: A Naturalistic Approach to Philosophy* (1986) and in a couple of more recent collections, *Philosophy after Darwin: Classic and Contemporary Readings* (2009) and *The Cambridge Handbook of Evolutionary Ethics*, coedited with Robert J. Richards (2017). I have looked at the relationship between Darwinism and Christianity in *Can a Darwinian Be a Christian? The Relationship between Science and Religion* (2001) and more broadly, making much use of the concept of metaphor, in *Science and Spirituality: Making Room for Faith in the Age of Science* (2010). I have defended my nonbelief in *Atheism: What Everyone*

19

I'll be looking at three major issues that typically arise in discussions about Christianity and science, namely, the relationship between science and Scripture, ways of thinking about God's actions in the world, and how we should understand the emergence of human beings.

Can Scripture Shape Science?

In the past, people have certainly thought Scripture could shape science, and many people think so now. People in the Middle Ages would have been shocked at the idea that the earth was not the center of the universe, given the church's teaching at the time. Today, young earth creationists (YEC) certainly think that physics must show how everything has happened in the past six thousand years or so, given their interpretation of the opening chapters of Genesis. I suspect that they would deny the motivation I ascribe to them, arguing that they are led to the age of the earth simply by science and not by religious wish-fulfillment. I'll believe you; millions wouldn't. While we are at it, I have a really nice bridge for sale.

Of course, respectable people—Episcopalians?—rather look down on the theologically unwashed, such as the YECs. They would never behave this way. But of course they do. The Church of England's Thirty-Nine Articles tell us that we are tainted with original sin:

> ORIGINAL Sin standeth not in the following of Adam, (as the Pelagians do vainly talk;) but it is the fault and corruption of the Nature of every man, that naturally is engendered of the

---

Needs to Know (2015) and then in *Darwin and Design: Does Evolution Have a Purpose?* (2003), *On Purpose* (2017), and in *A Meaning to Life* (2019) tried more positively to think about meaning and existence. In what has turned into a trilogy, I have looked at the often uncomfortable clash between Christianity and those Darwinians who would make a humanistic religion of their science: *The Evolution-Creationism Dispute* (2005); *Evolution as Religion: What Literature Tells Us about Evolution* (2017); and *The Problem of War: Darwinism, Christianity, and Their Battle to Understand Human Conflict* (2018). Much of my thinking in this trilogy is based on work that I did on the concept of progress in evolution: *Monad to Man: The Concept of Progress in Evolutionary Biology* (1996). I discuss evolution generally in *Darwinism and Its Discontents* (2006) and human evolution, its religious and philosophical implications, in *The Philosophy of Human Evolution* (2012). Finally, I wrote (what I think is) an entertaining little dialogue between five very different people on the evolution-religion relationship: *Evolution and Religion: A Dialogue*. I show, to my own surprise, sympathy for the pagans, something traceable to my research for *The Gaia Hypothesis: Science on a Pagan Planet* (2013). I rush to assure the reader, who will learn (perhaps with some regret), that I am not now into drawing down the moon or prancing around in the woods, stark naked, at midnight.

offspring of Adam; whereby man is very far gone from original righteousness, and is of his own nature inclined to evil, so that the flesh lusteth always contrary to the spirit; and therefore in every person born into this world, it deserveth God's wrath and damnation.

I am not sure how much biblical evidence there is for any of this, except the reporting of Saint Paul's fertile imagination. The claim is that Adam existed, before him there was no sin, and that we are all his descendants and thus tainted.

I have two comments to make about these claims. First, you are laying away nothing but trouble if you try this gambit. Again and again, you are going to be saying things on Sunday that you would never say on Monday. How can you possibly work for an oil company and take seriously the universality of Noah's flood? Or, let me put it more carefully—I am thoroughly convinced the more nonsensical an idea, the more administrators, even those outside universities, like it. How can you possibly do the science an oil company requires and take seriously the universality of Noah's flood? The same is true with original sin. How can you work for a museum or university and believe in it? None of its supposed foundation is true. There was no original Adam, we are descended from a group of people, and there were sinners before Adam, going back to the monkeys—and they weren't too well behaved either.

Related to this is that, by trying to be the strictest of the strict, the holiest of the holy, you are befouling the very nest in which you sit. Central to your religion is that we are made in the image of God. Not physically with genitalia, but intellectually and morally. To turn your back on science is to turn your back on your Godlike nature, for what is science but the exercise of the intelligence? This segues directly into my second comment. Scripture is not to be treated as a work of science. It was never intended as such. It is rather the story of the relationship between the Creator and his people. Augustine was very strong on this point. The ancient Jews were not literate people like the Romans—they were illiterate and ignorant of science. God could not speak to them in sophisticated language. Whatever the sun did for Joshua, it would be just silly to think the ancient Jews could have grasped the event in the language of Plato or Aristotle, let alone Ptolemy.

Can Science Shape the Interpretation of Scripture?

This is the reverse question to that just answered, and as you might infer, I am not too keen on interaction this way either. Obviously, in a negative sense, science is important. You cannot believe in Noah's flood as a worldwide phenomenon in light of modern geology. You cannot believe in the Pauline-Augustinian account of original sin given above in light of modern paleoanthropology. Let me stress what was implied above—in no way does this mean that the Bible is false. Whether you accept it or not, the Genesis story of creation is incredibly powerful and insightful about us and about our nature. But it's not a literal account of what happened to humankind a few centuries ago.

What about the more moderate strategy of using the big bang to confirm or round out the Genesis story of creation? What about using a comet or some such thing to explain the parting of the Red Sea? What about some actual heavenly body guiding the wise men? One problem with this sort of trick is that, as Karl Popper stressed, science has a nasty habit of changing its mind. It is falsifiable. That doesn't mean that it is false. It does mean that it is always in the business of being shown false. And often, as we know, it is shown false. Newton was wrong, at least in the sense that, for all the power of his theory, it doesn't truly capture the ultimate truth of things, for instance, about aspects of relativity. If you put too many religious eggs into this kind of scientific basket, you run the danger of ending up with your religion supported (supposedly) by false science, the sort of thing where it turns out that there was no such comet at the time of Moses or the wise men. My advice is not to get into this sort of game in the first place. This is not just tactical advice. As I noted earlier, the Bible is a work of religion, not science, and the books of Newton or Darwin are works of science, not religion.

Approaching Apparent Scripture-Science Conflicts

How do we approach apparent conflicts between science and Scripture? Ignore them! More seriously, recognize from the start that the conflicts are apparent, not real. Let me qualify this in one obvious way. Evangelicals are religious, just as much as Quakers—although not more so, as most of them think. Many evangelicals believe in a literal universal flood. Geology says no. This is a real conflict. My experience is that you explain gently—or loudly, your choice—why the science is right and leave it at that. You hope their kids will think differently—some are already starting to change on global warming—and leave things at that. You are not going to change their minds.

One place where you might perhaps be helpful is in showing alternative interpretations of Scripture. Take Noah's flood. For me, the most significant part is the conclusion of the story that you were not encouraged to read as a kid. The rude bit at the end—where Noah gets blind drunk and his son sees him naked and laughs at him. As I read the Noah story, it is not at all about ship building and bad weather. It is about the futility of simplistic solutions to complex problems. People are behaving badly, so God clears the decks except for Noah and his fellow travelers. It all goes smoothly according to plan. And what is the end result? The chap chosen to lead us to a brighter future turns out to be as flawed as those drowned. Would that Bush and Blair had read this part of Genesis before they marched blithely into Iraq.

You may not agree with my interpretation, and you can supply your own. But you can see how Genesis and geology are both true and profound. And I'm a nonbeliever!

The Role of Natural Theology

If you don't realize already, now is the time to tell you that although I am a nonbeliever, I am a very Protestant, conservative nonbeliever. I am with Luther on the subject of "that whore reason"! I joke that I was a Kierkegaardian before I had heard of Denmark. Karl Barth is my hero, my poster boy. Actually, I am a little more nuanced than that—probably more in the tradition of St. Thomas Aquinas than anything. What I am certain about is that natural theology—proving the existence of God through reason and evidence—is not and should not be the basis of religious belief. That is the role of faith and faith alone. "Now faith is the substance of things hoped for, the evidence of things not seen" (Hebrews 11:1 KJV). It is that unconditional awareness and acceptance of God and what that implies—for the Christian, the Trinity. It is like falling in love. It is totally overwhelming and impossible to resist. Jesus set the terms of the debate.

Then saith he to Thomas, Reach hither thy finger, and behold my hands; and reach hither thy hand, and thrust it into my side: and be not faithless, but believing.

And Thomas answered and said unto him, My Lord and my God.

Jesus saith unto him, Thomas, because thou hast seen me, thou hast believed: blessed are they that have not seen, and yet have believed. (John 20:27–29 KJV)

All the great theologians have endorsed this at one level or another. Aquinas thought that reason can get there in the end—"For certain things that are true about God wholly surpass the capability of human reason, for instance that God is three and one: while there are certain things to which even natural reason can attain, for instance that God is, that God is one, and others like these."[2] Note, however, that reason—where we could be wrong—is limited, and in the end, faith—where we cannot be wrong—is top dog. "The truth of the intelligible things of God is twofold, one to which the inquiry of reason can attain, the other which surpasses the whole range of human reason."[3] Ultimately, without faith you only get part of the story, and Aquinas makes clear that faith trumps all—how else could the ignorant or stupid or lazy get knowledge of God? John Paul II, in his encyclical *Fides et Ratio* (1998) affirmed this position strongly: "The results of reasoning may in fact be true, but these results acquire their true meaning only if they are set within the larger horizon of faith: 'All man's steps are ordered by the Lord: how then can man understand his own ways?' (Prov. 20:24)."[4]

What this means is that almost everyone who teaches the philosophy of religion, in the English-speaking world at least—and I include myself here—gets things backwards. Reason, then faith. We trot out the usual suspects, the ontological argument, and so forth, and happily move through the semester taking them apart and thinking that by the time the test comes around, the job is done. Whereas for the Christian,

2. St. Thomas Aquinas, *Summa contra Gentiles*, trans. V. J. Bourke (Notre Dame: University of Notre Dame Press, 1975), 5.

3. Aquinas, *Summa contra Gentiles*, 7.

4. John Paul II, *Fides et Ratio: Encyclical Letter of John Paul II to the Catholic Bishops of the World* (Vatican City: L'Osservatore Romano, 1998), 16.

the job hasn't really started! More pertinently, we have missed looking properly at what the arguments might tell us. This is a serious charge to make, even against philosophy professors, so let me say that I think we come by this mess naturally and reasonably honorably. The Elizabethan Settlement of the second half of the sixteenth century was a masterpiece of compromise and innovation. Henry VIII had declared England for the Protestants. His son, Edward VI, although Protestant, lived only a few years. Mary came to the throne, and as a good Catholic, set about persecuting her Protestant subjects. She died in 1558, and Elizabeth took over, reigning until 1603.

Although a Protestant, Elizabeth steered a careful course between Catholicism and the authority of the Church (not to mention all those proselytizing Jesuits determined on martyrdom) and the *sola scriptura* of the Calvinists (during the reign of Mary, many British Protestants found it prudent to move to Geneva). The fabric and customs of the Anglican Church, the buildings, the ceremony, the role of the priest, are Catholic. The theology is Calvinist. Already, in the Thirty-Nine Articles, we have seen evidence of this. Where the innovation came in was in promoting natural theology as the distinctive base of religious thought. This fit in nicely with the empiricist/scientific/technological mood and genius of the British—doing science was doing God's work—and explains incidentally the huge number of very gifted parson-naturalists. By collecting butterflies, one was doing service as much as tending to the sick and poor. Textbook writer Archdeacon William Paley, who was showing at the end of the eighteenth century that not only can natural theology get you to God, but that natural theology can confirm revealed theology or religion also, was no anomaly. It is a perversion of traditional Christianity, but the Brits came by it naturally, as they still do.

What then is the value of natural theology, or does it have none? I certainly would not want to say that. It helps us to clarify many issues of great importance and throws much light on faith and its objects, one of which is this whole intelligent design business that seems all the rage. John Henry Newman was clear about this. He writes:

> I have not insisted on the argument from *design*, because I am writing for the 19th Century, by which, as represented by its philosophers, design is not admitted as proved. And to tell the

truth, though I should not wish to preach on the subject, for 40 years I have been unable to see the logical force of the argument myself. I believe in design because I believe in God; not in a God because I see design.

He continues:

Half the world knows nothing of the argument from design— and, when you have got it, you do not prove by it the moral attributes of God—except very faintly. Design teaches me power, skill, and goodness, not sanctity, not mercy, not a future judgment, which three are of the essence of religion.[5]

This is not a man who has given up on natural theology. Just one who knows its true place.

Let us turn now to the three most common arguments for God's existence and to the argument generally thought the most negative against God. I am not insensitive, as you will learn, to Newman's crack just above about the "philosophers," and for those who feel that without divine fireworks something is lacking, I shall get to miracles later.

First, there is the ontological argument that derives God's existence from his definition—that than which none greater can be conceived. To deny the existence of God is to allow the possibility of an existent God, who would be greater, and thus, through a *reductio ad absurdum* argument, God exists necessarily.

Apart from Descartes, I am not sure that any sensible person in the thousand years since Anselm first formulated it has really thought the argument valid, although there have been countless attempts at philosophical glory by those who try to slip in innocuous-seeming modifications and then in triumph declare it valid. But it is a very powerful indicator of the need to think carefully about the nature of God's existence. We are contingent. Hard as it is to imagine a world without Bruce Gordon and Alister McGrath—even harder a world without Michael Ruse—it is possible. The point is that it is not possible to imagine a

---

5. J. H. Newman, *The Letters and Diaries of John Henry Newman*, vol. 25, eds. C. S. Dessain and T. Gornall (Oxford: Clarendon, 1973), 97.

world without God. You may think this a contradiction in terms. Hume did, and I am inclined to agree with him. But it is not a silly question to be answered, and it is a question that any good Christian—any good theist—should wrestle with. For instance, Anselm's argument rather focuses on logical possibility and impossibility—such as the possibility of a square with five sides, for example. Is this the only notion that can be formulated or that would work?

Moving on to the second of the big arguments for the existence of God—the causal argument—this brings us right to the heart of this already-raised issue of existence. Everything has a cause. The world is a thing. Therefore, the world had a cause. God! To which Richard Dawkins's response is: What caused God? Strange as this may seem to his fellow humanists, Christians had thought about this one before the *God Delusion* brought them to sober reality. Aquinas knew all about it. And he worried about it, because the alternative to God seemed to be an infinite regress of causes, always with an earlier one. The only way to stop this is to make God necessary.

Which at once leads to the really profound insight that "God as cause" is not like the "atomic bomb as cause" (of the destruction of Hiroshima and Nagasaki). God is more a sustaining cause, outside the regular causal chain. If you think of regular causal chains as being horizontal through time, God as cause is at right angles to this and active all the time. The deists think that God created and then headed to join Elvis in retirement in Florida. (No, I am not God, although the idea does have possibilities.) Theists think that God is ever immanent, always at work. Without God, there is nothing. The traditional analysis moves away from God as a logically necessary being to an empirically necessary being in some way. Aseity is the notion that God exists in and of himself, independent of anything and anyone else. Positively, God is self-sufficient. "I am who I am," as God self-confesses to Moses at the burning bush. Negatively, God requires no outside causes. He cannot not be.

Again, you might think that all of this is bunk. Richard Dawkins notwithstanding, it is important bunk. If nothing else, physics in the last century has shown us that existence is a lot more complex than pebbles in a jar. You tell me about Schrödinger's cat, which may or may not be alive, according to whether or not the door is opened. And this is before you get to questions about whether or not mathematics exists, and if so, where, and if not, why does it seem so necessary? Why isn't it like a novel where we can have a happy ending or not as we will? The fact is that existence is a tricky concept. I doubt in our thinking about it, we would have advanced as much as we have without a lot of heavy spadework by the theologians.

This brings me to the biggie, the one that Newman's philosophers were worrying about. The argument from design, or the teleological argument. The eye is like a telescope. Telescopes have designers. Hence, the eye must have had a designer, the Great Optician in the Sky. Before Darwin, as Richard Dawkins (to praise him) has presciently pointed out, it was impossible to be an intellectually fulfilled atheist. David Hume wrestled with this argument, but in the end, he gave up.

> That the works of Nature bear a great analogy to the productions of art, is evident; and according to all the rules of good reasoning, we ought to infer, if we argue at all concerning them, that their causes have a proportional analogy. But as there are also considerable differences, we have reason to suppose a proportional difference in the causes; and in particular, ought to attribute a much higher degree of power and energy to the supreme cause, than any we have ever observed in mankind. Here then the existence of a DEITY is plainly ascertained by reason: and if we make it a question, whether, on account of these analogies, we can properly call him a mind or intelligence, notwithstanding the vast difference which may reasonably be supposed between him and human minds; what is this but a mere verbal controversy?[6]

Charles Darwin, in the *Origin of Species*, gave the answer to this. Natural selection!

> Let it be borne in mind in what an endless number of strange peculiarities our domestic productions, and, in a lesser degree, those under nature, vary; and how strong the hereditary tendency is. Under domestication, it may be truly said that the

---

6. David Hume, *Dialogues Concerning Natural Religion*, ed. M. Bell (London: Penguin, [1779] 1990), 203–4.

whole organisation becomes in some degree plastic. Let it be borne in mind how infinitely complex and close-fitting are the mutual relations of all organic beings to each other and to their physical conditions of life. Can it, then, be thought improbable, seeing that variations useful to man have undoubtedly occurred, that other variations useful in some way to each being in the great and complex battle of life, should sometimes occur in the course of thousands of generations? If such do occur, can we doubt (remembering that many more individuals are born than can possibly survive) that individuals having any advantage, however slight, over others, would have the best chance of surviving and of procreating their kind? On the other hand, we may feel sure that any variation in the least degree injurious would be rigidly destroyed. This preservation of favourable variations and the rejection of injurious variations, I call Natural Selection.[7]

Note the crucial key to the whole Darwinian story. Selection makes for useful features or characteristics, things that will help their possessors in the struggle for existence—the eye, the hand, the leaf, and the root.

How have all those exquisite adaptations of one part of the organisation to another part, and to the conditions of life, and of one distinct organic being to another being, been perfected? We see these beautiful co-adaptations most plainly in the woodpecker and missletoe [sic]; and only a little less plainly in the humblest parasite which clings to the hairs of a quadruped or feathers of a bird; in the structure of the beetle which dives through the water; in the plumed seed which is wafted by the gentlest breeze; in short, we see beautiful adaptations everywhere and in every part of the organic world.[8]

Natural selection! You don't need God. Does that mean that God does not exist? Although, towards the end of his life, Darwin became an

7. Charles Darwin, *On the Origin of Species by Means of Natural Selection, or the Preservation of Favoured Races in the Struggle for Life* (London: John Murray, 1859), 80–81.
8. Darwin, *Origin*, 60–62.

agnostic, he didn't think that at all. This passage remained unchanged through all the editions (1859–72) of the *Origin*.

> Authors of the highest eminence seem to be fully satisfied with the view that each species has been independently created. To my mind it accords better with what we know of the laws impressed on matter by the Creator, that the production and extinction of the past and present inhabitants of the world should have been due to secondary causes, like those determining the birth and death of the individual. When I view all beings not as special creations, but as the lineal descendants of some few beings which lived long before the first bed of the Silurian system was deposited, they seem to me to become ennobled.[9]

Christians agreed with Darwin. This is the High-Church Anglican, Aubrey Moore:

> Science had pushed the deist's God farther and farther away, and at the moment when it seemed as if He would be thrust out altogether, Darwinism appeared, and, under the guise of a foe, did the work of a friend. It has conferred upon philosophy and religion an inestimable benefit, by showing us that we must choose between two alternatives. Either God is everywhere present in nature, or He is nowhere. He cannot be here, and not there. He cannot delegate his power to demigods called "second causes." In nature everything must be His work or nothing. We must frankly return to the Christian view of direct Divine agency, the immanence of Divine power from end to end, the belief in a God in Whom not only we, but all things have their being, or we must banish him altogether.[10]

If you are a believer, you can go right on believing in God after Darwin. You can give thanks to Darwin for telling you of God's magnificent powers of creation. (It doesn't prove creation, but it helps you to

---

9. Darwin, *Origin*, 488–89.

10. Aubrey Moore, "The Christian Doctrine of God," in *Lux Mundi*, ed. C. Gore (London: John Murray, 1890), 73–74.

understand God's wonderful world.) There may be an interesting asymmetry for the nonbeliever. If you are not in the faith business, and if you are not building a secular religious world picture based on Darwinism (usually through its supposedly progressive nature), as I think many humanists are, then I don't see why Darwinian selection theory cannot have any effect on your world picture. You have—or should have—rejected God on other grounds, so that is not at issue. But the bleakness of the world under Darwinism is a factor. The poet Thomas Hardy saw this. This is his poem "Hap" written around 1866, when he had lost his Anglican faith and had read Darwin:

> If but some vengeful god would call to me
> From up the sky, and laugh: "Thou suffering thing,
> Know that thy sorrow is my ecstasy,
> That thy love's loss is my hate's profiting!"
>
> Then would I bear it, clench myself, and die,
> Steeled by the sense of ire unmerited;
> Half-eased in that a Powerfuller than I
> Had willed and meted me the tears I shed.
>
> But not so. How arrives it joy lies slain,
> And why unblooms the best hope ever sown?
> —Crass Casualty obstructs the sun and rain,
> And dicing Time for gladness casts a moan. . . .
> These purblind Doomsters had as readily strown
> Blisses about my pilgrimage as pain.

It is all very existentialist. If you are going to make anything from your life, and I don't see Darwin's theory as forbidding this, then you are going to have to do so on your own. Even if God exists, he is indifferent. Of course, he isn't indifferent if you have faith, but if you don't, he is. Meaning comes from you and not from outside.

Finally, what about the big argument against God's existence, the problem of evil? How does one reconcile an all-powerful and all-loving God with the existence of suffering and pain? Darwin worried about this question and thought that his theory exacerbated the problem. In a well-known letter written (just after the *Origin*) to his American friend, the Harvard botanist Asa Gray, Darwin opined:

> With respect to the theological view of the question; this is always painful to me.—I am bewildered.—I had no intention to write atheistically. But I own that I cannot see, as plainly as others do, & as I shd. wish to do, evidence of design & beneficence on all sides of us. There seems to me too much misery in the world. I cannot persuade myself that a beneficent & omnipotent God would have designedly created the Ichneumonidae with the express intention of their feeding within the living bodies of caterpillars, or that a cat should play with mice. Not believing this, I see no necessity in the belief that the eye was expressly designed.[11]

Richard Dawkins, again, weighs in on this. Cheetahs seem wonderfully designed to kill antelopes. "The teeth, claws, eyes, nose, leg muscles, backbone and brain of a cheetah are all precisely what we should expect if God's purpose in designing cheetahs was to maximize deaths among antelopes."[12] Conversely, "we find equally impressive evidence of design for precisely the opposite end: the survival of antelopes and starvation among cheetahs."[13] One could almost imagine that we have two gods making the different animals and then competing. If there is indeed but one God who made both animals, then what is going on? What sort of God makes this sort of encounter? "Is He a sadist who enjoys spectator blood sports? Is He trying to avoid overpopulation in the mammals of Africa? Is He maneuvering to maximize David Attenborough's television ratings?"[14]

Let me say straight out that I think the problem of evil is a great barrier to religious belief. I am with Dostoevsky on this one—or at least with Alyosha Karamazov. Ivan asks his brother a question:

---

11. Charles Darwin, The Collected Correspondence of Charles Darwin, *Letters* (Cambridge: Cambridge University Press, 1985–), 8:224.

12. Richard Dawkins, *A River Out of Eden* (New York: Basic, 1995), 105.

13. Dawkins, *A River Out of Eden*, 105.

14. Dawkins, *A River Out of Eden*, 105.

"Tell me yourself, I challenge your answer. Imagine that you are creating a fabric of human destiny with the object of making men happy in the end, giving them peace and rest at last, but that it was essential and inevitable to torture to death only one tiny creature—that baby beating its breast with its fist, for instance—and to found that edifice on its unavenged tears, would you consent to be the architect on those conditions? Tell me, and tell the truth."

"No, I wouldn't consent," said Alyosha softly.[15]

A world of Adolf Hitler and Heinrich Himmler and the rest of that sorry crew—and the subsequent deaths of Anne Frank, Sophie Scholl, and Dietrich Bonhoeffer—is not for me the world of the theists. Nor does it help to look down the road and say God will make it all right in the end. There may be a god. Not the Christian God. Thank goodness. I don't want the Christian God to exist.

This said, note that I am not offering a scientific argument here; more a philosophical or theological argument. These days, my impression is that Christian philosophers tend to be rather smug about the evil issue. They feel they have the problem licked by explaining that free will speaks to moral evil and necessity speaks to natural evil. To be made in the image of God—the best of all possible choices—we had to be free, which allows the possibility of moral evil. To create, God had to make decisions—the best of all possible worlds—and that is why burning hurts, because it brings on instant action away from a significant danger.

Paradoxically, Darwinian evolutionary theory goes some considerable way to support these arguments.[16] With respect to the free will problem, having some form of flexibility is a very sophisticated and powerful adaptation that we humans have. We can live in varied and complex situations, adjusting rapidly when things change. If we were programmed like ants, we could not do so. When it rains and the pheromone trails get washed away, many foraging ants get lost and die. Mother ant compensates by having thousands of children. If some go,

15. Fyodor Dostoevsky, *The Brothers Karamazov* (London: Penguin, 2003), 5.4.

16. Michael Ruse, *Can a Darwinian Be a Christian? The Relationship between Science and Religion* (Cambridge: Cambridge University Press, 2001).

there are plenty more. Humans are not like this. Imagine if someone asked you how many kids you have. "I have three. No, one just went to McDonald's, and it's been raining. Better say two." That's a joke, because like the Mars Rover, we can deal with obstacles without outside instruction. As opposed to ants, who have gone the route of so-called r-selection—many offspring produced cheaply and let nature take care of itself (and us)—we have gone the route of so-called K-selection— few offspring because they need more energy to produce, and we'll take care of nature.[17] We need to be flexible in the sense of being able to reassess in the light of circumstances, and the reason for this is because, undoubtedly, part cause and part effect—we are very social, and being social means being flexible. If opportunities come up, you have to make decisions. Am I going to get involved in hunting and killing this giraffe? If I do so, what am I going to expect in the way of a share of the meat? And so forth. There is no one fixed answer, but answers are to be worked out according to circumstances.

As far as natural evil is concerned, Richard Dawkins (1983) of all people has argued that the only way you can naturally get design features is through natural selection. Lamarckism is false, and other alternatives, like saltations (jumps from one form to another), simply don't lead to adaptations. They exemplify Murphy's Law. If it can go wrong, it will go wrong. Unless there is a powerful counter-force, like natural selection, organisms won't work. Saltations lead to things like dwarfism or idiocy—in one leap or generation. So, this means at least some natural evil is indeed part of the Leibnizian trade-off. You want humans? Then you had better put up with fish eating fish, with birds eating rabbits, and with viruses causing all sorts of horrendous diseases. Natural selection doesn't explain all natural evil—such as the Lisbon earthquake—but it takes a big bite out of it, to use a pertinent metaphor!

So where do we come out in the end about natural theology? It is a very important enterprise and teaches us a lot about the world and our possible relationship to God. What it does not do is lead us to God, and most certainly not through science. That is the exclusive role of revealed religion. Faith.

---

17. R. H. MacArthur and E. O. Wilson, *The Theory of Island Biogeography* (Princeton: Princeton University Press, 1967).

Divine Action and Science

Let me change course a little now and start asking questions about God's (possible) actions in the world. First, do I think that God (assuming he exists) could act in the world, miraculously in some way? Second, would someone like me ever allow the authenticity of such an action? The answer to the first question is that of course God could intervene in his creation if he wanted to. He made it, he can change it! I should say at once, however, that were I a believer, I would be indifferent as to whether there were actual breaks in the course of nature. For me, the resurrection is not a matter of physiology, but of those dispirited disciples on the third day suddenly realizing that their Savior lived on. That's a miracle! When I was a kid, Dunkirk was thought a miracle. Normally so stormy, the Channel was like a millpond and the British Army was saved. If you asked someone if God intervened or if it was all regular meteorology, they would have thought you nuts—sincerely, nuts. The miracle was that God made it possible for us to continue the fight against Hitler. It is all a matter of meaning. How he did it is irrelevant.

This said, would I allow a miracle in the sense of a break or intervention in the natural chain? I am with Hume here. It's going to take an awful lot to persuade me. Certainly, I am not keen on those miracles the Catholic Church finds to make people saints. If someone says that God had to intervene directly—real water into real wine—I am happy to go with that, so long as they don't try to make me believe on evidence. Like saying that the resurrection must be literal because it was reported by women, and no one back then would say this unless it were true. That's just wishful thinking. Believe on faith and move on to helping your fellow humans.

Could anything make me believe a miracle? Say I am Lazarus's doctor, and I saw him last Thursday and he was just fine. Then on Saturday I am called over and he is very sick—expected because he was an alcoholic—and dies. On Sunday, I check in on the family and he is about to be buried, just as well because already he is a bit fetid. On Tuesday, I check back again and am greeted by Lazarus, who says, "Hi, Doc. Fancy seeing you. I just got a case of King David Merlot. How about a drink?" I check him and he is in good shape. I wonder if he has an identical twin brother. I never heard of one, so I check his teeth. I know he had a funny crack on the upper left molar. It is there. Unlikely that a twin would have the same. I insist on the tomb being opened. No Lazarus. What do I say now? Perhaps, "Oh well, if it is so important to you, you win." At the same time, I am going to say, "If you think this is going to make Jesus Christ my savior, you have another thing coming. Jesus Christ was not Dr. Frankenstein before his time. Beating David Copperfield at his own game has nothing to do with the death on the cross and my eternal salvation. It makes the whole thing a rather tawdry, Coney Island sort of thing. Not early morning sunlight on the Canadian Rockies."[18]

The Necessity of Methodological Naturalism for Science

These are really important questions. At the time of Newton, it was possible to appeal to divine forces in explanation. By the nineteenth century, much under the influence of Kant—"I had to deny knowledge in order to make room for faith"—science was and had to be methodologically naturalistic—blind laws all the way—and if that could not be, then it was not science. William Whewell, convinced that there could be no naturalistic explanation of species' origins, said simply that science says nothing but points upwards. Accordingly, even if intelligent design theory be true, it cannot be science because it appeals to nonnatural causes.

Does this then mean that science answers all the questions, or at least all the meaningful questions? Religion is out of luck? "The more the universe seems comprehensible, the more it also seems pointless." Although he did not quite intend this conclusion, the Nobel Prize winner Steven Weinberg knew whereof he spoke. The inference that science answers all is totally unwarranted. All the traditional Christian issues are still there awaiting answers.

I recognize that this is not a popular answer among my fellow nonbelievers. Generally, they take "scientism"—if it is science, it can answer, and if science cannot answer, it is not a meaningful or worthwhile question—for granted. Lawrence Krauss, for instance, writes a

---

18. Note that my conservative nonbelief is conservative Canadian nonbelief, not conservative American nonbelief, which is probably an oxymoron anyway.

whole book arguing that the question of existence—why is there something rather than nothing—is answered by the big bang.[19] One up on Wittgenstein, I guess, who, when he discovered he could not answer that question, went into a massive philosophical sulk and decided it was not a meaningful question.

> If I say "I wonder at the existence of the world" I am misusing language. Let me explain this: It has a perfectly good and clear sense to say that I wonder at something being the case, we all understand what it means to say that I wonder at the size of a dog which is bigger than anyone I have ever seen before or at any thing which, in the common sense of the word, is extraordinary. In every such case I wonder at something being the case which I could conceive not to be the case. I wonder at the size of this dog because I could conceive of a dog of another, namely the ordinary size, at which I should not wonder. To say "I wonder at such and such being the case" has only sense if I can imagine it not to be the case. In this sense one can wonder at, say, the existence of a house when one sees it and has not visited it for a long time and has imagined it had been pulled down in the meantime. But it is nonsense to say that I wonder at the existence of the world, because I cannot imagine it not existing.[20]

The trouble with this kind of argument is that many people, including myself, can imagine the world not existing. So, where do we go from here?

Something is wrong, and what is wrong is scientism. To see this, recognize that science is not out of *Dragnet*—"Just the facts, ma'am, just the facts." It is a matter of observation and interpretation, and that means metaphor. Force, work, attraction, genetic code, natural selection, selfish gene, Oedipus complex. Science has root metaphors, an overriding world vision—or "paradigm" in Kuhn's language. Before the Scientific Revolution, the root metaphor was the world is an organism. Then, it changed to the world is a machine—not a machine with purpose,

---

19. L. M. Krauss, *A Universe from Nothing* (New York: Atria, 2012).
20. Ludwig Wittgenstein, "A Lecture on Ethics," *The Philosophical Review* 74 (1965): 8–9.

but one endlessly going through cycles, governed by unchanging law. The thing about metaphors/paradigms, as Kuhn pointed out, is that they work by focusing you and declaring certain, quite meaningful questions off limits. My love is a red, red rose. She is beautiful. She is fresh and blooming (another metaphor!). She might, I am joking a bit, be rather prickly. Is she good at math? I don't know. It is a meaningful question. I am just not asking it. Same with the machine metaphor of science. Here are four genuine questions it doesn't ask.

Why is there something rather than nothing? Science is a bit like the nineteenth-century cookbook recipe for jugged hare: "First take your hare." You want to make a functioning automobile? First take your aluminum and steel. Where did the aluminum come from? Perhaps Quebec. But where did it come from before Quebec? Who cares? I want to know how the auto functions. And don't tell me, because Wittgenstein so tells me, that it is not a genuine question. Of course, it is a genuine question. Heidegger was right to label it the Fundamental Question of Metaphysics. Because I cannot answer it does not mean that it is bogus. Krauss and his pals are as mixed up about existence as are the critics—often one and the same—who go after Aquinas on the causal argument. We are talking about the very fact of existence, not what goes on once you have given the actuality of existence.

What is the ultimate foundation of morality? Science can explain why we are moral. Darwin offers one explanation:

> It must not be forgotten that although a high standard of morality gives but a slight or no advantage to each individual man and his children over the other men of the same tribe, yet that an advancement in the standard of morality and an increase in the number of well-endowed men will certainly give an immense advantage to one tribe over another. There can be no doubt that a tribe including many members who, from possessing in a high degree the spirit of patriotism, fidelity, obedience, courage, and sympathy, were always ready to give aid to each other and to sacrifice themselves for the common good, would be victorious over most other tribes; and this would be natural selection. At all times throughout the world tribes have supplanted other tribes; and as morality is one element in their success, the standard of

morality and the number of well-endowed men will thus every-where tend to rise and increase.[21]

We think that morality is objective, because if we didn't, we would start to cheat and it would break down. Science cannot say that morality really is objective.

What is consciousness? Leibniz was right about this one. Machines don't think.

One is obliged to admit that *perception* and what depends upon it is *inexplicable on mechanical principles*, that is, by figures and motions. In imagining that there is a machine whose construction would enable it to think, to sense, and to have perception, one could conceive it enlarged while retaining the same proportions, so that one could enter into it, just like into a windmill. Supposing this, one should, when visiting within it, find only parts pushing one another, and never anything by which to explain a percep-tion. Thus it is in the simple substance, and not in the composite or in the machine, that one must look for perception.[22]

Philosophers like Daniel Dennett,[23] who claim that, once you have given a physical description of what is going on, you have solved the problem, strike me as between silly and dishonest. They are taking comparisons between computers and minds a bit too seriously.

And finally, the meaning of it all. I am not surprised that Weinberg got no answers because he was not in a business that yields such answers. Many machines do have purposes or ends. Vibrators are for skin stimu-lation, or so I am told. I find them great for making mayonnaise. Really gets those ingredients to nuzzle up to each other. But in science we have cut down the metaphor so as not to answer questions about purpose because they are not helpful to science. We are always doing this. If I

---

21. Charles Darwin, *The Descent of Man, and Selection in Relation to Sex* (London: John Murray, 1871), 1, 161.

22. Gottfried W. F. Leibniz, *Discourse on Metaphysics and Other Essays: On the Ultimate Origination of Things, Preface to the New Essays, The Monadology* (Indianapolis: Hackett, 1989), 215.

23. D. C. Dennett, *Consciousness Explained* (New York: Pantheon, 1992).

say I am a bit sluggish this morning, it is a bit daft to ask if I have sludge in my blood as you might expect to find in a slow-moving river. You just rule out those kinds of physiological questions when you use the metaphor. You might ask if the sluggishness comes every day or in phases, but not if someone opened a factory waste pipe by mistake.

These are all questions that Christians try to answer. Creation? A good God. Morality? The will of that God. Consciousness? Being made in the image of that God. Purpose? Obedience and future happiness. I am not saying you should accept these answers. I don't! But I reject them not because of science but because of philosophy and theology. For a start, I cannot reconcile a Good God with the Dostoevsky challenge. And you should accept these answers, not because of science but because of philosophy and theology, meaning faith. Science tells us that we cannot take Genesis literally. It tells us nothing about whether Genesis is true.

Science and Miracles

Can we allow miracles occasionally—perhaps they occurred at the time of Christ—or more generally, miracles that are still happening today? I have spoken to these questions already. God could work in these ways. The question is whether he would. I have given what are for me convincing reasons—note, reasons mainly given on the basis of Christian belief and practice—that God would probably not do it generally and probably not at all. It isn't important! People who spend their time trying to prove that the resurrection really is a historically attested fact, reasonable to believe on empirical grounds, are doing bad science, bad history, and bad philosophy. Worse, theologically they are close to, if not already, over the line of heresy. Think about it. Does your eternal salvation really depend on whether Jesus literally turned water into wine? What if Jesus filled the host with shame that he was hoarding the best for himself and so the host decided to share? Which Jesus do you worship?

Science, Providence, and Sovereignty

Say it again. I believe in design because I believe in God, not God because I believe in design. This is not a motto for me, because I don't believe in God. But this is absolutely and totally the way for Christians to think about things spiritual and secular. It is a wonderful and mysterious world that we live in. Were I a Christian, it would fill my heart and mind with love and adoration. But this would happen because I am a Christian, not because design made me a Christian. I have the spirit of a Quaker, and I approve of Sophie Scholl of the White Rose Group because of her nobility and sacrifice under the Nazis. That nobility and sacrifice did not give me the spirit of a Quaker. It certainly does not make me believe in a Good God. My Good God would never have let Heinrich Himmler loose in the first place.

What about *Homo sapiens*?

We are at the final questions. What about *Homo sapiens*? Where do we come out in all of this? Let me answer the second question straight off. No, if you must appeal to divine action in your explanation, rather than assuming this on faith as your background, then you are not doing science. That is beyond question. We did appear. Naturally, I think, and I find nothing in Darwinian theory to make this exceptional. I think humans are exceptional, but this is my judgment, not biology's. Big brains demand a lot of energy, meaning large chunks of protein, generally from other animals. And this requires effort and more. Biology doesn't say it is the best. Paleobiologist Jack Sepkoski puts things colorfully: "I see intelligence as just one of a variety of adaptations among tetrapods for survival. Running fast in a herd while being as dumb as shit, I think, is a very good adaptation for survival."[24]

The interesting question for the Christian is whether we think humans are a one-off, or whether we think that generally, given life, we might expect human-like beings. For Christians, humans are special, so the question is whether the unique appearance of humans is rather special or whether the specialness lies in the mechanism that produces humans. I suppose if you have multiverses, generating infinite possibilities, then just as, finally, a monkey will type Shakespeare, we are going to have human-like beings. But does one want to do this at the cost of having billions of planets with all the also-rans—sub-human beings trying to produce unusable plays?

Some people do think that Darwinian evolution does point to

24. Michael Ruse, *Monad to Man: The Concept of Progress in Evolutionary Biology* (Cambridge, MA: Harvard University Press, 1996), 486.

progress towards humans. This was Darwin's position. He supposed that there are what today's evolutionists call arms races, with lines competing against each other and intelligence finally emerging.

> If we look at the differentiation and specialisation of the several organs of each being when adult (and this will include the advancement of the brain for intellectual purposes) as the best standard of highness of organisation, natural selection clearly leads towards highness; for all physiologists admit that the specialisation of organs, inasmuch as they perform in this state their functions better, is an advantage to each being; and hence the accumulation of variations tending towards specialisation is within the scope of natural selection.[25]

Today, Richard Dawkins stands in this tradition. "Directionalist common sense surely wins on the very long time scale: once there was only blue-green slime and now there are sharp-eyed metazoa."[26] The key lies in arms races. Dawkins notes that, more and more, today's arms races rely on computer technology rather than brute power. In the animal world, Dawkins finds this translated into ever bigger and more efficient brains. Dawkins invokes a notion known as an animal's EQ, standing for "encephalization quotient."[27] This is a kind of cross-species measure of IQ that factors in the brain power needed simply to get an organism to function (whales require much bigger brains than shrews because they need more computing power to get their bigger bodies to function), and that then scales according to the surplus left over. Dawkins (1986) writes: "The fact that humans have an EQ of 7 and hippos an EQ of 0.3 may not literally mean that humans are 23 times as clever as hippos! But the EQ as measured is probably telling us something about how much 'computing power' an animal probably has in its head, over and above the irreducible amount of computing power needed for the routine running of its large or small body."[28]

---

25. Charles Darwin, *The Origin of Species*, 3rd ed. (London: John Murray, 1861), 134.
26. Richard Dawkins and John R. Krebs, "Arms Races between and within Species," *Proceedings of the Royal Society of London* 205, no. 1161 (1979): 489–511.
27. Harry J. Jerison, *Evolution of the Brain and Intelligence* (New York: Academic Press, 1973).
28. Dawkins, *Blind Watchmaker*, 189.

A somewhat different approach to the humans-must-appear conundrum comes from paleontologist Simon Conway Morris—a Christian, but one who is seeking an entirely natural explanation. He argues that only certain areas of what we might call "morphological space" are welcoming to life forms. The center of the sun would not be, for instance. This constrains the course of evolution. Over and over, organisms take the same route into a pre-existing niche. The saber-toothed, tiger-like organisms are a nice example, where the North American placental mammals (real cats) were matched right down the line by South American marsupials (thylacosmilids). There existed a niche for organisms that were predators, with cat-like abilities and shearing/stabbing-like weapons. Darwinian selection found more than one way to enter it—from the placental side and from the marsupial side. It was not a question of beating out others but of finding pathways that others had not found.

Conway Morris argues that, given the ubiquity of convergence, the historical course of nature is not random but strongly selection-constrained along certain pathways and to certain destinations. Most particularly, some kind of intelligent being was bound to emerge. After all, our own very existence shows that a kind of cultural adaptive niche exists—a niche that prizes intelligence and social abilities. "If brains can get big independently and provide a neural machine capable of handling a highly complex environment, then perhaps there are other parallels, other convergences that drive some groups towards complexity." He continues: "We may be unique, but paradoxically those properties that define our uniqueness can still be inherent in the evolutionary process. In other words, if we humans had not evolved then something more-or-less identical would have emerged sooner or later."[29]

A third and final solution is not very Darwinian. Duke University colleagues, paleontologist Daniel McShea and philosopher Robert Brandon, promote what they proudly call "Biology's First Law."[30] Called the "zero-force evolutionary law," or ZFEL, its general formulation states: "In any evolutionary system in which there is variation and

---

29. S. Conway Morris, *Life's Solution: Inevitable Humans in a Lonely Universe* (Cambridge: Cambridge University Press), 196.

30. Daniel W. McShea and Robert N. Brandon, *Biology's First Law: The Tendency for Diversity and Complexity to Increase in Evolutionary Systems* (Chicago: University of Chicago Press, 2010).

heredity, there is a tendency for diversity and complexity to increase, one that is always present but that may be opposed or augmented by natural selection, other forces, or constraints acting on diversity or complexity."[31] McShea and Brandon see this law as something with the status in evolutionary biology of Newton's First Law of Motion. It is a kind of background condition of stability—perhaps better, continuity—against which other factors can operate.

The authors are fairly (let us say) generic on their understandings of complexity and diversity—number of parts, number of kinds. In any case, the claims to be made are grandiose.

Given the natural tendency of life to complexity—parts tend to be added on—this generates new organic variations and hence types. One thus gets a version of what the theoretical biologist Stuart Kauffman has called "order for free." It is not always obvious whether the claim is that adaptation is created in this way or if adaptation is now irrelevant. Probably more the former:

> . . . we raise the possibility that complex adaptive structures arise spontaneously in organisms with excess part types. One could call this self-organization. But it is more accurately described as the consequence of the explosion of combinatorial possibilities that naturally accompanies the interaction of a large diversity of arbitrary part types.[32]

Their feeling is that selection is mainly a negative force, cleaning up after the really creative work has been done. Naturally, all of this is going to lead to intelligence.

> The scope we claim for the ZFEL is immodestly large. The claim is that the ZFEL tendency is and has been present in the background, pushing diversity and complexity upwards, in all populations, in all taxa, in all organisms, on all timescales, over the entire history of life, here on Earth and everywhere.[33]

---

31. McShea and Brandon, *Biology's First Law*, 4.
32. Stuart A. Kauffman, *The Origins of Order: Self-Organization and Selection in Evolution* (Oxford: Oxford University Press), 124.
33. McShea and Brandon, *Biology's First Law*, 4.

What is there to say about these suggestions? Basically, the more Darwinian you get, the less likely you are to get humans. Arms races? There is undoubtedly some empirical evidence for them. For instance, as predators get better at boring into shells, the owners of those shells get better at producing ever stronger and thicker protection. However, the evidence is not uniformly positive. Fossils, for instance, do not show unambiguously that prey and predators have become ever faster. And even if arms races are ubiquitous, it does not follow that intelligence will always emerge. We have noted the costs and demands of big brains. There were no clever vegans in the Pleistocene. Being clever, however, isn't everything. Sometimes—as cows and horses demonstrate—it is just easier to get your food in other ways, especially if you are living on grassy savannahs. Remember the cautionary words of Jack Sepkoski.

Turning to the convergence suggestion, why should we or anyone else necessarily or even probably enter the culture niche? Life is full of missed opportunities. Maybe most times evolution would have gone other ways and avoided culture entirely. Warthogs rule supreme. Many wonder if it is right to think that niches are just waiting out there, ready to be conquered and entered.[34] Do not organisms create niches as much as find them? Until vertebrates like us humans came along, there was hardly a niche for head lice, for instance. Should we expect that there was a niche for culture, just waiting there, like dry land or the open air? Perhaps there are other niches not yet invented. We cannot imagine something other than consciousness, but that could be our problem, not a fault of objective reality. For all their talk about analogy, Christians tend to think that their God can get up to some clever tricks, way beyond their ken. Perhaps these are not all supernatural abilities, but simply abilities which were omitted from our evolution—like understanding the nature of consciousness or being able to handle teenagers. Perhaps, far from being the best, we are a short side-path and very limited in the true scheme of things. No more than in the case of arms races do we get much guarantee of either human emergence or a sense that we are in some way superior and for this reason we won.

ZFEL? One can only say that if you believe in this, then you are

---

34. Richard Lewontin, *The Triple Helix: Gene, Organism, and Environment* (Cambridge, MA: Harvard University Press, 2000).

ready for the tooth fairy. Ideas like this seem to appeal to, and only to, those who spend their days in front of computers. If they spent less time running simulated scenarios and more time looking at the real world, they would think otherwise. Blind law leads to blind results, and supposing that laws are not really blind is to suppose that there is some kind of intelligence behind it all. These days popular among philosophers is an Aristotelian force, an Unmoved Mover, to which everything strives teleologically. I just don't see the evidence for it, I just don't. In my world, Murphy's Law rules supreme. If it can go wrong, it will go wrong. I am not sure that either arms races or niches did do the job, but I can see how they could and how natural selection was vital. Suggestions like ZFEL strike me as trying to slip in some kind of (German Romantic) teleological force upwards to humans. I am not necessarily saying this is wrong—Aristotle did it, and anyone less shifty than he would be hard to imagine—but it is being done by sleight of hand.

I come back to where I went in. If I were a Christian paleoanthropologist—a student of the evolution of human beings—I would be absolutely fascinated by what we have learned. That we are more closely related to chimpanzees than they are to gorillas, for instance. Or that we got up on our hind feet and then our brains exploded, not vice versa. That there may have been at the same time as us a group of little beings in Indonesia, *Homo floresiensis*, the hobbit. That we Europeans are 5 percent related to Neanderthals. Not true of Africans. It is us white folk who are the cavemen. I would want to work out causes. Is there anything to arms races? What were the conditions that made us leave the jungle and move to the plains? A question of great importance to me, because I have been writing on Darwinism, Christianity, and war: Were we always killer apes or did that come later, for instance, with the move to agriculture? None of this would change my Christian faith in any way. Rather, God's wonderful work would inspire me in my work and tell me that I am contributing to his glory. What better tribute could one give to one's Creator?

ALISTER MCGRATH

It is a pleasure to respond to Michael's robust and immensely engaging approach to the relation of Christianity and the natural sciences, which raises some important questions. I envy him his easy and accessible style and his willingness to ask hard questions. In general terms, Michael's essay has four main sections: the relationship between science and the Bible, the idea of natural theology, the question of methodological naturalism, and how we should understand the emergence of human beings. I shall follow his order of presentation to make it easier for readers to follow our interaction. Michael's views are important, as the basic positions he so engagingly expounds will resonate with many in Western culture, and he helpfully identifies points of central importance.

I am committed to a model of dialogue between disciplines and individual thinkers, which allows for some difficult but highly rewarding conversations and forces me to make sure that I have understood someone's position before I criticize it. My own unsatisfactory and somewhat perfunctory engagements with Richard Dawkins and Christopher Hitchens persuaded me that they did not wish their stereotypes of religious belief to be challenged, not least because their antireligious polemic largely depended on misrepresentation of their target. Happily, Michael stands above this. This response to Michael picks up on some of our disagreements, while at the same time highlights some points at which we converge.

Science and the Bible

Michael's first major section explores the difficult yet immensely important question of the relation of the natural sciences and Scripture.

47

He opens with some critical reflections on the Christian idea of original sin, generously foregrounding the views of the Church of England (my own denomination) and those of Augustine of Hippo. This in itself is an interesting topic in relation to our overall theme.

Why did Augustine develop such a doctrine, and take it seriously? Michael suggests this may rest on a questionable overemphasis on Paul. As I read Augustine's works, I see something rather different, with important parallels with Aristotle's basic scientific principle of "saving the appearances [*phainomena*]."[1] The basic idea is that we identify observations and then proceed to ask what way of seeing the world—in other words, what *theory*—seems to integrate these observations into a satisfyingly coherent whole. Augustine's concern was to find a theory that weaves together as many biblical passages as possible, not relying on isolated and decontextualized "proof texts" but rather trying to identify the fundamental principles holding these passages together coherently. For Augustine, the notion of original sin—the idea that humanity is by nature broken, wounded, and damaged, requiring a healing and transformation that lies beyond our intrinsic capacities—is part of the outcome of this process of correlation and colligation.

Michael's main point, however, concerns the question of whether Scripture can shape science. In responding, let me initially return to the idea of original sin. Intellectual historian Peter Harrison notes the importance of early modern anxieties about the compromising of human faculties by sin as a trigger for developing the natural sciences. Scientific methods, he suggests, were originally devised to ameliorate the cognitive damage wrought by human sin, allowing us to recapture the knowledge of nature that Adam had once possessed. For Harrison, theological considerations were thus of considerable significance in the framing of the scientific method.[2]

Yet while Michael and I diverge on some important points here, I agree with his blunt assertion that "Scripture is not to be treated as a work of science" (p. 21) (assuming, of course, that the English word *science* here means "natural science"—the older Latin term *scientia* had

---

1. Martha C. Nussbaum, *The Fragility of Goodness: Luck and Ethics in Greek Tragedy and Philosophy* (Cambridge: Cambridge University Press, 1986), 240–63.

2. Peter Harrison, *The Fall of Man and the Foundations of Science* (Cambridge: Cambridge University Press, 2007).

a much broader meaning during the Middle Ages). Since science is an essentially reductive and methodologically naturalist method of inquiry, treating Scripture as "scientific" imposes an epistemic agenda on the reading of Scripture that can only lead to a dilution, if not distortion, of its distinct character and goals. John Wesley, for example, argued that Scripture was not to be read as a scientific textbook but as a disclosure of the nature and intentions of God.[3]

So does science shape the interpretation of Scripture? We all approach the reading of the Bible with a set of presuppositions. Many in the Middle Ages read the Bible in the light of a "common sense" cosmology, in which the earth stood at the center of the universe, and imposed this controlling assumption onto their reading of biblical texts. Some Protestant theologians have subsequently argued that scientific advance can call into question some older ways of interpreting certain biblical passages, showing that these interpretations are culturally and historically located. Benjamin B. Warfield's careful theological exegesis of this point led him to conclude that a perceived conflict between scientific theory and the prevailing interpretation of biblical texts should not lead to the rejection of a scientific account of nature, nor the doubt of the truth of Scripture, but to the interrogation of those controlling interpretative assumptions, to see if they needed to be reviewed.[4]

In discussing this issue, Michael makes a critically important point, which represents important common ground between us—an attentiveness toward the *provisionality* of scientific theorizing. "As Karl Popper stressed, science has a nasty habit of changing its mind." Michael's observation must be taken with the greatest seriousness. As an intellectual historian, I am amused by studying past theological attempts to accommodate to the scientific consensus of the day—only to find that, within decades, this consensus was displaced by something quite different.

Finally, we come to the question of how we deal with what might seem to be conflicts between science and the Bible. Michael's solution

---

3. John W. Haas, "John Wesley's Eighteenth-Century Views on Science and Christianity: An Examination of the Charge of Antiscience," *Church History* 63 (1994): 378–92.

4. For further exploration of this point, see David N. Livingstone, *Darwin's Forgotten Defenders: The Encounter between Evangelical Theology and Evolutionary Thought* (Grand Rapids: Eerdmans, 1987).

to this dilemma is completely consistent with the general approach he outlines: "Ignore them! More seriously, recognize from the start that the conflicts are apparent, not real" (p. 22). My commitment to a dialogical approach puts me in a more difficult position, although I firmly believe it is one that can be defended. My approach requires me to take such appearances of conflict with seriousness, even if—as Michael suggests—the perception of conflicts is likely to turn out to be apparent rather than real. It is completely fair to point out that the underdeveloped (by modern standards) concepts of "science" and "history" we find in the thought-worlds of the ancient Near East and the New Testament period cannot easily be mapped onto their modern equivalents. Yet I have no reason to doubt that the gospel writers (to mention one category of writer) believed both that they were writing history and that the writing of history was important. We might do things differently today; we must nevertheless respect earlier conventions and assumptions, as otherwise we will lose any link with the worlds of life and thought of the ancient world.

The Role of Natural Theology

Michael clearly has misgivings about natural theology, understood as an attempt to prove the existence of God using "natural" human reasoning, appealing to the beauty or complexity of nature. In some ways, the emergence of natural theology is a distinctively English phenomenon,[5] reflecting the rise of a scientific culture within a religious culture that was able to create conceptual space for this new development, which was presented in terms of a harmony between "God's two books"—the "book of nature" and the "book of Scripture."

As Michael makes clear, this development was not without its problems, not least of which was its tendency to overplay its hand— for example, in speaking ambitiously and somewhat prematurely about having "proved" God's existence on the basis of the observation of design within the nature world. The difficulty is well known: design is something that is inferred from observation, not something that is itself directly observed. Such an inference of design is at best a probabilistic

---

5. Scott Mandelbrote, "The Uses of Natural Theology in Seventeenth-Century England," *Science in Context* 20, no. 3 (2007): 451–80.

judgment. This issue regularly surfaces in studies of wooden or stone objects found in Neanderthal sites: Are these natural, or have they in some way been crafted for a purpose?[6]

I can see why Michael might worry that some forms of natural theology represent a "perversion of traditional Christianity" and agree that it might point merely toward a divine designer and constructor (what William Paley describes as an "artificer") of an orderly universe. The logic of Paley's arguments, framed at the time of the British Industrial Revolution, leads to the inference of a God who designs and constructs machines; while this is not entirely unhelpful, it arguably leads to a deist view of God that lacks certain core Christian characteristics—such as a capacity to relate to us. Paley, for example, found it difficult (and probably unnecessary) to include the notion of providence in his account of God's dealings with the world.[7] I agree with Michael that this is a theologically deficient and existentially inadequate conception of God, just as I also agree with him that it continues to serve some useful purposes.

One of those purposes seems to merit comment—its capacity to critique scientism, the view that regards the natural sciences as alone being able to tell us anything true or useful about ourselves and the world. Michael has some excellent quotes from British poets; let me add to these with some lines from English poet John Keats's rambling (but occasionally stunning and brilliant) 1820 poem *Lamia*:[8]

> Do not all charms fly
> At the mere touch of cold philosophy?
> There was an awful rainbow once in heaven:
> We know her woof, her texture; she is given
> In the dull catalogue of common things.
> Philosophy will clip an Angel's wings.

6. John F. Hoffecker, "The Complexity of Neanderthal Technology," *PNAS* 115, no. 9 (2018): 1959–61.

7. Alister E. McGrath, "Chance and Providence in the Thought of William Paley," in *Abraham's Dice: Chance and Providence in the Monotheistic Traditions*, ed. Karl Giberson (Oxford: Oxford University Press, 2016), 240–59.

8. For the importance of how Keats "saw" nature, see Paul Endo, "Seeing Romantically in *Lamia*," *ELH* 66, no. 1 (1999): 111–28.

Keats worried that a purely scientific account of nature both robbed it of its beauty and eliminated its capacity to act as a sign of the transcendent. The "philosophy" to which Keats refers is "natural philosophy," a term widely used around this time as a near equivalent to the "natural sciences."[9] Keats here complains of the effect of reducing the beautiful and awesome phenomena of nature to the cold abstractions of scientific theory. Such a strategy, he argues, is aesthetically impoverishing, emptying nature of its beauty and mystery, and reduces it to something cold and clinical. In doing so, of course, he evoked the ire of Richard Dawkins,[10] who somewhat condescendingly dismissed Keats's concerns precisely because Dawkins's blinkered scientism prevented him from realizing that there was a genuine problem here. A natural theology affirms a semiotic relationship between the world and God, the creation and creator—and in doing so, blocks the notion that a scientific account of the natural world is the *only* legitimate way of understanding it. Other perspectives and approaches need to be invoked and integrated to give a proper account of our world.

Michael also offers a helpful overview of attempts to prove God's existence by argument, making some pertinent criticisms. My own view is that such arguments are helpful in displaying the rationality of religious belief and are in many cases best seen as a demonstration of the capacity of a Christian way of thinking to accommodate scientific observations. Such arguments need not compel belief in God; they nevertheless indicate the potential capacity of such a belief to explain our world, whether epistemically or ontically.

Methodological Naturalism and Science

Like Michael, I take the view that the natural sciences make use of an empirical method generally known as "methodological naturalism." This distinguishes the empirical sciences from other forms of human knowledge production, such as philosophy and theology. Some, of course, take the view that scientific knowledge is the *only* valid form of knowledge. Science thus offers a monopolistic and privileged access to

---

9. For the subtlety of this distinction, see David Cahan, ed. *From Natural Philosophy to the Sciences: Writing the History of Nineteenth-Century Science* (Chicago: University of Chicago Press, 2003).

10. Richard Dawkins, *Unweaving the Rainbow: Science, Delusion and the Appetite for Wonder* (London: Allen Lane, 1998).

truth. I can see no reason for believing this rather dogmatic statement, which often seems to reflect anxieties within some sections of the scientific community over the continuing influence of the humanities on wider cultural discussions.

Michael's critique of scientistic writers such as Lawrence Krauss is well taken, and I am in agreement with him on this point. Science is simply not equipped to deal with the category of the "supernatural" and hence has no authority to speak on the issue. There is a spectrum of human knowledge, and "scientific knowledge" constitutes a range within that spectrum. I try to avoid using the phrase "the scientific method," as it is clear there are multiple scientific methods—but it is clear that these methods all, though in different ways, develop their ideas using the principle of methodological naturalism. That's what distinguishes scientific forms of knowledge from other forms of knowledge. It does not define or determine what is true knowledge, as if other claims to "knowledge" are disqualified on account of the method(s) they use in developing their ideas.

Scientific knowledge, in the first place, takes the form of an accumulation of observations—Aristotle's "phenomena," which are integral to the scientific method. It is misleading to describe these as "facts," in that this fails to take into account the entanglement of theory and observation, which means that something is a "fact" when seen from one specific (if unacknowledged) theoretical perspective. We might think here of the philosopher Alasdair MacIntyre's famous quip that "facts, like telescopes and wigs for gentlemen, were a seventeenth-century invention."[11]

Yet science then proceeds to a second stage of the reflective process, in which it asks what larger picture or more general way of looking at things is best able to accommodate these observations. In other words, science seeks a theory—a way of beholding things—that colligates (to use William Whewell's term) these observations, as if they were empirical pearls held together by a theoretical string. This helps us understand why scientific knowledge is provisional: new observations (often due to technological advances) have to be accommodated within existing theories, which often require modification in their light. Think,

---

11. Alasdair C. MacIntyre, *Whose Justice? Which Rationality?* (Notre Dame: University of Notre Dame Press, 1988), 357. For further reflections, see Martin Carrier, "Values and Objectivity in Science: Value-Ladenness, Pluralism and the Epistemic Attitude," *Science & Education* 22 (2013): 2547–68.

for example, of the discovery of the redshifting of galactic spectra in the 1920s and the slow realization of its implications for our understanding of the origins of the universe.

Up to this point, Michael and I are taking a similar trajectory. Yet I now find myself facing a problem that does not arise with Michael's approach—namely, how to connect the different regions of the spectrum of human knowledge. My dialogical approach *requires* me to engage and correlate, to bring into conversation, two spectral zones—science and Christianity. Yet my own personal reluctance to be restricted by disciplinary frontiers makes me want to find some way of trying to correlate *multiple* regions of this spectrum. So how might I do this?

In my original article, I explore the Renaissance metaphor of God's two books—the "book of nature" and the "book of Scripture." Yet while this imaginative analogy offers a helpful way of framing the "scientific" and "Christian" zones of the spectrum of human knowledge, it has little to offer to wider attempts to correlate other regions. Such a broader range of interdisciplinary dialogue is, however, encouraged by thinking of specific disciplines offering different "perspectives" on a complex reality, or engaging different "levels" of this reality. These frameworks allow for at least a degree of correlation, although they are frustratingly resistant to the kind of precision some would regard as essential to the process of knowledge production.

It is, of course, clear that some scientists consider a commitment to an ontological materialism to be integral to the scientific enterprise. This is perhaps surprising; why should an essentially empirical discipline be thought to entail an *a priori* philosophical commitment of this sort? For most scientists, the natural sciences are philosophically agnostic, presupposing no metaphysical beliefs, even if they may point to some as a result of empirical investigation. Yet such ensuing beliefs would then be *a posteriori*, arising from scientific investigation, without themselves being its necessary presuppositions. A *methodological* naturalism does not entail an *ontological* naturalism. As British philosopher of science Roy Bhaskar pointed out relentlessly, epistemology does not determine ontology.[12] It is also interesting to note that old-fashioned scientific

---

12. For Bhaskar's views on this, see Roy Bhaskar, *The Possibility of Naturalism: A Philosophical Critique of the Contemporary Human Sciences*, 3rd ed. (London: Routledge, 1998).

materialists have yet to catch up with the "new materialism" of writers such as Bruno Latour,[13] which raises some awkward questions about the approaches to materialism that are uncritically accepted as the received wisdom in scientistic circles, which so often seem to be wedded to an eighteenth-century mechanistic materialism.

What about Homo Sapiens?

The question of the place of humanity within nature remains complex, not least because from a scientific perspective we have to see ourselves as natural creatures attempting to understand the natural world of which we are part. This paradox has often been widely regarded, perhaps most intriguingly by Max Planck, as the foundational figure of quantum theory: "Science cannot solve the ultimate mystery of nature. And that is because, in the last analysis, we ourselves are part of nature and therefore part of the mystery that we are trying to solve."[14]

Michael is quite clear in stating that science offers an account of the origins of humanity that does not make reference to divine action. While I agree with him, this is perhaps a truth of definition, in that the natural sciences are here defined (or at least characterized) in terms of their use of, and dependence upon, a methodological naturalism. It is important to recognize that this principle takes different forms in different scientific disciplines. I remain resistant to the phrase "*the* scientific method," preferring to speak of "scientific methods" in the plural, or "a scientific method" in the singular. Yet despite such disciplinary variation, there are sufficient commonalities to allow us to apply this method to the question of human origins. To put the outcome bluntly: science does not recognize a divine role in the emergence of humanity.

Yet that blunt statement must be read slowly, and appreciated—both in terms of what it says and what it does *not* say. Strictly speaking, science does not recognize any divine role in the functioning of the natural world; it does not—indeed it *cannot*—exclude this, on the basis of its core methods. Scientific accounts of the world, including the origins of humanity, can be accommodated within an agnostic, theistic, or atheistic framework. None is demanded by science; none is endorsed

13. Simon Choat, "Science, Agency and Ontology: A Historical-Materialist Response to New Materialism," *Political Studies* 66, no. 4 (2018): 1027–42.

14. Max Planck, *Where Is Science Going?* (New York: W. W. Norton & Co., 1932), 217.

by science. Darwin himself was quite clear about this, even if he is misrepresented by those who want to present him as a New Atheist guru. While Darwin was critical of Christianity at points, it is important to note that he did not see his evolutionary theories as raising fundamental difficulties for religious belief.[15] Leading theologians of the Church of England in the 1870s shared that view, even if this scholarly observation is often obscured by the superficial populist atheist polemic so regrettably deployed by Richard Dawkins.

What science does exclude is the idea, resting on a highly questionable biblical hermeneutic, that the world was created about six thousand years ago.[16] This belief, which gained much support in England during the Elizabethan and Jacobean periods, rests on a specific and deeply problematic way of reading the Old Testament,[17] making certain controlling assumptions that can now be seen to be wrong and that are not demanded or legitimated by the biblical texts themselves. This spurious dating of the origins of the world and humanity rests on a flawed interpretation of the Old Testament and is not in any way normative for Christians. For biblical writers, the doctrine of creation does not concern the date of the inception of the universe but its meaning and place in the purposes of God. This theological interpretation of purpose and place of the universe and humanity does not depend on chronological specificity.

In this short response to Michael, I have tried to critically and constructively engage some of his core ideas. He insists on the independence of Christianity and science; I insist on acknowledging and respecting their distinctiveness while believing they can and should be brought into dialogue with each other. If, as Amy Lee suggests,[18] religion and science can be thought of as two distinct languages, I have tried to become bilingual. The strength of Michael's position is that it isolates both science and religion, thus allowing both autonomy and freedom from

---

15. For a good account by an atheist writer, see Raymond Tallis, *Aping Mankind: Neuromania, Darwinitis and the Misrepresentation of Humanity* (London: Routledge, 2014).

16. Patrick Wyse Jackson, *The Chronologers' Quest: Episodes in the Search for the Age of the Earth* (Cambridge: Cambridge University Press, 2006), 14–27.

17. James Barr, "Why the World Was Created in 4004 BC: Archbishop Ussher and Biblical Chronology," *Bulletin of the John Rylands University* 67 (1984–5): 575–608.

18. Amy H. Lee, "Science and Religion as Languages: Understanding the Science–Religion Relationship using Metaphors, Analogies, and Models," *Zygon* 54, no. 4 (2019): 880–908.

external interference. Scientists can do science without religious interference; Christians can get on with their lives without feeling science undermines their faith.

Yet my overall conclusion is that the strength of Michael's position is also its weakness. We are left with two disconnected ways of thinking and bodies of knowledge, which can easily lead to the marginalization of religion in a scientific culture, and science in a religious culture. In my original article, I noted John Dewey's concern that we seem unable or unwilling to integrate our "thoughts about the world" with our thoughts about "value and purpose."[19] My own approach tries to secure—or at least to lay the groundwork for securing—such an integration, however limited and incomplete, while being alert to the difficulties associated with this enterprise. Edward O. Wilson speaks for many in despairing about the human failure to respect the complexity of our world and to draw on both science and faith in trying to inhabit it meaningfully. "We are drowning in information, while starving for wisdom."[20] I am not sure whether, as Wilson suggests, we can (or should) achieve a unification of human knowledge. But creating conceptual space for a productive conversation seems to be a good start—even if much more needs to be done!

19. John Dewey, *The Quest for Certainty* (New York: Capricorn, 1960), 255.
20. E. O. Wilson, *Consilience: The Unity of Knowledge* (New York: Vintage, 1999), 294.

BRUCE GORDON

I've known Michael personally for about twenty years, though it's been a while since I've had the pleasure of interacting with him. He hasn't changed much—his lighthearted, irreverent conviviality are still very much on display. But what should we make of this advice, from a non-believer no less, on how Christians should think about the relationship between their faith and modern science? It's certainly playful and, one suspects, contains elements that are tongue-in-cheek, but let's take it seriously. Since I have limited space, I'll focus on just three themes: (1) the relationship between faith and reason (science) and Michael's thesis of their "independence;" (2) the question of natural theology, natural selection, and the argument from evil; and (3) whether methodological naturalism is central to science and should preclude arguments for miracles (the resurrection of Jesus especially) as "bad science, bad history, and bad philosophy" (p. 40).

On Faith and Reason

Michael's consideration of faith and reason begins with an easy target—the kind of biblical literalism that leads to young-earth creationism and puts the beliefs of some Christians in conflict with science—and moves to the conclusion that belief in God should rest on faith, not reason. After all, he tells us, Jesus said to Thomas, who had to see to believe, that those who believe *without* seeing are the ones who are really blessed (John 20:29). Now, we should note both that Jesus gave Thomas the evidence he needed (John 20:27) and that in the very next verses John reports, "Jesus performed many other signs in the presence of his disciples, which are not recorded in this book. But these are written *that you may believe* that Jesus is the Messiah, the Son of God" (John 20:30–31, emphasis added). So evidence *is* provided as a basis for belief. This undermines what Michael tries to sell us, which seems to be that faith has nothing to do with knowledge; rather, it's better than knowledge because it "cannot be wrong" (p. 24). This idea that faith cannot be wrong fits well with Michael's conception of Christianity and science as "independent." It suggests that faith is a purely private matter immune to public rationality. But faith in God isn't a way of *knowing* God exists; it's a *trust* in God, resting on reason and knowledge while simultaneously supporting them.

Let's backtrack a bit. It's a modern misconception to see faith as a path to belief that's an alternative to reason. This insulates Christianity's intellectual content from reasoned criticism or support. The social effect, of course, is to make Christian belief unreasonable, isolate it from knowledge, render it private and personal, and destabilize its content. This misconception arises from the modernist attitude that says science is objective and everything else, especially moral and spiritual knowledge, is opinion. But this attitude undermines science itself. Believing that science is a pathway to knowledge assumes the world is ordered in a way that's intelligible to the human mind. This belief has no scientific justification. Furthermore, scientific rationality is grounded in human reason, but why think human reasoning leads to truth? Providing reasons for its truth-conduciveness begs the question by assuming it. We have no choice but to trust (have faith in) our reason from the outset. Is there any basis, though, for thinking that reason gets us truth about the world? Reid's response to Hume is relevant:

> Reason, says the sceptic, is the only judge of truth, and you ought to throw off every opinion and every belief that is not grounded on reason. Why, sir, should I believe the faculty of reason more than that of perception?—they both came out of the same shop, and were made by the same artist; and if he puts one piece of false ware into my hands, what should hinder him from putting another?[1]

---

1. Thomas Reid, *Thomas Reid's Inquiry and Essays*, eds. Keith Lehrer and Ronald E. Beanblossom (Indianapolis: Bobbs-Merrill, 1975), 84–85.

For instance, if we can't say perception produces true beliefs rather than beliefs merely useful for survival, why think reason fares better? Christian theism beats Michael's evolutionary naturalism as a ground for trusting human reason.

What about Christian spiritual knowledge? It is knowledge, but there are conditions on its availability. Blaise Pascal wisely observed:

> [W]ishing to appear openly to those who seek him with all their heart and hidden from those who shun him with all their heart, he has qualified our knowledge of him by giving signs which can be seen by those who seek him and not by those who do not.[2]

If we do not see these signs, yet desire them, how do we begin? We can't make ourselves believe something. Pascal counsels:

> You want to find faith and you do not know the road . . . learn from those who were once bound like you . . . follow the way by which they began. They behaved just as if they did believe, taking holy water, having masses said, and so on. . . . This diminishes the passions which are your great obstacles. . . . What harm will come to you from pursuing this course? You will be faithful, honest, humble, grateful, full of good works, a sincere, true friend . . . at every step. . . . Your gain is so certain and your risk so negligible that in the end you will realize that you have wagered on something certain and infinite for which you have paid nothing.[3]

So behave as if you believe and walk the path that believers walk. Adapting Pascal's practices to Michael's "very Protestant, conservative nonbelief" (p. 23) would minimally include study of and meditation on Scripture, prayer, private and corporate worship, and giving of one's time and resources in service to others.[4] It is the path of *imitatio Christi*

---

2. Blaise Pascal, *Pensées*, trans. A. J. Krailsheimer (New York: Penguin, 1966), fragment 232 (p. 101) and fragment 149 (p. 80).
3. Pascal, *Pensées*, fragment 418, p. 152.
4. See Dallas Willard's discussion of Christian spiritual knowledge in *Knowing Christ Today: Why We Can Trust Spiritual Knowledge* (San Francisco: HarperOne, 2009); and Richard

that transforms character and perception. It changes attitudes, initiates relational contact with God, and reliably promotes growth in spiritual knowledge.[5] Rightly so, for God promises "you will seek me and find me when you seek me with all your heart " (Jer. 29:13), but if you suppress the truth in unrighteousness, your thinking will become futile and your foolish heart will be darkened (Rom. 1:18, 21). Seeking God is a condition for knowing his reality and being rightly related to him, for "without faith [trust] it is impossible to please God, because anyone who comes to him must believe that he exists and that he rewards those who earnestly seek him" (Heb. 11:6).

Biblical faith is not blind assent to propositions for which there is no evidence. It is trusting God based on knowledge of who he is and what he has done. The disciples' knowledge of who Jesus was grounded their faith and the Spirit's empowerment of them to "make disciples of all nations" (Matt. 28:19), birthing the Christian church and transforming the world. We trust God because of what we *know* when facing what we do not know. This is the correct understanding of passages like 2 Corinthians 5:7 (KJV): "We walk by faith, not by sight," and Hebrews 11:1: "faith is confidence in what we hope for and assurance about what we do not see." Faith rests on prior knowledge of God, grounding this trust. That's why Jesus chastised Thomas. Thomas knew Jesus. Before his crucifixion, Jesus had told his disciples that he would die and rise again (Matt. 16:21). When Thomas heard that Christ had risen and that

---

J. Foster's classic *Celebration of Discipline: The Path to Spiritual Growth* (San Francisco: Harper Collins, 1988).

5. "What about different religions?" is the inevitable question. In matters where world religions make inconsistent claims, they cannot all be true. Concluding they're all false is unwarranted, however. All world religions attain *some* spiritual and moral knowledge through their practices, and all of them produce spiritual effects. From a Christian standpoint, however, when these are incompatible with core Christianity, what has been learned has not been understood correctly. Christianity offers a better explanation. Can such disputes be settled by rational argumentation? Yes, partly. The truth, internal coherence, and explanatory power of different religions can be compared. Historical religions such as Christianity have advantages in this regard and, potentially, disadvantages. Their historical claims are evaluable against the evidence of history and science. If they pass muster, this counts in their favor. Furthermore, each religion has a conceptual structure. Does it make sense and is it internally consistent? If so, this too counts in its favor. Finally, each religion makes claims about the nature of reality and the purpose of humanity. Which provides the best explanation for the universe's existence, human nature and purpose, and the very possibility of rational explanation itself? Looking at world religions this way helps us evaluate which one provides the best path to growth in spiritual knowledge. For parallel reflections, see Willard, *Knowing Christ Today*, 169–91.

other disciples had seen him, Thomas's prior knowledge should have been sufficient for belief. He'd have been blessed if he'd believed rather than having to be shown. Similarly, we're blessed when we trust God for the future on the basis of what we *do* know and *have* seen.

Michael's "independence" model is problematic. The implication is that science and Christianity have their own domains and their claims do not overlap: Christianity occupies the realm of *faith* and *value*; science occupies the realm of *reason* and *factuality*. This is both naive and false. Doing science requires prior faith in the orderliness of the universe and its amenability to human reason, along with faith in the truth-conduciveness of human cognition, none of which is scientifically justifiable without begging the question. Scientists also have faith in certain epistemic, aesthetic, and moral values that aren't scientific: explanatory simplicity, mathematical symmetry, coherence with accepted science, predictive and retrodictive power, unifying power, programmatic fecundity, and honesty in handling data, to name a few. Furthermore, biblical Christianity is a historical religion, so its central claims overlap with scientific and historical investigation. It affirms that our universe had a beginning and isn't self-sufficient (Gen. 1:1; Job 38:4–7; Isa. 42:5; John 1:3; Acts 17:24–25, 28; Col. 1:16–17; 2 Tim. 1:9; Titus 1:2; Heb. 1:2–3; Rev. 4:11); that God's existence is evident in creation (Ps. 19:1–4; Rom. 1:20); that gospel accounts of Jesus's life, teaching, death, and resurrection are based on eyewitness testimonies capable of being carefully investigated (Luke 1:1–4); that Jesus's resurrection is a widely corroborated historical event central to Christianity's truth (1 Cor. 15:3–8, 12–18); and that biblical writers, properly interpreted, speak of events in space-time history that are investigable with scientific, archaeological, and historical tools (1 John 1:1).

On Natural Theology, Natural Selection, and the Problem of Evil

Michael loosely discusses the ontological, cosmological/causal, and teleological arguments, undermining the last with an equally casual discussion of natural selection and the argument from evil. A more careful treatment reveals a cumulative consilience of natural theological arguments. Anselm's ontological argument, Michael notes, proceeds from the definition of God, as the being than which none greater can be conceived, to his existence. Leibniz's ontological argument focused on the *possibility* of

God's existence as a necessary being. Plantinga uses Leibniz's strategy, rendering Anselmian divine perfections as great-making properties. Using Leibniz's idea of worlds that might possibly exist, inclusive of ours, which actually exists, Plantinga assumes the Anselmian conception of God is metaphysically possible, so God exists in some possible world. God is therefore a being who is *maximally excellent* in every possible world in which he exists, where maximal excellence entails maximal properties such as omniscience, omnipotence, aseity, necessary being, and moral perfection. Maximal properties have *intrinsic maxima*—they couldn't be any greater. For instance, God is omnipotent; he can do everything that is logically and metaphysically possible to do. God's essential possession of *only* maximal properties avoids the necessary existence of perfect islands, for example, because such things lack objective properties with intrinsic maxima (we can't say how long its beaches are or how many coconuts it has). Furthermore, God is unique; the existence of another being like him would, for example, compromise his omnipotence. God therefore possesses what Plantinga calls *maximal greatness*. We then argue:[6]

1. It's possible a maximally great being exists (the maximal property of necessary existence is possibly exemplified).
2. If it's possible a maximally great being exists, it exists in some possible world.
3. If a maximally great being exists in some possible world, it exists in *every* possible world (because it exists necessarily).
4. If a maximally great being exists in every possible world, it exists in the actual world.
5. If a maximally great being exists in the actual world, a maximally great being exists.
6. Therefore, a maximally great being exists.

Since this argument is valid, Michael needs to reject one of its premises. The only noninferential premise is the first, asserting it's possible there's a maximally great being. Why should this be true? Perhaps it

---

6. See Alvin Plantinga, *The Nature of Necessity* (Oxford: Clarendon, 1974), chapter 10, and Bill Craig's discussion on pp. 914–17 of "Theism Defended" in Bruce Gordon and William Dembski, eds. *The Nature of Nature: Examining the Role of Naturalism in Science* (Wilmington, DE: ISI, 2011), 901–17.

isn't. We're owed an argument either way. What's been shown, therefore, is that God's existence is either necessary or impossible. To cast doubt, Michael needs to argue (he doesn't) that it's impossible for a maximally great being to exist and we need to argue it's possible there's a maximally great being who necessarily exists.

Is God's necessary existence possible? This is where cosmological arguments become relevant. Consider any contingent state of affairs— for instance, the existence of our universe—and let p be a proposition representing this state of affairs. Every state of affairs is representable by a (suitably complex) proposition, and every contingent proposition represents a contingent state of affairs. We now argue:[7]

1. For all p, if p is a contingently true proposition, it's *possible* there's a proposition q such that q completely explains p.
2. (1) is uncontroversial: given any contingently true proposition, it's merely *possible* there exists an explanation for its being true.
3. The fact that q explains p entails both p and q, since q cannot explain p if q isn't true, and p must be true if it's explained.
4. For a contradiction, assume that p has no explanation.
5. Let p^* be the following proposition: p is true and there's no explanation for p.
6. Since p is contingently true, so is p^*.
7. By (1), there's a possible world W at which p^* has a complete explanation, q.
8. If a conjunction has been completely explained, so has each conjunct.
9. Since p is a conjunct of p^* and q completely explains p^* at W, q explains p at W.
10. But q also explains p^* at W, so p^* is true at W, thus there's *no* explanation for p at W.
11. Hence, p both has and lacks an explanation at W, a contradiction.
12. The supposition that p has no explanation leads to a contradiction and therefore is false.
13. Thus, for any contingently true proposition p, p has an explanation.

7. See Richard Gale and Alexander Pruss, "A New Cosmological Argument," *Religious Studies* 35 (1999): 461–76, and Alexander Pruss, *The Principle of Sufficient Reason: A Reassessment* (Cambridge: Cambridge University Press, 2006), 234–35.

Since every contingently true proposition represents a contingent state of affairs that's actual, and every contingently true proposition has an explanation, every contingent state of affairs has an explanation. This principle of sufficient reason is necessarily true. Since what is contingent cannot ultimately be explained by another contingent thing—infinite regresses of contingent explanations (were such possible) would themselves be contingent—ultimate explanations must terminate upon something noncontingent, i.e., necessary. It's a necessary truth, therefore, that a necessary being is the ultimate explanation for contingent states of affairs, including our universe's existence.

What is this necessary being? It transcends and explains the contingent existence of space, time, matter, and energy, so it's logically and ontologically prior to the universe, sufficient unto itself, nonspatiotemporal, and immaterial. It cannot be an abstract object such as a mathematical equation, for such things are causally inert. What's left? A timeless immaterial necessarily existent being capable of creating a universe has to be an immensely powerful and knowledgeable *personal* being possessed of a rational will. This is certainly suggestive of God's maximally excellent attributes.

The activity of such a being might be evidenced by features of nature that indicate design or purpose. This moves us to the teleological argument. As Aquinas recognized and Hume belabored, the teleological argument doesn't get you to theism or the uniqueness of the designer. Nonetheless, it has an important place. Michael's response to it ("Natural selection! You don't need God.") is inadequate. Even if natural selection *could* explain the evolution of life in terms of differential reproductive success, it *wouldn't* explain the existence of the universe; the life-permitting fine-tuning of the initial conditions, laws, and constants of nature; or the origin of life.

But natural selection isn't even adequate to explain the undirected evolution of life. My primary essay demonstrates this by examining the shortcomings of anatomical and molecular homology and the waiting-time problem (among other considerations). Michael's essay does nothing to ameliorate these considerations. He never argues that natural selection as a blind watchmaker is sufficient to do away with teleology. He merely asserts it. He considers three explanations involving natural selection (pp. 29–34) he finds inadequate—evolutionary arms races, evolutionary convergence,[8] and the zero-force evolutionary law—but never shows how natural selection does the job without divine assistance. In light of my argument that it can't, he needs to make his case with some nontrivial examples.

This leads to the crux of the issue for Michael: the problem of evil and suffering. A world of nature red in tooth and claw, with monsters like Adolf Hitler, with earthquakes and tsunamis and massive loss of life, and with seemingly purposeless pain and suffering, is not, for Michael, a world with an omnipotent, omniscient, and omnibenevolent God. Natural selection might explain a lot of the world's suffering, but a good God wouldn't make such a world. Michael dismisses as "smug" best-possible-world theodicies that explain moral evil using free will and natural evil using natural processes that make earth habitable and natural regularities as a background for rational expectations (p. 33). He rejects eschatological theodicies where "God will make it all right in the end." He says, "I don't want the Christian God to exist" (p. 33). Needless to say, the charge of smugness is *ad hominem* and does nothing to undermine free will or natural regularity theodicies, and Michael's dislike of Christianity is no more relevant to eschatological theodicies and God's existence than math phobia is to the truths of arithmetic. Furthermore, beyond these theodicies lie many more: soul-making theodicies, greater-good theodicies, *felix culpa* theodicies, christological theodicies, and (despite my reservations) skeptical theist theodicies. There's no shortage of Christian resources for addressing the problem of evil and suffering.

More revealing is the very foundation of good and evil. Michael thinks science explains human behavior—that the just-so stories of sociobiologists, evolutionary psychologists, and evolutionary ethicists

---

8. Evolutionary convergence is a genuine phenomenon with a lot of evidence for it. Interestingly, it creates further problems for evolutionary arguments from anatomical and molecular homologies. Homology is standardly interpreted as being explained by and as evidence for universal common descent. But evolutionary convergence provides many examples of the same structures occurring in different evolutionary lineages where the last common ancestor *lacked* the homologous feature. Common descent cannot be the correct explanation for homology in such cases, nor can homologous structures be evidence for evolution here. So what does homology really show? Consider Fazale R. Rana, "Molecular Convergence: Repeated Evolution or Repeated Designs?" in Gordon and Dembski, eds. *The Nature of Nature*, 460–82.

explain why we have the moral beliefs and behaviors we do,[9] even though science can't ground objective morality (pp. 41–46). Those familiar with Michael's other writings also know he thinks "morality is an illusion fobbed off on us by our genes."[10] If so, nothing's really wrong with someone killing Michael and taking credit for his work; it's just that Michael is evolutionarily conditioned to think there is. Nonsense. The certainty of our objective moral obligations to one another vastly exceeds that of the just-so stories of evolutionary ethics. Furthermore, even if the stories were true, they could be natural reinforcements of objective morality just as plausibly as grounds for its dismissal. Since the objectivity of evil seems so compelling, however, perhaps we should argue this way: If God does not exist, our belief that pain and suffering is objectively evil is illusory. But pain and suffering *are* objectively evil, so our belief is not illusory. Therefore, God exists. What you take the "problem of evil" to be depends on what you think the proper conclusion is. We can go further. Everything God created was good, Augustine says, and since evil isn't good, it wasn't created by God. But since God created *everything* and God did not create evil, evil isn't a real thing. What is it, then? Augustine argued it's a privation of the good caused by the will turning from the highest good (God himself) to that which is lesser. It's not the lesser object, but the turning, that is evil. This turning affects everything, including angelic and demonic activity, and (I'd argue) manifests itself transhistorically.

On Methodological Naturalism and Miracles

Michael insists on methodological naturalism (MN) in philosophy and history, not just science. How else should we interpret his remark that arguments for the resurrection of Jesus are "bad science, bad history, and bad philosophy" (p. 40)? His claim is so obviously false I'm inclined to dismiss it as ill-advised bravado. We cannot, with a straight face, call Richard Swinburne, N. T. Wright, Bill Craig, Craig Evans, Craig

---

9. David Berlinski criticizes such explanations compared to "the model for what science should be" in "The Origins of Mind," in Gordon and Dembski, eds. *The Nature of Nature*, 713–25. On the inadequacy of naturalistic ethics, see Dallas Willard's "Naturalism's Incapacity to Capture the Good Will," in Gordon and Dembski, eds., *The Nature of Nature*, 865–79.

10. Michael Ruse and Edward Wilson, "The Evolution of Ethics," in James E. Huchingson, ed., *Religion and the Natural Sciences: The Range of Engagement* (Orlando: Harcourt, 1993), 310.

Blomberg, and many other competent, credentialed, and well-published thinkers, bad philosophers and irresponsible historians. So let's call his bluff.

I argued in my essay that no naturalistic account of physical regularities was philosophically or quantum-mechanically tenable (pp. 136–39); physical regularities are grounded in something that transcends physical reality. The best explanation is they're regularities of divine action: nature's regularity is an active expression of divine faithfulness. Miracles aren't therefore a matter of God violating autonomous laws of nature, but of God acting in extraordinary rather than ordinary ways. Furthermore, departures from the ordinary course of nature aren't just possible, they're sometimes evidentially detectable as deviations from what nature's ordinary course would permit. But if the behavior of nature doesn't have a natural explanation when it's regular, let alone when it isn't, MN is obviously the wrong way to do science. I've critiqued MN here (pp. 145–50) and quite extensively elsewhere;[11] I won't repeat myself. Suffice to say that if MN were a *requirement* of science, science *couldn't be done* in its absence. Since this isn't true, MN isn't required. All science requires is a broad uniformitarianism allowing inferences to the best explanation that include, when needed, intelligent causation (pp. 157–64).

Academic historical reasoning also frequently argues that one among multiple competing explanations of an event is superior. Since there's no reason to support MN in history when it's not even required by science, insisting on MN when evaluating the evidence for Christ's resurrection simply begs the question against it and the significance that Christians attribute to it. *This* is poor philosophy and poor history! If space permitted, I would argue for the historicity of Christ's resurrection and the New Testament's interpretation of it as true and the best explanation

---

11. See Bruce Gordon, "Is Intelligent Design Science?" in W. Dembski and J. Kushiner, eds., *Signs of Intelligence*, 2001, 193–216; Bruce Gordon, "In Defense of Uniformitarianism," *Perspectives on Science and the Christian Faith* 65, no. 2 (2013): 79–86; and Bruce Gordon, "Scientific Explanations are Not Limited to Natural Causes," and "Gordon's Response to Bishop," in Steven Cowan, ed. *Problems in Epistemology and Metaphysics: An Introduction to Contemporary Debates* (New York: Bloomsbury Academic, 2020). See also Stephen Meyer, "Sauce for the Goose: Intelligent Design, Scientific Methodology, and the Demarcation Problem," in Gordon and Dembski, eds. *The Nature of Nature*, 95–131.

by far for what is known. But space does not permit, so I'll leave you with some good resources instead (see footnote)[12] and hope that Michael will take the time to discover just how *good* the history and philosophy defending Jesus's resurrection and its significance are!

---

12. In no particular order: Richard Swinburne, *The Resurrection of God Incarnate* (Oxford: Oxford University Press, 2003); Richard Swinburne, *Was Jesus God?* (Oxford: Oxford University Press, 2008); N. T. Wright, *The Resurrection of the Son of God* (Minneapolis: Fortress, 2003); William Lane Craig, *Assessing the New Testament Evidence for the Historicity of the Resurrection of Jesus* (Lewiston: Edwin Mellen, 1989); William Lane Craig, *Reasonable Faith: Christian Truth and Apologetics*, 3rd ed. (Wheaton: Crossway, 2008), 207–404; Gary R. Habermas and Michael R. Licona, *The Case for the Resurrection of Jesus* (Grand Rapids: Kregel, 2004); Michael R. Licona, *The Resurrection of Jesus: A New Historiographical Approach* (Downers Grove, IL: InterVarsity Press, 2010); Lydia McGrew, *Hidden in Plain View: Undesigned Coincidences in the Gospels and Acts* (Chillicothe, OH: DeWard, 2017); Craig L. Blomberg, *The Historical Reliability of the New Testament* (Nashville: B&H Academic, 2016); Richard Bauckham, *Jesus and the Eyewitnesses: The Gospels as Eyewitness Testimony*, 2nd ed. (Grand Rapids: Eerdmans, 2017); and Craig S. Keener, *Miracles: The Credibility of the New Testament Accounts* 2 vols. (Grand Rapids: Baker Academic, 2011). There are *many* other excellent resources.

REJOINDER

MICHAEL RUSE

O n rereading what I have written, and what my two coauthors-cum-commentators have written on the subject of science and religion, I am struck forcibly how I and they are so very much in different worlds, paradigms if you like. They are believing, practicing Christians. Sometimes I sense they are further apart from each other than either is from me. But they are in, and I am not. Let me underline this. I am not a non-Christian saying: "Oh gosh! Oh gosh! I wish I could believe." I might say this about getting into Oxford or Harvard; but while (to take a very pertinent and up-to-date reference) I lie awake at night worrying about the well-being of my middle son, who is a first responder in the virus pandemic, my nonbelief does not make me lie awake at night worrying about my immortal soul. Perhaps Saint Paul was right—if you don't believe, you are in *big trouble*. Can't say I care.

So I am a person apart in this dialogue. I ask myself why this should be. A traditional Calvinist, like Alvin Plantinga, would say that it is because, in a way not true of Alister and Bruce, I am tainted with original sin.[1] Perhaps so, and I am quite prepared to say that I am sinful in a way—probably many ways—that Alister and Bruce are not. I doubt they, as teenagers, ever told a girl that it was her mind that attracted them to her. I do, however, take umbrage at the suggestion that I am more sinful than the defrocked, former cardinal Theodore McCarrick,

---

1. Alvin Plantinga, *Warranted Christian Belief* (New York: Oxford University Press, 2000).

who relinquished his red hat when it emerged that for over forty years he had systematically abused young men and boys, some not yet teenagers.

Perhaps I am the person apart because in this society, especially the kind of secular academic society within which I live and work, Christianity is so obviously a minority position, not much regarded by most of my fellows. I don't want to be a person apart. Well, possibly I don't want to be, but being in an unfashionable minority is nothing new. I am an evolutionary epistemologist and an evolutionary ethicist, and that is about as popular in proper-thinking analytic philosophy circles as a Salvation Army lassie in a house of ill repute.[2] I am also a nonstop accuser of Darwinians, making a secular religion of their science, and that goes over in humanist circles like the proverbial lead balloon.[3]

Perhaps it is because I am just not interested in these things. My wife and children are not so much nonbelievers as a-believers. My wife doesn't know the relationship between Abraham and Isaac and doesn't particularly want to know. The only one of my children out of five who has any scriptural knowledge is one who spent a year at a church school. He knows quite a bit, but it is all wrong. Don't ask him about the relationship between Abraham and Isaac. Gay partners? I won't tell you what kind of church school he went to, but I will note that many such schools in our neck of the woods are Anglican. I, to the contrary, am obsessed with these questions. I have been since my childhood Quaker upbringing. I think and talk about them nonstop.[4] What do you think I am doing right now? But it doesn't bring me any closer to belief; it really doesn't.

So where does that leave me? Well, I could just say different paradigms and leave it at that. Incommensurables. Alister and Bruce can

2. Michael Ruse, *Taking Darwin Seriously: A Naturalistic Approach to Philosophy* (Oxford: Blackwell, 1986); *A Philosopher Looks at Human Beings* (Cambridge: Cambridge University Press, 2021).

3. Michael Ruse, *The Evolution-Creation Struggle* (Cambridge, MA: Harvard University Press, 2005); Michael Ruse, *Darwinism as Religion: What Literature Tells Us About Evolution* (Oxford: Oxford University Press, 2017); Michael Ruse, *The Problem of War: Darwinism, Christianity, and Their Battle to Understand Human Conflict* (Oxford: Oxford University Press, 2018).

4. Michael Ruse, "A Darwinian Pilgrim's Early Progress," *Journal of Cognitive Historiography* 4 (2019): 151–64; Michael Ruse, "A Darwinian Pilgrim's Middle Progress," *Journal of Cognitive Historiography* 4 (2019): 165–79; Michael Ruse, "A Darwinian Pilgrim's Late Progress," *Journal of Cognitive Historiography* 4 (2019): 180–98.

and must wrestle with the relationship between science and religion. My approach is that of a person to whom science is open and religion is closed. It is not so much, for me, that religion and science cannot be reconciled. It is, for me, that there is nothing to reconcile. Which is all very well, but I cannot stop here. I have huge respect for people like Alister and Bruce. In some very important way, I feel we are travelers together through what John Keats called the vale of soul-making. Can I at least get closer to them by turning to what I refer to as my extreme Protestant nonbelief? What would be my attitude were I a believer? As one raised a Quaker, I am about as far from theistic personalism—God is one of the chaps—as it is possible to be.[5] I am drawn to mysticism. Now I see through a glass darkly. (Sorry, editors, there are times when only the King James Version will do.) I am very much into apophatic theology—I can say what God isn't; I cannot say what he is. With this kind of belief system—faith that cannot be justified or driven by reason but that demands a leap into the absurd—problems like that of evil fade away. Not the evil itself, obviously, but the need to reconcile its existence with the Creator. Simply, God moves in a mysterious way, his wonders to perform.

Let's push this approach for a minute. My counterfactual mystical approach to God applies to a problem nigh as great as that of evil. How do we reconcile our belief in Jesus as the incarnation with the very different beliefs of those outside our culture? Nineteenth-century evangelicals had no doubt that they were right and others were wrong.

> The heathen, in his blindness,
>   Bows down to wood and stone.
> Can we, whose souls are lighted
>   With wisdom from on high,
> Can we, to men benighted,
>   The lamp of life deny?

I just don't have the self-righteous confidence of those Victorians. My fellow philosopher (and incidentally a product of the same Quaker

---

5. Brian Davies and Michael Ruse, *Taking God Seriously* (Cambridge: Cambridge University Press, 2021).

school as I am) John Hick wrestled with this one, doing sterling work on interfaith projects in Birmingham, England (the city of my birth). He found the answer in the kind of theology I—he—endorse(d). Why would you expect people of different cultures to share religious beliefs? God knows what he is doing.[6]

Now, here is my point, or rather my question. Can my nonbelief be covered under this umbrella? I would not expect it to extend to a New Atheist, but I am not one of those. I am an agnostic. I just don't know. Unfortunately, I cannot in honesty say that this is enough. I don't believe. I don't have a God, however unknown, however mysterious. I just don't. My nonbelief is not in the same category as Islam and Buddhism and all the other religions. So then how do I deal with the comments of Alistair and Bruce on the topic of science and religion, both what they say positively and what they say critically of one such as me? It pains me to say that I think them fundamentally wrong. I don't mean they don't have the guts for nonbelief. There are lots of Christians far gutsier than I am. Start with Sophie Scholl of the White Rose group in Munich in 1943. She, as a Christian, lost her life opposing Hitler. The fact remains, however, that I think Alistair and Bruce are self-deceiving, desperate to avoid Albert Camus's conclusion that life is absurd. William James knew the score. On the one hand, the "sanest and best of us are of one clay with lunatics and prison inmates, and death finally runs the robustest of us down." On the other hand, thanks to religion, thanks to faith, "what we most dreaded has become the habitation of our safety, and the hour of our moral death has turned into our spiritual birthday. The time for tension in our soul is over, and that of happy relaxation, of calm deep breathing, of an eternal present, with no discordant future to be anxious about, has arrived."[7]

So that, I am afraid, is how I approach their arguments in these pages. They are papering over the untenable. In my world, my paradigm, if you like, they are doomed before they start. Let me take a couple of examples, one from each critic, to show what I mean. To be honest, I have some difficulty in finding one in Alister's response because he finds so much agreement between our positions! But there is the divide.

6. John Hick, *God Has Many Names* (Philadelphia: Westminster, 1980).

7. William James, *Varieties of Religious Experience: A Study in Human Nature* (New York: Longman, 1902), 47.

Right at the end he speaks of the strength and the *weakness* (I italicize) of my position. "We are left with two disconnected ways of thinking and bodies of knowledge, which can easily lead to the marginalization of religion in a scientific culture, and science in a religious culture." If I were in the God business, in the way I have sketched earlier in this response, I would simply say that you have entirely missed what I am about. I just don't see science and religion as things of the same nature at all.[8] One could not marginalize the other. Faith is not a bunch of claims, like "the earth goes around the sun." The whole point is that I don't know what God is like.

As it happens, I am not in the God business, so I do see science and religion in many respects in the same ballpark. I think there are ways of getting around the problems—I have shown how I think one might deal with Noah and the flood. But if you are going to keep pushing science and religion as going head to head, then you are absolutely right that science is going to marginalize religion—at the very least, it is going to make religion do what it is told. Original sin and atonement theory? Depends on a literal Adam and Eve. Adam sinned, his descendants, which include us, are tainted, the incarnation occurred so the Son of God could be crucified and atone for our sins—buy off God with his blood on the cross. Sorry, modern science says, no can do. There was never an original Adam and Eve, and every time you pick out candidates, they had parents just as good and bad as they were. No forbidden fruit. No God getting mad. No—thank God (and I mean this literally)—blood sacrifices. Now there are alternatives. Incarnation theory, older than atonement theory, sees Jesus on the cross as the embodiment of perfect love for us to emulate. No problem with literal Adams and Eves. But note, religion is doing what it is told, what it is allowed. Science need never do what religion tells it. I just don't see this as a weakness of my position.

Turning to Bruce, I have rather less difficulty in picking out our basic disagreement. Without prejudice, I see Bruce taking a much more traditional approach to science (or reason and evidential things in general) and religion (meaning here the Christian religion). Bruce does see

---

8. Michael Ruse, *Science and Spirituality: Making Room for Faith in the Age of Science* (Cambridge: Cambridge University Press, 2010).

them much more in the same business. Different ends perhaps, but on parallel tracks that can merge and help each other. For instance, Bruce refers to my treatment of the interaction of Darwin's theory with the argument from design. He sees me as using Darwin to try to undermine the argument, which of course (in principle) it could do if they were in the same business. In fact, I am not dissing the argument from design. If I were a Christian, I would be absolutely convinced that I see design in God's creation. The smile of a child, the freshness of a daisy, the early morning sunlight on the Canadian Rockies. It is just that, as John Henry Newman says, I don't see the one trying to do the job of the other. Darwin couldn't undermine the argument as I read it, because it is just not the sort of thing that could be undermined by science.

I should say I don't find any of this as blood-pressure raising. When Bruce apparently endorses that favorite of Alvin Plantinga, *felix culpa* arguments—God let the bad happen so great good could be the consequence—the measurement goes off the scale.[9] God let Adam eat the fruit so Jesus could die in agony on the cross so we can be saved. The evil of eating the forbidden fruit was outweighed by the good of having nails hammered into your hands. Oh, and incidentally, it just so happens that along the way people tainted with original sin did some dreadful things. Tough luck on Anne Frank dying of typhus in Bergen-Belsen. I just simply don't know what to say. I thank God we are in different paradigms. I am not surprised that at the end of his response, Bruce recommends for my further reading no less than eleven books proving the historical authenticity of the resurrection and adds "there are *many* other excellent resources." My instant reaction? "The lady doth protest too much methinks." The point is that I think they are all irrelevant. As one for whom science is prior, which means universal coverage by natural law, such works are rather sad exercises in self-deception. In any case, whether Jesus physically rose from the dead simply doesn't matter. What does matter is that the disciples, who had absolutely no reason to be other than downcast—their leader and friend had just died in the most painful and degrading manner—suddenly felt in their hearts that their Redeemer liveth. (Sorry, editors, KJV again.)

---

9. Alvin Plantinga, "Supralapsarianism or 'O Felix Culpa'" in *Christian Faith and the Problem of Evil*, Peter Van Inwagen, ed. (Grand Rapids: Eerdmans, 2004), 1–25.

I am going on, my time and space exhausted. When I was a kid, there were always within the Meeting (the Quaker term for congregation) several rather self-important members, known, not entirely affectionately, as "Weighty Friends." They would get up and hold forth at length, using the self-created theology that is both the strength and weakness of Quakerism, on some topic of burning significance. I fear I am turning into a Weighty Friend. I will shut up.

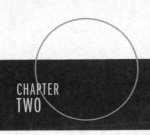

ALISTER MCGRATH

Clarifying the possible relationships of Christianity and the natural sciences is undoubtedly one of the most important and interesting questions facing the academy and the church. Yet any discussion of the relationship between Christianity and the natural sciences has been made problematic by the lingering influence of past controversies and popular misreadings of complex historical episodes.[1] Modern scholarship has successfully deconstructed popular historical accounts of many of these controversies, exposing the power dynamics and cultural agendas of many of those who seek to portray science and Christianity as locked in mortal combat.

In a series of important and influential historical studies of science and religion in the 1990s and beyond, focusing especially on the nineteenth century, Oxford scholar John Hedley Brooke has argued that serious scholarship in the history of science has revealed "so extraordinarily rich and complex a relationship between science and religion in the past that general theses are difficult to sustain. The real lesson turns out to be the complexity."[2] Brooke's analysis has found widespread support within the scholarly community. Peter Harrison has pointed

---

1. For a good overview, see Ronald L. Numbers, ed. *Galileo Goes to Jail and Other Myths About Science and Religion* (Cambridge, MA: Harvard University Press, 2009).

2. John Hedley Brooke, *Science and Religion: Some Historical Perspectives* (Cambridge: Cambridge University Press, 1991), 6.

out that "study of the historical relations between science and religion does not reveal any simple pattern at all,"[3] such as the monomyth of the "conflict" narrative. It does, however, disclose a "general trend"—that for most of the time, religion has *facilitated* scientific inquiry.

There is no "right" or privileged way of understanding the relationship of Christianity—or any other religion—to the natural sciences. Instead, we find a rich range of possibilities, some of which are declared to be normative by those with special interests in the matter. The tendency to essentialize both "science" and "religion" has led many to neglect the importance of historical and cultural context in shaping perceptions about how Christianity and the natural sciences should—or might—relate to each other.[4]

Christianity and the natural sciences are to be recognized as methodologically and conceptually distinct approaches to understanding and inhabiting our strange and complex world. Yet, as the writings of Rowan Williams indicate,[5] recognizing this point does not necessarily entail a meaningful dialogue between them; it might simply encourage a minimalist engagement between the two with no expectation of any positive or constructive outcome. This chapter, written by a natural scientist turned theologian, argues that while these differences between Christianity and the natural sciences must be respected and safeguarded, there are important and productive areas of dialogue, allowing for the potential enrichment of each participant. I argue that Christianity and the natural sciences can—and should—engage in a critical yet constructive dialogic relationship.

The term *dialogue* is too easily understood as a cozy and uncritical conversation, often tending toward an agreeable yet unwarranted assimilation of ideas. That is not the view I advocate in this chapter. I understand a dialogue to be an interaction and exchange that is

---

3. Peter Harrison, "Introduction," in *The Cambridge Companion to Science and Religion*, ed. Peter Harrison (Cambridge: Cambridge University Press, 2010), 4.

4. E.g., see Peter Dear, "Reason and Common Culture in Early Modern Natural Philosophy: Variations on an Epistemic Theme," in *Conflicting Values of Inquiry: Ideologies of Epistemology in Early Modern Europe*, eds. Tamás Demeter, Kathryn Murphy, and Claus Zittel (Leiden: Brill, 2014);" Peter Harrison, *The Territories of Science and Religion* (Chicago: University of Chicago Press, 2015).

5. For Williams's position, see Peter N. Jordan, "Minimalist Engagement: Rowan Williams on Christianity and Science," *Zygon* 51 (2016): 387–404.

critical in its nature, even if it might be constructive in its outcomes. A dialogue between Christianity and the natural sciences needs to be robust, probing deep and potentially threatening questions concerning the authority and limits of each participant and discipline. A dialogue is characterized by epistemic virtue, requiring each participant to take the other seriously, attempting to identify strengths and weaknesses while at the same time being willing to learn from the other and to face up to one's own limits and vulnerabilities. In defending this approach, I shall develop a sketch map that identifies and affirms the distinct domains of Christianity and the natural sciences, which helps us understand how conflict can arise on the one hand and how conceptual enrichment might result on the other.

Mapping the Landscape: Christianity and the Natural Sciences

Every community develops practices of reasoning and investigation that are adapted for its own specific tasks and purposes, often reflecting its distinct form of engagement with reality.[6] This view has become commonplace in the natural sciences. Biologist Steven Rose, for example, insists that while we live in a world that is an "ontological unity," we must nevertheless adopt "an epistemological pluralism" in investigating it.[7] This raises the important question of how we correlate or colligate the insights that arise from the different methodologies of specific disciplinary communities.

In general terms, the natural sciences represent a cluster of disciplines that choose to investigate our universe using empirical methods. Such a "methodological naturalism" is a specific lens, an angle of approach, that is characteristic of the natural sciences. Science has established a set of tested and reliable practices and norms by which it investigates reality, and "methodological naturalism" is one of them. Yet in laying down the means by which the natural sciences explore our universe, they are not *limiting* reality to what can be uncovered in this way. After all,

---

6. For a detailed discussion, see Alister E. McGrath, *The Territories of Human Reason: Science and Theology in an Age of Multiple Rationalities* (Oxford: Oxford University Press, 2019), 75–92.

7. Steven Rose, "The Biology of the Future and the Future of Biology," in *Explanations: Styles of Explanation in Science*, ed. John Cornwell (Oxford: Oxford University Press, 2004), 128–9.

the prevailing consensus within the scientific community is that a mere 4 percent of the universe is observable: 23 percent of the universe is now thought to consist of dark matter, and 73 percent of dark energy. Thus, 96 percent of our universe lies beyond the scope of scientific investigation.[8]

It is true that some argue that the explanatory successes of science imply an underlying ontological materialism.[9] Yet this is only one of several ways of interpreting these successes, and there are others commanding considerable support within the scientific community. Eugenie Scott, a former director of the National Center for Science Education, made this point succinctly: "Science neither denies nor opposes the supernatural, but *ignores* the supernatural for methodological reasons."[10] Science is thus best seen as a *nontheistic*, not an *antitheistic*, method of engaging reality, which is nevertheless porous to theological engagement. As philosopher Alvin Plantinga so rightly observes, the fundamental conflict is not, as is so often thought to be the case, between "science" and "Christianity" but between a dogmatic metaphysical naturalism and belief in God.[11]

Although the Enlightenment argued for a universal method of investigation, common to all areas of human research, the notion of a culturally invariant methodology, independent of specific disciplines, is now viewed with suspicion. Most would now hold that each academic discipline— including theology—develops its own methods adapted to the specific object of its investigation.[12] This does not in any way preclude some degree of conceptual overlap with, or tension with, the natural sciences. It does, however, hold that the eighteenth-century Enlightenment was fundamentally wrong in attempting to impose a single methodology on each intellectual discipline—including Christian theology.

---

8. For the problems this creates, see Pavel Kroupa, "The Dark Matter Crisis: Falsification of the Current Standard Model of Cosmology." *Publications of the Astronomical Society of Australia* 29 (2012): 395–433.

9. For an assessment, see Yonatan I. Fishman and Maarten Boudry, "Does Science Presuppose Naturalism (or Anything at All)?" *Science & Education* 22 (2013): 921–49.

10. Eugenie C. Scott, "Darwin Prosecuted: Review of Johnson's *Darwin on Trial*," *Creation/Evolution Journal* 13, no. 2 (1993): 43 (emphasis in original).

11. Alvin Plantinga, *Where the Conflict Really Lies: Science, Religion, and Naturalism* (New York: Oxford University Press, 2011), 168–74.

12. For an influential discussion, see Thomas F. Torrance, *Theological Science* (London: Oxford University Press, 1969). More recently, see McGrath, *The Territories of Human Reason*.

One outcome of the now defunct Enlightenment monomyth of a single universal method of investigation was to view religion as a deficient and primitive form of natural science. In his *The Golden Bough* (1890), social anthropologist James George Frazer portrayed religion as offering explanations of the world that had since been rendered obsolete by modern science.[13] On the basis of this outdated and deficient understanding of religion, science and Christianity are, in Frazer's view, obliged to compete for the same logical space and are to be judged by the same empirical criteria. Yet this negative evaluation of Christianity is dependent on the reliability of Frazer's widely ridiculed conceptual map,[14] which maps religion in a specific—and ultimately indefensible—way. It is no accident that Richard Dawkins made Frazer's discredited "general principles" of religion central to his evolutionary debunking arguments.

Christian apologists need to avoid this trap, lest they end up defending a spiritually impoverished, reduced, and theologically distorted Christianity. If Christianity is portrayed, either by its critics or its well-meaning apologists, as a form of science, its distinct identity and insights are ultimately distorted, if not denied. As Marilynne Robinson points out, this way of understanding the methods and goals of Christianity reduces it to "a crude explanatory system, an attempt to do what science actually could do, that is, account for the origins and the workings of things."[15] Thomas Aquinas, like many medieval theologians, rightly described theology as a *scientia* ("science"), meaning that theology was an intellectual discipline with its own criteria and methods.[16] In modern English, however, the word *science* has now come to mean a specific type of intellectual discipline that is based on an empirical method.

Christianity grounds its understanding of our world in Scripture—and the long process of reflection on Scripture throughout Christian

13. Jason Ānanda Josephson-Storm, *The Myth of Disenchantment: Magic, Modernity, and the Birth of the Human Sciences* (Chicago: University of Chicago Press, 2017), 125–52.

14. This work is now seen by anthropologists as "a cautionary tale of a grand project blighted by its poor anthropological theory and methodology." See Victor Kumar, "To Walk Alongside: Myth, Magic, and Mind in The Golden Bough." *Hau: Journal of Ethnographic Theory* 6, no. 2 (2016): 233–54.

15. Marilynne Robinson, *What Are We Doing Here? Essays* (New York: Farrar, Straus & Giroux, 2018), 257.

16. Rudi A. te Velde, *Aquinas on God: The 'Divine Science' of the Summa Theologiae* (Burlington, VT: Ashgate, 2006), 18–28.

history. It adopts neither the same starting point nor the same methods as the natural sciences but seeks to unfold the intellectual, spiritual, and moral consequences of the narrative of Jesus Christ, which is both articulated and interpreted in the Christian Bible. Proposing a dialogue between the natural sciences and Christian theology is thus not conceptually incoherent or contradictory. As Steven Rose suggests, the different perspectives offered by multiple scientific disciplines, including theology, per Aquinas, can be brought together to yield a richer and deeper account of reality than any single perspective allows. While this process of alignment and discernment is not without its difficulties, it is profoundly worth undertaking.

A Relational Metaphor: The Two Books

Complex relationships are often best envisaged using metaphors, which are now recognized as more than rhetorical embellishments to make our language more interesting and are rather seen as powerful cognitive tools for our conceptualization of the world.[17] Such metaphors are helpful in the imaginative representations of disciplinary boundaries, the mapping of complex structures, and the framing of potential relationships. The most influential metaphor used to conceptualize the relation of Christianity and the natural sciences is that of their intrinsic and necessary "conflict" or "warfare."[18] Though long discredited by historical scholarship, the metaphor retains an appeal that ensures its constant and uncritical repetition in the popular media.

Yet there are alternative metaphors within the Western intellectual tradition in which the potential for productive and meaningful conversations between Christian theology and the natural sciences is acknowledged and actualized. The most important of these is the "two books" metaphor, which emerged during the early medieval period[19]

---

17. Zoltán Kövecses, "Conceptual Metaphor Theory," in *The Routledge Handbook of Metaphor and Language*, eds. Elena Semino and Zsófia Demjén, 13–27 (London: Routledge, 2016).

18. For the historical emergence of this rhetorical trope, see Brooke, *Science and Religion*; Harrison, *Territories of Science and Religion*.

19. Constant J. Mews, "The World as Text: The Bible and the Book of Nature in Twelfth-Century Theology," in *Scripture and Pluralism: Reading the Bible in the Religiously Plural Worlds of the Middle Ages and Renaissance*, eds. Thomas J. Heffernan and Thomas E. Burman, 95–122 (Leiden: Brill, 2005).

(though it can be traced back to the patristic age) and was further developed during the Renaissance.[20] This metaphor invites us to see God as the author or creator of two distinct yet related "books"—the natural world and the Bible—and thus to imagine nature as a readable text that requires interpretation,[21] in a manner comparable to the Christian interpretation of the Bible.

One of the clearest statements of this approach is found in the writings of Sir Thomas Browne (1605–82), particularly his idiosyncratic work *Religio Medici* (1643): "There are two Books from whence I collect my Divinity; besides that written one of God, another of His servant Nature, that universal and publick Manuscript, that lies expans'd unto the Eyes of all: those that never saw Him in the one, have discovered Him in the other."[22]

The metaphor of the two books was widely used to affirm and preserve the distinctiveness of the natural sciences and Christian theology on the one hand yet to affirm their capacity for dialogue on the other. Both, it was argued, were written by God; might God be known, in different ways and to different extents, through each of these books individually, and even more clearly through reading them side by side? Although the concept of natural theology is complex and contested, many in the Renaissance viewed natural theology as a knowledge of God drawn from the "book of nature," in contrast to a knowledge of God disclosed in the "book of Scripture."[23]

This metaphor served several important functions during the emergence of the natural sciences from about 1500 to 1750. In particular, it emphasized the importance of interpretation in the scientific investigation of the world. John Calvin's *Institutes of the Christian Religion* was envisaged as a tool to help Christians discern the "bigger picture" enfolded within the biblical text. Early Reformed confessions of faith—such as the Belgic Confession (1561)—affirmed that "the universe is

20. Kenneth J. Howell, *God's Two Books: Copernican Cosmology and Biblical Interpretation in Early Modern Science* (Notre Dame, IN: University of Notre Dame Press, 2002).

21. For a superb study of this point, see Hans Blumenberg, *Die Lesbarkeit der Welt* (Frankfurt: Suhrkamp, 1986).

22. Thomas Browne, *Religio Medici* (London: Pickering, 1845), 39–40.

23. Fernando Vidal and Bernard Kleeberg, "Knowledge, Belief, and the Impulse to Natural Theology," *Science in Context* 20 (2007): 381–400; Alister E. McGrath, *Re-Imagining Nature: The Promise of a Christian Natural Theology* (Oxford: Wiley-Blackwell, 2016), 41–68.

before our eyes like a beautiful book," designed to encourage us to "ponder the invisible things of God" while simultaneously emphasizing that the Bible both clarified and extended this knowledge of God, setting it on a more reliable foundation.

The Scientific Revolution highlighted the need to do more than merely *observe* nature; the key objective was to *understand* its deeper structures, which often—as in the case of astronomer Johannes Kepler—involved the correlation of scientific and theological insights.[24] Calvin's "big picture" of the Christian faith explicitly encouraged a dialogue between the natural sciences and theology, recognizing both the parallels and divergences between the two books. "The knowledge of God, which is clearly shown in the ordering of the world and in all creatures, is still more clearly and familiarly explained in the Word."[25]

The metaphor of God's two books rests on a fundamental belief that a God who created the world is also the God who is disclosed in and through the Christian Bible. Without this underlying and informing assumption, the two books need be seen as nothing more than two disconnected entities. The link between them is established and safeguarded by the Christian theological assumption of a creator God who is revealed in the Bible. The validity and intuitive plausibility of this metaphor during the Renaissance era reflect the cultural hegemony of Christianity at this time. Yet while this might now be seen to undermine the general cultural acceptability of this metaphor, it nevertheless remains a valid and valuable conceptual tool for the Christian community, as it seeks to frame and engage the natural sciences.

The metaphor of the two books originated within a historical context that sought to hold together the various elements of human knowledge, seeing this both as a cultural virtue and a spiritual duty. As has often been noted, one of the motivations for the serious scientific study of nature was a profound sense that this would enrich the believer's appreciation of the beauty and wisdom of God as creator. Yet the specific

---

24. Giora Hon, "Kepler's Revolutionary Astronomy: Theological Unity as a Comprehensive View of the World," in *Conflicting Values of Inquiry: Ideologies of Epistemology in Early Modern Europe*, eds. Tamás Demeter, Kathryn Murphy, and Claus Zittel (Leiden: Brill, 2014), 155–75.

25. John Calvin, *Institutes of the Christian Religion*, I.x.1. See further Stephen John Grabill, *Rediscovering the Natural Law in Reformed Theological Ethics* (Grand Rapids: Eerdmans, 2006), 70–97.

historical location of this metaphor does not render it inapplicable to today's discussions and reflections. It continues to offer an imaginative framing of the relation of Christianity and the natural sciences that has the potential to engage questions under consideration today, rather than restrict us to those that preoccupied Renaissance thinkers.

Recent thinking on metaphors has noted their potential to open up new ways of visualizing abstractions and framing relationships, rather than "freezing" us into any specific mode of understanding—such as that of a bygone age.[26] We may thus retain this Renaissance metaphor, without being trapped in the controversies and limited scientific understandings of that age, provided we are attentive to the process of "reimagination" that is integral to any contemporary application of such a historic metaphor.

The metaphor of God's two books has the potential to illuminate three significant aspects of the relation of Christianity and the natural sciences.

1. It emphasizes that the natural world and the Christian faith are distinct and that they must not be conflated or assimilated. Each has its own distinct topics and methods of investigation, representation, and systematization.

2. It creates an expectation of a meaningful, if limited, dialogue between science and Christianity that is grounded in a theological insight—namely, that God is the "author" of each of these two books. Although this theological insight was capable of being framed within a reductive and assimilationist deism, it remains an essentially Christian insight, suggesting that Christianity might itself provide a theological foundation or an informing theological context for this dialogue.

3. It underscores the point that the "reading" of either of these two books involves hermeneutical conventions. The interpreter of either book tends to approach it with certain preconceptions, which need, at least in principle, to be challenged by the process of engagement.

---

26. See the analysis in Brian F. Bowdle and Dedre Gentner, "The Career of Metaphor," *Psychological Review* 112, no. 1 (2005): 193–216.

A Dialogic Approach to Christianity and Science: Two Possibilities

The approach outlined in this chapter creates a space for a principled and responsible two-way dialogue between Christianity and the natural sciences. While such a dialogue depends on a degree of intellectual humility on the part of the two dialogue partners, it does not presuppose or demand any surrender or compromise of identity or distinctiveness on the part of either. It does, however, raise the question of what frameworks of interpretation or models might be used to frame this conversation between two distinct disciplines. In this section, we shall consider two such imaginative frameworks, both of which are widely used in broader interdisciplinary and transdisciplinary conversations.

1. Science and Christianity Offer Different Perspectives on Reality

The notion that science and religion offer different, yet potentially complementary, perspectives on reality has been widely explored.[27] Complex structures look different when seen from different angles; a full account of the structure aims to integrate these multiple perspectives. Oxford theoretical chemist Charles A. Coulson used this image in a number of his writings, seeing it as a heuristic device that allowed the fundamental coherence of science and faith to be affirmed and explored.[28] As an enthusiastic mountaineer, Coulson illustrated his own approach by inviting his readers to imagine Ben Nevis, Scotland's highest mountain. Seen from the south, the mountain presents itself as a "huge grassy slope"; from the north, as "rugged rock buttresses." Those who know the mountain are familiar with these different perspectives. "Different viewpoints yield different descriptions." A full description of the same mountain requires these different perspectives to be brought together and integrated into a single coherent picture.[29] For Coulson, our experience of reality is complex, requiring and mandating both scientific and religious approaches. "The two worlds are one, though seen and

---

27. See especially Watts, "Science and Theology as Complementary Perspectives." For related approaches, see Wolterstorff, "Theology and Science"; Rueger, "Perspectival Models and Theory Unification."

28. C. A. Coulson, *Science and Christian Belief* (London: Oxford University Press, 1955); C. A. Coulson, *Science and the Idea of God* (Cambridge: Cambridge University Press, 1958); C. A. Coulson, *Christianity in an Age of Science* (London: Oxford University Press, 1953).

29. Coulson, *Christianity in an Age of Science*, 20.

described in appropriate terms; and it is only the man who cannot, or will not, look at it from more than one viewpoint who claims an exclusive authority for his own description." [30]

This general approach clearly has weaknesses, most notably the need to negotiate intellectual boundaries and methodological privileges. Are all standpoints or angles of approach of equal value and utility? Or might one serve in effect as a privileged or normative standpoint, offering a conceptual framework on the basis of which others might be evaluated, positioned, and coordinated?

A second concern relates to the inability of such an approach to do justice to the complex texturing of reality. Coulson's perspectival approach reflects a somewhat "flat" view of the world, which seems inattentive and insensitive to the possibility of multiple levels or "strata" of reality. For example, religion is a complex social phenomenon that possesses and is characterized by multiple dimensions or levels.[31] So how can we do justice to the multiple layers of the Christian faith—such as its symbols, narratives, practices, and virtues? This brings us to the second approach to be considered, which sees Christianity and the natural sciences as engaging with different levels of reality.

2. Science and Christianity Engage Different Levels of Reality

This second approach suggests that the natural sciences and Christianity operate at different levels. The famous analogy of two explanations of why a kettle is boiling makes this point clearly:[32] one answer is that energy conversion is taking place, raising the water to its boiling point; the second answer is that someone wanted to make a cup of tea. Both answers are correct; they deal with different levels of the phenomenon and are thus part of a greater integrated response to the question "Why is the kettle boiling?" that is more satisfying and complete than either individual answer.

Some suggest, a little simplistically, that this distinction in levels of

---

30. Coulson, *Christianity in an Age of Science*, 21.

31. Aku Visala, "Explaining Religion at Different Levels: From Fundamentalism to Pluralism." In *The Roots of Religion: Exploring the Cognitive Science of Religion*, eds. Roger Trigg and Justin L. Barrett (London: Routledge, 2016), 55–74.

32. F. H. T. Rhodes, "Christianity in a Mechanistic Universe," in *Christianity in a Mechanistic Universe and Other Essays*, ed. D. M. MacKay (London: InterVarsity Fellowship, 1965), 11–48.

explanation is grounded in the sciences' tendency to ask "how" questions and in faith's tendency to deal with "why" questions. While this view requires some nuancing, it is perfectly defensible to suggest that the natural sciences are primarily concerned with establishing how the natural world works, where Christianity is primarily concerned with questions of meaning—such as the "ultimate questions" of human purpose, identity, agency, and value. There is a significant distinction between clarifying the functionality of our world and determining its meaning. Although there is a closer correlation between functionality and meaning than some appreciate, these are to be distinct levels of explanation that can be woven together into an integrated account of the world.

The natural sciences make extensive use of the notion of "levels of explanation," a stratified approach to the natural world that counters inappropriate reductionist tendencies. This approach emphasizes that there might be explanations of *some* aspects of a system that could not be applied to *every* aspect of that system, or to the system *as a whole*.[33] The interaction of such levels is complex, and it is becoming increasingly clear that causation exists and operates at multiple levels and in multiple directions within complex biological systems.[34] Whereas reductionist approaches prematurely argue that the more fundamental levels—such as physical reality—determine the properties and behaviors of higher levels, it is now clear that such "bottom-up" approaches need to be modified by recognizing the importance of "top-down" mechanisms.[35]

Such a stratified approach to the natural sciences and Christianity is capable of preserving and accommodating their complexity and stratification. It recognizes that Christianity is a multilayered phenomenon that cannot be reduced to any of its communal, symbolic, narrative, or ideational elements—a significant problem, incidentally, in relation to naturalist explanations of religion, which often reduce the phenomenon of religion to one of its levels, such as prosocial behavior. Given

---

33. Angela Potochnik, "Levels of Explanation Reconceived," *Philosophy of Science* 77, no. 1 (2010): 59–72; Bechtel, "Levels of Description and Explanation in Cognitive Science"; William Bechtel, "Levels of Description and Explanation in Cognitive Science," *Minds and Machines* 4, no. 1 (1994): 1–25.

34. Peter Fazekas and Gergely Kertész, "Causation at Different Levels: Tracking the Commitments of Mechanistic Explanations," *Biology and Philosophy* 26 (2011): 365–83.

35. See the evidence assembled in George Ellis, *How Can Physics Underlie the Mind? Top-Down Causation in the Human Context* (Heidelberg: Springer, 2016), 1–28, 133–209.

the complexity and stratified nature of religion, it proves resistant to explanation on evolutionary grounds in its totality.[36] This approach is also capable of accommodating the shifting historical and cultural understandings of what the terms *science* and *religion* designate.[37]

The two approaches noted in this section both offer a heuristic framework within which the distinctive identities of Christianity and the sciences can be respected. Religion is neither forced nor permitted to become a science, any more than science is forced or permitted to become a religion. These approaches facilitate a dialogue that engages philosopher John Dewey's concern that the "deepest problem of modern life" is our collective and individual failure to integrate our "thoughts about the world" with our thoughts about "value and purpose."[38]

These two correlating approaches are *imaginative*, inviting us to visualize the interaction of science and Christianity in a way that creates conceptual space for a principled dialogue. Recent studies have emphasized the importance of such mental images in theory development and scientific progress.[39] But neither of these approaches offers a framework by which possible interactions of science and Christianity may be regulated or interrogated—for example, in relation to boundary issues. What happens, for example, when science and religion seem to compete for explanatory hegemony? Does a scientific account of explanation trump a theological account? Or do we have to predetermine that the rules of engagement demand that each perspective be given equal weight or attentiveness, as a matter of principle? Nor do they clarify how science and Christianity might each "explain" aspects of our world. Given the importance of this point, we shall consider this in greater detail.

Science and Christianity: Some Explanatory Considerations

The capacity to explain our world is widely seen as virtuous, despite the obvious difficulties in defining what explanation might be in the first place, and how scientific explanation might differ from other forms of

---

36. Benson Saler, *Conceptualizing Religion: Immanent Anthropologists, Transcendent Natives and Unbounded Categories* (Leiden: Brill, 1993).

37. Harrison, *The Territories of Science and Religion.*

38. John Dewey, *The Quest for Certainty: A Study of the Relation of Knowledge and Action.* Gifford Lectures (London: Allen & Unwin, 1930), 255.

39. Hsiao-Chi Ho, Chia-Chi Wang, and Ying-Yao Cheng, "Analysis of the Scientific Imagination Process," *Thinking Skills and Creativity* 10 (2013): 68–78.

explanation. Science is ultimately a quest for understanding how our world functions, although it naturally leads into technology—the practical application of the deeper principles that are discerned as lying behind our world. Christianity is a religion of salvation, offering its own distinct understanding of what is wrong with human beings and the world and what can be done about this. Some theologians, taking their cues from Wittgenstein, tend to see Christianity as having no explanatory ambition or capacity. Others—including the present writer—see Christianity as possessing a derived explanatory capacity that arises from the metanarrative that emerges from the integration of multiple biblical narratives.[40] Philosopher Basil Mitchell thus holds that, in its intellectual aspects, "traditional Christian theism may be regarded as a worldview or metaphysical system which is in competition with other such systems and must be judged by its capacity to make sense of all the available evidence."[41]

Although both the natural sciences and Christianity are often said to "explain" aspects of our world, it is important to appreciate that the concept of explanation remains frustratingly vague. The two most common models of explanation in the philosophy of science at present are based on "ontic" and "epistemic" approaches.[42] Ontic approaches are essentially causal, holding that explanation is essentially offering an account of how something took place. To say that A explains B is essentially to say that A causes B. Despite its significant traction within the scientific community, this approach is rendered problematic by the absence of a generalized account of causation in the first place. David Hume's concerns about the notion have never been properly resolved; although many solutions have been proposed, none has secured widespread acceptance.[43] Yet most

---

40. For two excellent studies, see Willibald Sandler, "Christentum als große Erzählung. Anstöße für eine narrative Theologie," in *Religion—Literatur—Künste. Ein Dialog*, ed. Peter Tschuggnall (Anif: Müller-Speiser 2002), 523–38; Gunda Schneider-Flume, "Die vielen Geschichten der biblischen Tradition und die eine Geschichte Gottes. Zur Frage nach Einheit und Mitte der Schrift," in *Dogmatik erzählen? Die Bedeutung des Erzählens für eine biblisch orientierte Dogmatik*, eds. Gunda Schneider-Flume and Doris Hiller (Neukirchen-Vluyn: Neukirchener Verlag, 2005), 31–50.

41. Basil Mitchell, *The Justification of Religious Belief* (London: Macmillan, 1973), 99.

42. Wesley C. Salmon, *Causality and Explanation* (Oxford: Oxford University Press, 1998); Philip Kitcher, "Explanatory Unification and the Causal Structure of the World," in *Scientific Explanation*, eds. P. Kitcher and W. Salmon, 410–505 (Minneapolis: University of Minnesota Press, 1989); Margaret Morrison, *Unifying Scientific Theories: Physical Concepts and Mathematical Structures* (Cambridge: Cambridge University Press, 2000).

43. Phil Dowe, *Physical Causation* (Cambridge: Cambridge University Press, 2000).

natural scientists adopt a pragmatic approach, noting that the explanatory potential of the notion of causation warrants its continued use.

Epistemic approaches to explanation ascribe an essential role to the conceptual structures by which an explanation is conveyed and tend to understand explanation as a cognitive achievement. The most significant example of such an approach at present is the unificationist conception of explanatory understanding, which holds that science achieves explanation by uncovering a unified picture of the world. A scientific explanation can thus be understood as providing a unified account of a range of different phenomena. To understand any given phenomenon is to discern the "bigger picture" within which certain phenomena take place, and thus the fundamental unity that underlies the apparent diversity of the phenomena themselves.[44]

While Christian theological explanations tend to be epistemic rather than ontic in character, it is important to appreciate that the Christian vision of reality does make ontic claims—for example, in relation to the doctrine of creation. The theological frameworks set out by writers such as Augustine of Hippo and Athanasius of Alexandria rest on a core belief that a rational God created a coherent and rational (*logikos*) universe, whose structures reflect the character of its creator and are capable of being grasped by the human mind.

This framework of belief incorporates both ontic and epistemic elements. In the first place, it affirms that the being of the universe ultimately derives from the being of God; in the second, it affirms that humanity, in bearing the image of God, has a created capacity to engage, interpret, and understand the universe. More specifically, it affirms that the Christian "belief system" is capable of accommodating our observations and experiences within an intelligible and coherent greater whole. On this approach, it is possible to argue that the Christian metanarrative or a theistic metaphysics offers a framework within which many observable features of the world—such as the intelligible order of the universe and a fruitful cosmic history—can be accommodated.[45]

---

44. For the partial overlap of ontic and epistemic approaches, see Phyllis Illari, "Mechanical Explanation: Integrating the Ontic and Epistemic," *Erkenntnis* 78 (2013): 237–55.
45. For this approach, see John C. Polkinghorne, "Physics and Metaphysics in a Trinitarian Perspective," *Theology and Science* 1 (2003): 33–49.

Natural Theology: An Informed Reading of the Two Books

It is impossible to talk about the relation of science and Christianity without talking about natural theology, just as it is impossible to discuss this meaningfully without taking account of the multiple understandings of natural theology encountered within the Christian tradition. A careful study of the genealogy of the term *natural theology* suggests that there are multiple ways of understanding its meaning.[46] Greater care should be taken to avoid the simplistic equation of the complex and rich enterprise of natural theology with one of its multiple historical forms. One example is the idea that natural theology can be defined exclusively in terms of proving the existence of God without recourse to revealed premises (an idea that would have been totally alien to Raimundo de Sebonde [d. 1436], who reintroduced the term *natural theology* in the fifteenth century, framing it in terms of God's "two books"). To avoid such foreclosures of a potentially interesting discussion, we shall frame natural theology as the general enterprise of exploring symbolic and discursive correlations between the natural world and God.

As understood by philosophers, the intellectual trajectory of natural theology is from nature to God. This approach is particularly to be seen in the enterprise of "physicotheology," which was particularly influential in western Europe during the late seventeenth and eighteenth centuries. Here, the ordering and complexity of the physical and biological worlds is seen as corroborating the existence and character of God.[47] In eighteenth century England, such approaches to natural theology helped both to defend the natural sciences in a Christian context and to defend Christianity in a scientific context. The "book of nature" is seen as the starting point for the discovery and exploration of the "book of Scripture."

Such approaches, which played an important role in the thought of early Reformed theologians at Geneva—including John Calvin and Theodore Beza—remain important for Christian apologetics, although

---

46. See McGrath, *Re-Imagining Nature*, 11–35. Cf. David Fergusson, "Types of Natural Theology," in *The Evolution of Rationality: Interdisciplinary Essays in Honor of J. Wentzel van Huyssteen*, ed. F. LeRon Schults, 380–93 (Grand Rapids: Eerdmans, 2007).

47. Peter Harrison, "Physico-Theology and the Mixed Sciences: The Role of Theology in Early Modern Natural Philosophy," in *The Science of Nature in the Seventeenth Century*, eds. Peter Anstey and John Schuster, 165–83 (Dordrecht: Springer, 2005).

many would now resist any suggestion that they "prove" the existence of God, seeing them rather as resonating or chiming in with a Christian way of thinking. These early Genevan Reformed approaches to natural theology gave way to more rationalist approaches during the eighteenth century, when the rise of rationalism stimulated the emergence of approaches focusing on the natural verification of theological rationality.[48] Although Karl Barth's criticism of this form of natural theology has been influential within some sections of Protestantism, Barth's failure to distinguish the role and place of natural theology in systematic theology and in apologetics has weakened the force of such criticisms in an increasingly post-Christian age.

An alternative direction of intellectual travel should also be noted: from God to nature. Here, natural theology would be understood as the way of seeing the natural order from within the Christian tradition—what some might term a "theology of nature." Apologetically, this invites the evaluation of the Christian way of seeing the world—a *theoria*—in terms of its correspondence or resonance with observations of the world. Just as a scientific theory can be assessed by its capacity to accommodate observations, so the reliability of Christianity as a way of thinking about and envisioning our world can be evaluated through the quality of its rendering of reality.[49]

These debates have often become entangled with unhelpful angles of approach, such as that associated with William Paley's *Natural Theology* (1802). Paley argued that the observation of "contrivance"—that is to say, intelligent design and construction—in nature constituted grounds for belief in God. "Contrivance, if established, appears to me to prove everything which we wish to prove."[50] Paley's insistence that the observation of design in nature provides warrant for belief in God raises many difficulties, of which the most problematic is this: "design" is not something that is *directly observed* but rather is something *inferred from observation*.

English theologian John Henry Newman was severely critical of

---

48. See especially Martin Klauber, "Jean-Alphonse Turrettini (1671–1737) on Natural Theology: The Triumph of Reason over Revelation at the Academy of Geneva," *Scottish Journal of Theology* 47 (1994): 301–25.

49. McGrath, *Re-Imagining Nature*, 173–81.

50. William Paley, *Natural Theology*, 12th ed. (London: Faulder, 1809), 408. The important phrase "proof of contrivance" occurs five times in *Natural Theology*: see pp. 7, 21, 269, 323, 417.

Paley's approach to natural theology. While noting that such a line of argument from the ordering or beauty of nature could reinforce an *existing* belief in God, Newman was skeptical about its intellectual capacity to bring someone to faith in the first place.[51] While natural theology may support faith, it lacks the capacity to create that faith. It is meaningful to speak of proving something in logic or mathematics, in which human reason masters reality. God resists such intellectual subjugation. We may indeed aim to show that belief in God is reasonable; that belief, however, cannot be proved by an appeal to reason or the natural world. Newman declared that he believed in design within creation because he believed in God, rather than believing in God because he saw design in the natural world.[52] In other words, Newman's apologetic argument focused on the capacity of the Christian faith to enfold scientific observation, rather than arguing that scientific observations "proved" the Christian faith, in whole or in part. There is merit in Newman's point; however, it is a well-established fact that many people do indeed come to faith through a perception that nature possesses an intricacy or complexity that is best accounted for in terms of divine design.

In the twenty-first century, a Christian reading or rendering of nature opens up three important areas of reflection. First, it lays the groundwork for a "spirituality of nature," a way of engaging with the natural world that sees it as extending the scope and enriching the quality of the Christian perception of nature.[53] For example, consider Psalm 19, which affirms that "The heavens declare the glory of God" (v. 1). This was not suggesting that the night sky provided a proof of God's existence, but rather that it offered an expansion of Israel's appreciation of this God. There was no question of an unknown God being disclosed through the night sky. Rather, contemplation of the night sky was seen as offering an imaginative enrichment of Israel's vision of God. Paul, of course, asserted that all people have access to a basic knowledge of God through creation (Rom. 1:18–21; Acts 14:16–17). Yet Israel was special: it already possessed a revealed theological framework that enabled it to

---

51. Stuart Peterfreund, *Turning Points in Natural Theology from Bacon to Darwin: The Way of the Argument from Design* (New York: Palgrave Macmillan, 2012), 109–30.

52. Noel K. Roberts, "Newman on the Argument from Design," *New Blackfriars* 88 (2007): 56–66.

53. McGrath, *Re-Imagining Nature*, 163–8.

see nature as the creation of its covenant God—and which thus mirrored God's glory, in however tempered a form.

A second aspect of the Christian engagement with nature is of particular importance in an age troubled by the possibility of climate change—the affirmation that nature is God's possession, not ours, which we are called on to tend and cherish. Although some have argued that the Christian metanarrative encourages an attitude of human dominion over nature, the predominant tendency within Christianity is to recognize that the natural world is God's possession that has been entrusted to us and thus to act as stewards of it.[54]

Yet it is the third aspect of a Christian engagement with nature that needs further discussion—the Christian critique of rival ideologies or alternative worldviews. In a famous essay of 1929, Emil Brunner spoke of the "other task of theology"—namely, an "eristic" dimension to theology, in which it offered not merely a systematic presentation of Christian ideas but an ensuing critique of other ways of conceiving and inhabiting our world.[55] One such ideology has come to be known as "scientism," an ideology underlying the "New Atheism" of Richard Dawkins and Sam Harris, which is generally understood as "a totalizing attitude that regards science as the ultimate standard and arbiter of all interesting questions; or alternatively that seeks to expand the very definition and scope of science to encompass all aspects of human knowledge and understanding."[56] The approach set out in this chapter respects the contributions of the natural sciences but challenges any claims to privilege or ultimacy in regard to what Karl Popper called "ultimate questions"—such as the meaning of life.

Christianity and Science: A Critical Dialogue

Critical dialogues are uncomfortable, and many prefer monologues or disengagement for that reason. This is not a serious intellectual option for those committed to a dialogic conception of the relation of science

---

54. There is a huge literature: a good starting point is Max Oeschlaeger, *Caring for Creation: An Ecumenical Approach to the Environmental Crisis* (New Haven: Yale University Press, 1994).

55. Alister E. McGrath, *Emil Brunner: A Reappraisal* (Oxford: Wiley-Blackwell, 2014), 62–74.

56. Massimo Pigliucci, "New Atheism and the Scientistic Turn in the Atheism Movement," *Midwest Studies in Philosophy* 37, no. 1 (2013): 144.

and Christianity, which, if anything, sees such discomfort as a virtue. In this section we shall consider some questions that might illuminate the opportunities and limits of the dialogic approach set out in this chapter.

What Is the Relationship between Scripture and Science?

The dialogic approach I have outlined thus far is informed by the classic metaphor of the two books of God, which both provides an imaginative and conceptual framework for considering the relation of Scripture and science and which has an established history of use in the Renaissance and early modern period. Each book has the same author, yet the hermeneutical methods required to interpret and understand the "book of nature" and "book of Scripture" are different, reflecting *and respecting* their distinct identities and forms.

Christian theology represents an integration of biblical insights, as a series of threads woven together into a tapestry. Individual biblical texts must be interpreted within this greater framework rather than be allowed to function as decontextualized and fragmented "proof" texts. The development of Christology during the patristic age is a model case for understanding how good theology preserves biblical insights while seeking to incorporate them into a coherent and consistent framework. Athanasius of Alexandria's interpretative method holds together as biblically warranted what some considered to be philosophically irreconcilable—such as the humanity and divinity of Christ.[57]

The issue is therefore not how individual biblical texts relate to the natural sciences but how the greater Christian "big picture" of reality encourages and informs the scientific enterprise. It is, of course, interesting to note how individual biblical verses feature in scientific debates—such as the role of Psalm 104:5 (God "set the earth on its foundations; it can never be moved") in the Copernican debates.[58] Historically, there is a general consensus that the Christian worldview,

---

57. James D. Ernest, *The Bible in Athanasius of Alexandria* (Boston: Brill, 2004); Margaret Beirne, "St Athanasius and the Scriptures: Exemplified in His Letter to Marcellinus," *Phronema* 28, no. 2 (2013): 89–106.

58. The best discussion is now Charlotte Methuen, "On the Threshold of a New Age: Expanding Horizons as the Broader Context of Biblical Interpretation," in *Hebrew Bible, Old Testament: The History of Its Interpretation*, ed. Magne Saebo (Göttingen: Vandenhoeck & Ruprecht, 2008), 671–84.

especially its view of an ordered creation accessible to the human mind, played a significant role in catalyzing the emergence of the natural sciences.[59] But it is also important to note how accommodationist approaches to biblical interpretation—such as that developed by John Calvin in the 1550s—played an important role in framing biblical texts in ways that recognized the historical context of divine revelation, thus allowing modern interpreters of Scripture to interpret its insights within the context of a scientific culture. The dangers of such an enterprise, however, need to be recognized in that it is not clear what criteria should guide such approaches to interpretation, which can too easily lapse into subjective judgments.[60]

It is instructive to consider the approach to the relation of biblical interpretation and the natural sciences adopted by some within the "Old Princeton" school of theology (1812–1929), which generally followed a traditional Reformed approach to the natural sciences that was grounded in the notion that God testified to himself through two books, the book of Scripture and the book of nature. Since these two books shared the same divine author, for Charles Hodge and Benjamin B. Warfield, these two sources therefore could not be in conflict with each other, if they were correctly interpreted. Any conflict between the actual facts revealed in nature (as opposed to extravagant scientific speculation about nature) and the biblical texts should lead the responsible exegete not to reject a scientific account of nature nor to doubt the truth of Scripture but to seek a better interpretation of Scripture in the light of these facts.[61]

Warfield was thus prepared to accommodate evolution within this framework and reread the opening chapters of Genesis in its light. Yet Warfield was clear that this rereading entailed the rejection of any account of evolution that eliminated or disregarded God's primal action or continuing involvement with the created order or that understood evolution as a random process. Warfield thus offers a theological

---

59. See, for example, James Hannam, *God's Philosophers: How the Medieval World Laid the Foundations of Modern Science* (London: Icon, 2010); Michael Hanby, *No God, No Science? Theology, Cosmology, Biology* (Hoboken, NJ: Wiley, 2013).

60. Note the points made by Jon Balserak, *Divinity Compromised: A Study of Divine Accommodation in the Thought of John Calvin* (Dordrecht: Springer, 2006), 163–83.

61. For the difficulties this approach raises, see David P. Smith, *B. B. Warfield's Scientifically Constructive Theological Scholarship* (Eugene, OR: Wipf & Stock, 2011), 88–119.

framework and hermeneutical method within which Darwinism can both be accommodated and criticized.[62]

How Does God Act in the World?

Since the early modern period, the natural sciences have interpreted the functioning of the world in terms of general principles, often (though unhelpfully) referred to as the "laws of nature," which are best seen as enumerative summaries of observations of regularity that were easily assimilated into the theological notion of God as lawmaker through the act of creation.[63] The specific terminology of physical "laws of nature" became prominent only in the seventeenth century and is now seen to reflect Descartes's belief, first published after his death in 1664, that God, having created matter, then imposed laws on it that determined all of its subsequent behavior.[64]

The regularity of God's actions within the natural world was not necessarily seen as contradicting the idea of special divine action, often described as "miracles" in popular literature. It is, however, important to note that David Hume's influential—but deeply problematic—definition of a miracle as a "violation of the laws of nature" is historically situated and (in the proper sense of the term) *anachronistic*; this definition would have made no sense to religious believers before Descartes, who enthusiastically discussed the category of the "miraculous" without reference to some presumed "laws of nature."[65]

The rise of deism in the eighteenth century, which many believe was catalyzed by Newton's "mechanical philosophy,"[66] led to theological ambivalence about the notion of divine action in the world. God acted to create the laws of nature, by which the world subsequently governed

62. David N. Livingstone and Mark A. Noll, "B. B. Warfield (1851–1921): A Biblical Inerrantist as Evolutionist," *Isis* 91 (2000): 283–304.

63. Peter Harrison, "The Development of the Concept of Laws of Nature," in *Creation: Law and Probability*, ed. Fraser Watts, 13–36 (Aldershot: Ashgate, 2008).

64. John Henry, "Metaphysics and the Origins of Modern Science: Descartes and the Importance of Laws of Nature," *Early Science and Medicine* 9 (2004): 73–114.

65. Aviezer Tucker, "Miracles, Historical Testimonies, and Probabilities," *History and Theory* 44 (2005): 373–90.

66. But see the cautionary comments in Stephen D. Snobelen, "The Myth of the Clockwork Universe: Newton, Newtonianism, and the Enlightenment," in *The Persistence of the Sacred in Modern Thought*, ed. Chris L. Firestone and Nathan Jacobs, 149–84 (South Bend, IN: University of Notre Dame Press, 2012).

and maintained itself.[67] Theologians in the eighteenth century generally considered God's presence and action in the world to be expressed and safeguarded by the notion of the "laws of nature." This concept served two important functions. First, it emphasized that God was not capricious or whimsical; God was best seen in the regularities of actions within the world—such as the movements of the planets. And second, it emphasized that God's original act of creation established a causal framework that was open to empirical study. Since God did not act under compulsion from external considerations, the regularities of the world might be studied to learn more of God's nature and ways. This point is made by mathematician Roger Cotes in his preface to the second edition of Newton's *Principia Mathematica* (1713): "Surely, this World—so beautifully diversified in all its forms and motions—could not have arisen except from the perfectly free will of God, who provides and governs all things. From this source, then, have all the laws that are called laws of nature come, in which many traces of the highest wisdom and counsel certainly appear, but no traces of necessity. Accordingly, we should not seek these laws by using untrustworthy conjectures, but learn them by observing and experimenting."[68]

The issue here is this: divine action—whether this is considered "general" or "special"—is not an empirical concept. An action or event is *observed*; this is then *interpreted* as divine action. It is not meaningful to speak of divine action as "detectable;" the issue is whether a detectable event is to be interpreted as divine action. This judgment will be shaped by a number of issues, including, as Charles Taylor has pointed out, the prevailing worldview of the observer. Taylor notes that people in the early 1600s had little difficulty in "naturally" thinking of divine action within the world. Yet the prevailing social imaginary of that period affirmed and consolidated this "natural" interpretation. Today's secular western "immanent frame," representing the social dominance of a cluster of modern prejudices, challenges any such interpretation, holding that it is more "natural" to interpret events within a closed immanent system.[69]

---

67. For the issues, see Alister E. McGrath, "Hesitations About Special Divine Action: Reflections on Some Scientific, Cultural and Theological Concerns," *European Journal for Philosophy of Religion* 7, no. 4 (2015): 3–22.

68. Isaac Newton, *The Principia*, ed. and trans. I. Bernard Cohen and Anne Whitman (Berkeley: University of California Press, 1999), 397.

69. Charles Taylor, *A Secular Age* (Cambridge, MA: Belknap, 2007), 25.

The dialogic framework set out in this chapter offers a helpful way to think about divine action in both scientific and theological contexts, using the notions of multiple perspectives or levels. An action—such as the rustling of leaves in a tree or the healing of a wound—may be observed, then located within several possible interpretative frameworks. It can be located within a framework offered by various forms of methodological naturalism, which seek to explain the natural world only in terms of the observable. (Some forms of naturalism, of course, exclude any possibility of the divine; this, however, is a *metaphysically freighted* naturalism, rather than the more generous empirical naturalisms that are widely encountered in the sciences.) It can also be interpreted within a theological framework as an example of God working in and through the created order. Or, to change the imagery, we might think of the natural sciences and Christian theology as offering different maps of reality, which can be superimposed on the world of observation and experience.

A natural scientist might use only a naturalist map or lens to interpret what is observed in the world, and thus limit reality to what that map or lens discloses. A theologian will use a quite distinct lens, which is attuned to the idea of God acting in and through the natural order and human experience. Yet both maps and lenses can be used, allowing a deeper rendering of our world. This approach is used routinely in the natural sciences. For example, both physiological and psychological maps can be used to explain why someone experiences anxiety in an unfamiliar situation. It is an idea that Christian theology has long worked with. Consider, for example, the biblical accounts of the crucifixion of Jesus Christ and its wider significance. The New Testament itself offers at least three maps or levels of meaning for this event: historical (the event took place at a specific date and time near Jerusalem), legal (Christ's death was an execution), and theological (Christ's death is the basis of God's redemptive transformation of humanity). Affirming any one of these three levels or maps does not entail the negation of the other two. For a Christian, the richest and deepest account of the significance of this event will incorporate all three.

So can this be referred to as a dialogue? Some might reasonably express concern that it is simply an enumeration of possibilities, without any engagement or modification as a result of a respectful informed discussion. Yet dialogue needs to be encouraged. Entrenched naturalists, such as Richard Dawkins, regard such dialogue as pointless in terms of its outcomes and compromising in terms of its assumptions. Two points are of particular importance.

First, it is clear that Dawkins does not understand what Christians mean by their distinct language or why they regard belief in God as "reasonable." A dialogue in this context might take the form of explaining what Christians believe and why they believe it. Dawkins might not choose to agree with the ideas that have been explained; but at least he would have a better grasp of what the ideas mean to those who value them. Second, such a dialogue often brings up unexpected points of similarity—for example, in relation to the limits of proof in science and faith or the important role of analogies, models, or metaphors in making sense of a complex reality. Such a dialogue might, for example, help a theologian understand how scientists develop and interpret models. And the theologian might allow this practice to illuminate how theology could develop such themes—for example, in relation to the question of the collation of multiple models.[70]

A Test Case: *Homo Sapiens*

So how does the dialogic approach set out in this chapter deal with the appearance and nature of *Homo sapiens*? Can we be content with a purely scientific account of this development, making reference only to natural laws and material entities? Any such discussion is, of course, going to become mired in technical difficulties relating to the not-quite-so-innocent term "natural." But it is possible to sketch out a response to this important question, which indicates the potential of this approach for engaging such issues.[71]

Let us begin by noting that human existence is critically dependent on several elements of the universe—especially carbon, nitrogen, and oxygen. Yet the emergence of these elements is widely conceded to be the outcome of processes that are critically dependent on the fundamental constants of the universe.[72] Although such "anthropic" arguments

---

70. For an excellent exploration of this theme by a scientifically conversant theologian, see Ian T. Ramsey, *Models and Mystery* (London: Oxford University Press, 1964).

71. See also the excellent collection of essays on such themes gathered together in Stanley Rosenberg and Michael Burdett, eds., *Finding Ourselves after Darwin: Conversations on the Image of God, Original Sin, and the Problem of Evil* (Grand Rapids: Baker, 2018).

72. See Martin J. Rees, *Just Six Numbers: The Deep Forces That Shape the Universe* (London: Phoenix, 2000); Alister E. McGrath, *A Fine-Tuned Universe: The Quest for God in Science and Theology* (Louisville, KY: Westminster John Knox, 2009), 111–201.

are too easily overstated, it is perfectly reasonable to suggest that the universe appears to be fine-tuned for the emergence of humanity—and that such an observation is entirely consistent with a Christian doctrine of creation.

Yet such a Christian doctrine of creation is not static. God did not create a world that was already shaped in its final form. As Augustine of Hippo pointed out in 401, the most natural reading of the Genesis creation accounts is that God's fashioning of the world involves both event and process—that is to say, a primary act of creation, followed by a secondary ongoing process of emergence and complexification, directed by divine providence.[73] Augustine rejected the notion of a purely random process of development, arguing that God remains involved within the shaping of this process of development. Although some writers (such as William Paley) resisted the idea of God endowing the material world with an innate created capacity to develop, such ideas are already present in the patristic tradition of biblical interpretation. Victorian theologian and novelist Charles Kingsley expressed this point neatly in his well-known aphorism: "We knew of old that God was so wise that he could make all things; but, behold, he is so much wiser than even that, that he can make all things make themselves."[74]

A purely scientific account of humanity can indeed be given; yet such an account is inadequate and incomplete. The use of multiple perspectives and levels is necessary if we are to do justice to human complexity. Furthermore, reductionist approaches to humanity encounter significant difficulties through the phenomenon now known as "emergence." While everything that exists in the world of space and time is composed of basic fundamental physical particles, physics proves inadequate to explain how this material came into being, or how it comes to be structured. When ensembles or aggregates of material particles attain an appropriate level of organizational complexity, genuinely novel properties begin to emerge, which cannot be reduced to, or predicted from, the lower level phenomena from which they emerge.[75]

Finally, we note that *Homo sapiens* seem to be endowed with an innate desire to quest for something that lies beyond us. Cognitive

73. McGrath, *A Fine-Tuned Universe*, 95–108.
74. Charles Kingsley, *Westminster Sermons* (London: Macmillan, 1874), xxv.
75. See especially the detailed analysis in Ellis, *How Can Physics Underlie the Mind?*

science of religion suggests that we find it natural to interpret the world in terms of a God or gods. Empirical psychology suggests that we are meaning-seeking creatures, who recognize the significance and value in living out meaningful lives. Science helps us figure out how the world works. But we seem to want to know what the world means—and what we mean. The Christian doctrine of humanity bearing the image of God offers a theological account of this innate desire and its true goal, which offers an interpretation of this experience and its significance,[76] supplementing scientific insights at this point.

Conclusion

This chapter has sketched a dialogic approach to the relationship of science and Christianity that clearly needs much more fulsome exposition and application. I have argued that a comprehensive Christian vision of reality provides a lens through which we can see nature properly and learn our responsibilities as its stewards. This also provides an apologetic framework in which a "natural theology" can play its appropriate role, not as a means of proving God's existence without an appeal to divine revelation but rather as an *a posteriori* confirmation of the consonance of a Christian worldview with the beauty and order that we observe in the natural world. I have used visual images—such as perspectives, levels, and maps—to emphasize not simply the importance of the human imagination in both science and Christianity but also in creating conceptual space for conceiving how they might relate to each other.[77] Any attempt to relate science and Christianity will need to go far beyond the imagination-emaciated rationalism of the Enlightenment if we are to hold them together persuasively. The program so briefly outlined in this chapter is fundamentally a call for the reimagination of our world, in which Christians set God's "two books" alongside each other and allow them to enrich and inform their readers.

---

76. On this, see especially Rosenberg and Burdett, *Finding Ourselves after Darwin*, 27–109.

77. See Mary Gerhart and Allan Melvin Russell, *New Maps for Old: Explorations in Science and Religion* (New York: Continuum, 2001).

RESPONSE TO ALISTER MCGRATH

MICHAEL RUSE

When I was a child, I spake as a child, I understood as a child, I thought as a child: but when I became a man, I put away childish things" (1 Corinthians 13:11 KJV). I can forgive Saint Paul a lot for his glorious paean to love. As I read Alister McGrath's chapter, again and again I thought of this verse (13:11). That might make me seem unbelievably condescending, so let me rush to assure you that it was not Alister I had in mind. It was me! As I said in my own chapter, I was raised very intensely as a Quaker—and let me assure you, I was into it with enthusiasm—and then, around the age of twenty, my faith died, never to return. It was not a road to Damascus experience in reverse. It was more a silent slipping away. "For the snark was a boojum, you see." I have spent the subsequent sixty years—by the time you read these words, I will be eighty—assuring myself that what happened to me was perfectly natural. I lost my childhood fondness for stamp collecting, I took up girls, and God was no more. Apart from anything else, I had left my Christian (Quaker) boarding school, and I joke that having had one headmaster in this world, I am damned if I want another in the next. Except it isn't a joke.

Warfare or Two Books?

And yet, here I am faced with an author at least as intelligent and quali-fied as I am—one from whom I have learned so much (starting with his exemplary introductions to Christian theology)—taking a completely different stance. It is true that, compared with my great age, Alister McGrath is but a little lad. He has not even reached the biblically allot-ted span of three score and ten. I doubt the years to come will make any difference. He is a totally committed Christian. He believes in the creator God of the Bible, he believes that humans are special—made in the image of God—and he believes that Jesus died on the cross for our sins. These beliefs are not wonky, as too often my internet connection tends to be. He is not a Charles Darwin, agnostic with flashes of belief. For Alister McGrath, his God and his love for his human creation is as real as Alister's professorship at Oxford. A lot more eternal than that professorship, one might add. I am convinced that Brexit will mean abject poverty for the country of my birth. On grounds of economy, all the institutions of higher education will have to be closed.

So, what is going on? Clearly faith is involved here. Alister has faith and I do not.[1] Yet I think it not unfair to say that Alister's contribution to this volume is not overly focused on faith. Natural theology gets a much bigger role. Alister dismisses the warfare between science and religion metaphor. I agree with him that fifty years of scholarship, featuring such historians as Ronald Numbers and Alister's professorial predecessor, Peter Harrison, have shown the warfare metaphor to be mainly a figment of the imaginations of nineteenth-century, anti-Christian polemicists, not to mention the most old-fashioned polemicist of them all, Richard Dawkins.[2] As often as not, science emerges from religion rather than despite it. (I would start with my own field of study, described in my *Darwinian Revolution*.[3])

Instead of the warfare metaphor, Alister endorses the two-books metaphor. Showing off, by recalling the compulsory Church of England instruction of my (English) state primary school, I share this:

---

1. Why is this? Pope John Paul II had the answer: faith is backed by reason. "According to the Apostle, it was part of the original plan of the creation that reason should without difficulty reach beyond the sensory data to the origin of all things: the Creator. But because of the disobedience by which man and woman chose to set themselves in full and absolute autonomy in relation to the One who had created them, this ready access to God the Creator diminished" (John Paul II, *Fides et Ratio: Encyclical Letter of John Paul II to the Catholic Bishops of the World* [Vatican City: L'Osservatore Romano, 1998], 22). Alister believes because in this respect he is not tainted by original sin. I do not believe because I am tainted by original sin. Hmm.

2. Peter Harrison, *The Bible, Protestantism, and the Rise of Natural Science* (Cambridge: Cambridge University Press, 2001); David C. Lindberg and Ronald Numbers, "Beyond War and Peace: a Reappraisal of the Encounter between Cambridge Christianity and Science," *Church History* 55 (1986): 338–54.

3. Michael Ruse, *The Darwinian Revolution*, Elements in the Philosophy of Biology (Cambridge: Cambridge University Press, 2019).

There is a book, who runs may read,
　　Which heavenly truth imparts,
And all the lore its scholars need,
　　Pure eyes and Christian hearts.
The works of God above, below,
　　Within us and around,
Are pages in that book to show
　　How God Himself is found.[4]

Now Alister is too experienced and cagey a scholar to say things outright—if all else fails, take back the claims of the text in a footnote—but it is not unfair to say that this is the conceptual background against which he approaches things (at least in this essay). He goes as far as to say that, for all the qualifications one might make, the two-books metaphor "nevertheless remains a valid and valuable conceptual tool for the Christian community, as it seeks to frame and engage the natural sciences" (p. 84).

Dialogue

Alister feels able to speak, in the terms of Ian Barbour, of a "dialogue" between science and religion.[5] Christianity and science are not the same, but they are on the same playing field as it were, and they can speak to and interact with each other. "Christianity and science are not the same." What does that mean? Alister does not spend a lot of time discussing science, mainly, I suspect, because, as one trained in the sciences and who has written much on the subject, he has little controversial to say. Science is a body of laws, trying to explain and understand the natural (physical and mental) world, without recourse to outside forces or causes. Approvingly, he quotes Eugenie Scott, former director of the National Center for Science Education: "Science neither denies nor opposes the supernatural, but *ignores* the supernatural for methodological reasons." The scientist as scientist is not committed to metaphysical naturalism, which denies any forces other than those of science. "Science is thus best seen as a *nontheistic*, not an *antitheistic*,

---

4. John Keble (1792–1866).
5. Ian Barbour, *Religion in an Age of Science* (New York: Harper and Row, 1990).

method of engaging reality," adding, "which is nevertheless porous to theological engagement" (p. 80).

What is this "theological engagement"? On the one hand, religion must be something *different* from science, or there is no need or place for engagement. As nonbelievers like me point out nonstop, if God and Jesus are one, it is hard to see how there can be any relationship between them. On the other hand, religion must be *similar* to science, or there is no possibility of engagement. *The Marriage of Figaro* is a great opera, but it is not about to engage with quantum mechanics. What then is religion if it is not a methodologically naturalistic approach to reality? Alister makes it clear that, for him, Christianity is all about us humans and our relationship to God. "Christianity is a religion of salvation, offering its own distinct understanding of what is wrong with human beings and the world and what can be done about this" (p. 90). Well, that certainly gives us the difference. The *Origin of Species* is not a sermon about what is wrong with human beings and what can be done about this. Nor, for that matter, is the *Descent of Man*. Perhaps Freud's *Three Essays on the Theory of Sexuality* qualifies, but would one really want to say this is a book of straight science?

What about the similarity? It is here, presumably, that natural theology steps up to the plate. The world is design-like. Design implies a creator. Hence, God. And note the interaction. Take the hand or the eye. Darwinism looks at these and speaks in terms of adaptation brought on by natural selection. Christianity looks at these and speaks of the designed creation of a good God. They are talking about the same things—a hand is a hand, not a Darwinian hand or a Christian hand—and they are both giving answers. The point is that they give answers that do not and could not conflict. Dialogue, not warfare.

I think it fair to say that, whatever you call it, Alister is aware that the discussion must go beyond the topics one finds in introductory philosophy texts—ontological argument, cosmological argument, and so forth. You must get involved in what usually comes under the heading of "revealed theology." "Christianity grounds its understanding of our world in Scripture—and the long process of reflection on Scripture throughout Christian history. It adopts neither the same starting point nor the same methods as the natural sciences but seeks to unfold the intellectual, spiritual, and moral consequences of the narrative of Jesus

Christ, which is both articulated and interpreted in the Christian Bible" (p. 82).

But that's okay. We are still in the dialogue business. "Proposing a dialogue between the natural sciences and Christian theology is thus not conceptually incoherent or contradictory" (p. 82).

One more bit of exposition of Alister McGrath's thinking. What about all the objections to natural theology? For instance, isn't the teleological argument worthless in the light of Darwin? We don't need God to explain the hand and the eye. And who is going to believe in the miracle at Cana in this day and age? Nice as it would be to have a source of unlimited bordeaux—or whatever it was that they drank in the Holy Land in those days—it is all pie in the sky. Or, rather, fantasy at the wedding. Alister anticipates these kinds of objections. Natural theology is not in the business of offering definitive proofs. It is more a matter of fleshing out the spiritual meaning of the material or natural. "In the twenty-first century, a Christian reading or rendering of nature . . . lays the groundwork for a 'spirituality of nature,' a way of engaging with the natural world that sees it as extending the scope and enriching the quality of the Christian perception of nature" (p. 94). He gives as an example of the right approach John Henry Newman's attitude to the design argument: we should believe in design because we believe in God, rather than in God because we believe in design.[6] Alister doesn't have much time either for the miracle doubters. Any serious person knows that it has been long since miracles were simply thought of as violations of the laws of nature. God is not constrained in this way.

Response

Well, what does someone like me say about all this? At one level, as you will realize, if you have read my essay, I am sympathetic to much that Alister claims. He makes much of how restricted is the reach of modern science. "After all, the prevailing consensus within the scientific community is that a mere 4 percent of the universe is observable: 23 percent of the universe is now thought to consist of dark matter, and 73 percent

---

6. John Henry Newman, *The Letters and Diaries of John Henry Newman*, 25 (Oxford: Oxford University Press, 1973), 97. The reader will note that I myself make reference to this argument in my essay. The reader will realize from what I am about to say that Newman's is precisely the attitude I would take, were I a Christian.

of dark energy. Thus, 96 percent of our universe lies beyond the scope of scientific investigation" (p. 80). I am not sure I buy into the implication that it will forever be beyond the scope of science, but I do agree that there is much that we do not know. How quantum entanglement works beats me, as I gather that, at the moment, it beats everyone else.

More importantly, I agree that there are problems forever beyond the scope of science as we know it—the body-mind problem, for example.[7] Alister mentions emergence, but that seems to me to be miracle-mongering of the most blatant kind. Putting a bunch of molecules together does not explain consciousness. Possibly some updated version of Spinoza's monism, panpsychism, will do the trick, seeing consciousness as part of the fabric of the universe.[8] But this is an idea, not an explanation. Perhaps a new paradigm will lead to some breakthroughs, but I doubt it can do so for everything. I am with J. B. S. Haldane on these matters. "Now my own suspicion is that the Universe is not only queerer than we suppose, but queerer than we can suppose."[9] In the wise words of Saint Richard of Oxford, "Modern physics teaches us that there is more to truth than meets the eye; or than meets the all too limited human mind, evolved as it was to cope with medium-sized objects moving at medium speeds through medium distances in Africa."[10]

Here I stand. I can do no other. Less theologically, I can go this far with Alister McGrath. But now, I am standing, not moving forward. Alister thinks that the way is now open for Christianity. Not for me it isn't. I am prepared to say that the unanswered—perhaps unanswerable—questions make me no atheist. Why is there something rather than nothing? I dunno. Could be a god, I guess. Could just be, without explanation. I end up as an agnostic or a skeptic. (I prefer the second term over the first because too often being an agnostic means you are uninterested in the question. In the tradition of Thomas Henry Huxley and of his grandson, Julian Huxley, I am very interested—without in any sense having desperate yearnings to move on to religious commitment.)

7. Michael Ruse, *Science and Spirituality: Making Room for Religion in the Age of Science* (Cambridge: Cambridge University Press, 2010).

8. Michael Ruse, *On Purpose* (Princeton: Princeton University Press, 2017), 286.

9. J. B. S. Haldane, *Possible Worlds and Other Essays* (London: Chatto and Windus, 1927).

10. Richard Dawkins, *A Devil's Chaplain: Reflections on Hope, Lies, Science, and Love* (Boston: Houghton Mifflin, 2003), 19.

So why am I not able to go with Alister McGrath on that major leap forward from doubt to belief? In part, I suspect, because for all his supposed openness and friendliness, Alister takes natural theology a lot more seriously than he rather pretends. Take the argument from design. I may be mistaken, but I sense altogether too much enthusiasm for the so-called anthropic principle, arguing that the constants of the universe are so remarkably tuned that this could not be chance; it must point to design or, rather, to Design.

> Let us begin by noting that human existence is critically dependent on several elements of the universe—especially carbon, nitrogen, and oxygen. Yet the emergence of these elements is widely conceded to be the outcome of processes that are critically dependent on the fundamental constants of the universe. Although such "anthropic" arguments are too easily overstated, it is perfectly reasonable to suggest that the universe appears to be fine-tuned for the emergence of humanity—and that such an observation is entirely consistent with a Christian doctrine of creation (p. 102).

I don't think it at all reasonable to suggest this. The whole argument strikes me as on a par with "think of a number, double it, and the answer you want is a half." Apart from the very dicey maneuver of arguing from just one example, Nobel Prize–winner Steven Weinberg points out that in fact the constants are not necessarily designed, as is often claimed.

> Recent developments in cosmology offer the possibility of an explanation of why the measured values of the cosmological constant and other physical constants are favorable for the appearance of intelligent life. According to the "chaotic inflation" theories of André Linde and others, the expanding cloud of billions of galaxies that we call the big bang may be just one fragment of a much larger universe in which big bangs go off all the time, each one with different values for the fundamental constants.
>
> In any such picture, in which the universe contains many parts with different values for what we call the constants of

nature, there would be no difficulty in understanding why these constants take values favorable to intelligent life. There would be a vast number of big bangs in which the constants of nature take values unfavorable for life, and many fewer where life is possible. You don't have to invoke a benevolent designer to explain why we are in one of the parts of the universe where life is possible: in all the other parts of the universe there is no one to raise the question.[11]

I am not sure Weinberg is right. I am not sure Weinberg thinks he is right. But it certainly gives me pause for thought before I declare victory and turn up for communion on Sunday morning.

I think there is also something fishy about Alister's treatment of the Bible and the creation issue, especially the Adam and Eve issue. He is pretty confident about the whole thing. "The issue is therefore not how individual biblical texts relate to the natural sciences but how the greater Christian 'big picture' of reality encourages and informs the scientific enterprise" (p. 96). I ask, how does the story of Adam and Eve "encourage and inform" what we have learned about human evolution from the fossil record, from the genetic variations in humans today, and most recently from the discovery and use of ancient DNA? "The Christian doctrine of humanity bearing the image of God offers a theological account of this innate desire and its true goal, which offers an interpretation of this experience and its significance, supplementing scientific insights at this point" (p. 103). The fact is that it doesn't; it just doesn't. The theological tradition to which Alister, as a practicing Anglican, belongs believes that we are tainted by the fall of Adam and this original sin could only be countered by Jesus's death on the cross, substitutionary atonement. From Article 9: "Original sin standeth not in the following of Adam, (as the Pelagians do vainly talk;) but it is the fault and corruption of the Nature of every man, that naturally is engendered of the offspring of Adam; whereby man is very far gone from original righteousness, and is of his own nature inclined to evil, so that the flesh lusteth always contrary to the Spirit; and therefore in every

---

11. Steven Weinberg, "The Future of Science, and the Universe," *New York Review of Books* 48, no. 18 (2001): 58–63.

person born into this world, it deserveth God's wrath and damnation."
From Article 31: "The Offering of Christ once made is that perfect
redemption, propitiation, and satisfaction, for all the sins of the whole
world, both original and actual; and there is none other satisfaction for
sin, but that alone."[12] Substitutionary atonement!

None of this can possibly be true. As I said in my essay, there were
no unique Adam and Eve; the protohuman population may have been
small, but it was never fewer than a few thousand. And everyone was
given to sin—parents, children, and grandchildren. It did not just arrive
because one protohuman ate a forbidden fruit. I don't think that science, including and especially Darwinian science, makes impossible all
religious belief. I think you can be a Christian and be a Darwinian.[13]
However, I just don't see Christianity fleshing out Darwinism in such a
way that the Darwinian ought to accept Christianity. I think it is going
to be Christianity taking its cues all the way. Substitutionary atonement
is out, apart from being theologically rather repellent. Why should fruit-
eating merit the appalling death on the cross, and what, in any case, is
it to me? With no literal Adam and Eve, you must opt for some other
theological tradition like incarnation theology, where Jesus's death on
the cross is seen as an exemplar of unconditional love, or some such
thing. Perhaps this works, but nothing makes this compulsory for the
nonbelieving scientist.

And this all is before you get to the problem of evil, a topic conspicuously missing from Alister's essay. I spoke to this problem in my essay.
Paradoxically, I think that modern science goes some way to explain why
we have the phenomenon we describe as evil. That doesn't mean it isn't a
problem and one that the God of Christianity should have tackled. And
if he couldn't, then he shouldn't have gotten into the creation business
in the first place. I am a bit of a Kantian on these things. I am not much
impressed if you tell me that Anne Frank's death of typhus in Bergen-
Belsen in 1945 turned out to be a good thing because most, or a good
number, can thereby enjoy eternal happiness. I don't think God should
have ever let death in a concentration camp happen to Anne Frank.
To think otherwise is to adopt the philosophy of the Doctor of Death,

---

12. https://anglicancommunion.org/media/109014/Thirty-Nine-Articles-of-Religion.pdf.
13. Michael Ruse, *Can a Darwinian Be a Christian?* (Cambridge: Cambridge University
Press, 2001).

Josef Mengele. I admit that the operations on twins was pretty hard cheese on my subjects, but it's okay, folks, because we all can now enjoy better health thanks to my findings. Thanks, but no thanks.

Two Protestant Theologies

A word by way of conclusion. I doubt that Alister McGrath and I are going to find a meeting place any time soon. The true reason, I suspect, is that we start from very different theological positions. If I say I see him as a conventional Anglican, I mean no slur. He takes seriously the Bible, and while he is certainly not a crude biblical literalist, he does believe that the Bible contains essential truths that cannot be compromised: the significance of Adam and Eve, the fall, the consequent original sin, Jesus's atoning sacrifice on the cross. Although a nonbeliever, I come from a very different Protestant tradition. Alister is not at all keen on that Kierkegaard-Barth tradition, one that goes back to Luther, who spoke of "that whore reason," that downplays natural theology, feeling that faith is compromised by proof—it must be a leap into the absurd. "Although Karl Barth's criticism of this form of natural theology [the theology of someone like Archdeacon Paley] has been influential within some sections of Protestantism, Barth's failure to distinguish the role and place of natural theology in systematic theology and in apologetics has weakened the force of such criticisms in an increasingly post-Christian age" (p. 93).

For me, this is where you start: faith, not reason; faith, not evidence; faith, not proof; faith because it compels and you can do no other; the faith that struck down Saul on the road to Damascus. Hardly reasonable, given that he ended up having his head lopped off! I combine this—and here you can see the Quaker influence—with a feeling for apophatic theology. You can define God only negatively, by saying what he is not. For me, science and religion cannot clash because I don't think they are in the same ballpark. It is not surprising that Quakers are much into mysticism.

Let me make clear what I am saying and why. I am not now admitting to conversion and to Christianity. I am saying that, for me, it is faith or nothing. I don't have faith, and so for me it is nothing—nothing in the sense of ignorance, not of firm nonbelief. If I did have faith, especially given my reluctance to pin down God to specific features,

I see no obstacle at all from science to being a Christian. What I don't think works is the kind of halfway position of Alister McGrath. He wants Christianity, but he is not prepared to elevate faith and give up on reason. That is the point I make. I return to 1 Corinthians 13:13 (KJV): "Now abideth faith, hope, charity, these three; but the greatest of these is charity." I don't have faith, and I am not sure hope is something I want to have. I want to live my life now for what it is rather than for the hope of true happiness in the hereafter.

> The lust after life in the chills of its lust
>   Claims a passport of death.
> The lover of life sees the flame in our dust
>   And a gift in our breath.[14]

Will Alister McGrath have charity toward such a nonbelieving sinner as I?

---

14. George Meredith, "In the Woods," *Fortnightly Review* 8 (1870): 179–83.

RESPONSE TO ALISTER MCGRATH

BRUCE GORDON

This book affords me the pleasure of interacting with Alister for the first time, though I've certainly been aware of his prodigious scholarly output. Since we're both Christians who love science and theology and desire the rational advancement of Christian claims, I hope for a fruitful exchange. Consequently, I'll start below with points of agreement before responding to disagreements. Regarding the latter, Alister says some interesting things about the need for epistemological pluralism despite the world's ontological unity. I mostly agree in respect of the division of labor but significantly disagree on the role that methodological naturalism plays at these different levels of analysis. Secondly, as we move up the explanatory hierarchy from fundamental physics through chemistry and biology to neurophysiology and consciousness, Alister thinks "emergence" explains the origin of higher levels of complexity and "top-down causation" explains how higher levels affect the lower ones. In this regard, I gave reasons in my main essay (I have lots more) for thinking inanimate nature is causally passive. Thus, aside from top-down *mental* causation, I find notions of emergence and top-down causality—even when precise mathematical *descriptions* can be given—explanatorily vacuous. I'll illustrate this in three ways: (1) by exploring the physical and metaphysical implications of God's timeless creative act, (2) by discussing how classical physics is recovered (emerges) from quantum physics and why this does nothing for naturalistic emergence, and (3) by talking about consciousness and the brain. Some final reservations about the dialogue view in science and theology will provide a conclusion.

How Pleasant It Is for Brethren to Dwell in Unity

With a nod to Psalm 133, even Christian mutual-congratulation societies are boring, so I'll be brief. Alister and I agree there's conceptual overlap between theology and the natural sciences (p. 80) and the two-books metaphor highlights the unity of reality, so Christianity and science are mutually relevant (p. 104). We agree that nature and Scripture each need interpretation and this is a central task of both science and theology (pp. 98–101). We agree the interaction between science and theology involves nonreductionistic integration of different levels of analysis to find a coherent picture (pp. 86–89), though our understanding of how this should be done diverges. We agree explanatory power is virtuous and worldview systems may be evaluated by comparing their explanatory power (p. 61). We agree that Christianity makes ontic and epistemic claims relevant to science, particularly with respect to its doctrine of creation (p. 41). We both think natural theology is important not only as support for Christians but also as a challenge to non-Christian views of the world, especially scientism (pp. 95–98). We both think Charles Taylor's account of secularization is useful and the "social imaginary" of secular modernity is prejudicially trapped in the "immanent frame" (p. 100); I also think preoccupation with methodological naturalism is symptomatic of this. Finally, we're both concerned the dialogue view—in its treatment of different perspectives, levels of analysis, and levels of meaning—can reduce to "an enumeration of possibilities, without any engagement or modification as a result of respectful discussion" (p. 101). While dialogue *can* address misunderstandings and reveal unexpected points of similarity, how readily does it free minds trapped in the immanent frame?

On Epistemic Pluralism and Methodological Naturalism: Some Critical Observations

Emergentism parses the world into ontological strata investigated using different methods. Each successive level has a special science dealing with complex structures distinguished by the causal characteristics of that level. Higher-level causal patterns supervene on lower-level interactions but aren't reducible to them, and emergent nomological structures irreducible to lower-level laws exercise "downward causation" on lower-level phenomena. At each level, Alister regards methodological naturalism (MN) as a constraint on *scientific* investigation (p. 79). I've argued in my essay (pp. 145–50) and elsewhere[1] that MN isn't necessary to science and that science functions better with a uniformitarianism that allows for intelligent causation. I won't repeat those arguments here. Instead, I'll focus on Alister's treatment of MN, since he thinks it requires observability (p. 80, 100), and he illustrates this point using dark matter and dark energy as embarrassments in cosmology.

While the standard Λ-CDM model in cosmology[2] requires these things and scientists are looking for them, Alister's equation of methodological naturalism with observability is mistaken, as is his belief that science "seeks to explain the natural world only in terms of the observable" (p. 100). Universally accepted and well-confirmed scientific theories postulate unobservable entities all the time. No one has seen a quark, for example, but its existence is accepted because it provides a testable explanation that has survived testing. The tests themselves involve a variety of theories *also* postulating unobservable entities known only through observable effects. The literature in philosophy of science discussing the observational-theoretical distinction, the ontological status of theoretical entities, and the theory-ladenness of observation is vast, and Alister's remarks show no sensitivity to it.[3] Similarly, there's a well-developed mathematical theory of design detection that allows

---

1. Bruce Gordon, "Is Intelligent Design Science? The Scientific Status and Future of Design-Theoretic Explanations," in William Dembski and James Kushiner, eds., *Signs of Intelligence: Understanding Intelligent Design* (Grand Rapids: Brazos, 2001), 193–216; Bruce Gordon, "In Defense of Uniformitarianism," *Perspectives on Science and the Christian Faith* 65, no.2 (2013): 79–86; and Bruce Gordon, "Scientific Explanations are Not Limited to Natural Causes" and "Gordon's Response to Bishop," in Steven Cowan, ed., *Problems in Epistemology and Metaphysics: An Introduction to Contemporary Debates* (New York: Bloomsbury Academic, 2020, forthcoming). See also Stephen Meyer, "Sauce for the Goose: Intelligent Design, Scientific Methodology, and the Demarcation Problem," in Bruce Gordon and William Dembski, eds., *The Nature of Nature: Examining the Role of Naturalism in Science* (Wilmington, DE: ISI, 2011), 95–131.

2. In the Λ-CDM model, the Λ (lambda) represents the cosmological constant, interpreted as the dark energy hypothesized to explain the accelerating expansion of the universe, and the CDM represents the "cold dark matter" (cold, slow-moving particles that don't interact with electromagnetic radiation and thus resist detection) hypothesized to explain the gravitational behavior of ordinary matter. If general relativity is correct, then only 5 percent of the universe consists of ordinary mass-energy, while 95 percent of the universe must be composed of dark matter and dark energy.

3. Those wanting to get up to speed on these issues will find it helpful to read the articles on theoretical terms in science, theory and observation in science, ontological commitment,

defeasible empirical testing for intelligent causation.[4] A successful design test licenses inference to an intelligent cause as the best explanation for a natural phenomenon. This intelligent cause is an unobserved theoretical entity postulated to explain observed effects. It has the same scientific status as any other unobserved theoretical entity postulated to explain observable effects (e.g., quarks). Two things follow: (1) observability doesn't function as a demarcation criterion separating science from nonscience, and (2) MN doesn't serve science well; uniformitarianism does a much better job.

The Exclusivity of Mental Causation and the Explanatory Vacuity of Emergence

Alister thinks emergence and top-down causation have *natural* explanatory power in science; I don't so much. Citing mathematical physicist George Ellis,[5] Alister emphasizes "levels of explanation" (p. 88) and "secondary ongoing processes of emergence and complexification directed by divine providence" (pp. 102–103). This direction is understood as intrinsic to the created order by way of novel systemic properties arising at "appropriate" levels of organizational complexity that can't be reduced to or predicted from lower-level phenomena (p. 103). Correspondingly, Alister quotes with approval Charles Kingsley's remark that God is so wise he can "make all things make themselves" (p. 102). Maybe, but the empirical question is whether he *did*. Ellis is a brilliant physicist, but his book involves a lot of handwaving, appeals to quantum indeterminacy to create wiggle room for the magic of emergence, and invocations of mind-independent abstracta (Platonic forms) with top-down causal powers.

As I explained in my main essay, invoking quantum indeterminacy in naturalistic explanation violates the principle of sufficient reason to disastrous effect. Furthermore, since abstraction is a *mental* process, attributing mind-independent existence and causal power to abstracta is

---

scientific realism, and other related entries in the *Stanford Encyclopedia of Philosophy* (https://plato.stanford.edu/index.html).

4. See my main essay (pp. 136–50, et passim) for discussion and references.

5. See George Ellis, *How Can Physics Underlie the Mind? Top-Down Causation in the Human Context* (Berlin: Springer, 2016). Incidentally, Ellis is a Quaker Christian, like Michael was before his early lapse.

simply a category mistake. Augustine was right: abstracta are independent of *human* minds but dependent on the mind of God. They have no causal power but derive their applicability to nature from God's design. Finally, Ellis's explanatory strategies do not address cosmological fine-tuning or overcome the obstacles to undirected biological evolution I discussed in my essay. Nor do they provide a plausible naturalistic account of the origin of consciousness, something I will say more about at the end of this section.

Reflect with me on two things that may seem odd at this point: God's relationship to time and the nature of time itself. Bear with me and the fruit will be evident. The classical Christian doctrine of creation is that God brought the universe into existence out of *nothing*. This means God created not only what we call matter and energy but space and time as well. Logically and ontologically prior to creation, there was no time, only a timeless eternity. This leads to the classical understanding of God as beyond space and time: God is an immaterial being without spatial location who is timelessly eternal. As Augustine famously stated in Book XI of his *Confessions*, "There can be no time without creation . . . and you [God] are before all times, the eternal creator of all times, and [those] times are not coeternal with you."[6]

God created the universe *with* time, not *in* time. As such, in a singular timeless act, God brought all time and space and everything happening in it into existence through an act of thought. What we time-bound creatures call the past, the present, and the future exist timelessly in the mind of God. From the divine perspective, then, we should speak not of space and time but of spacetime, for the whole of our three-dimensional space and its extension in time was a singular act of divine creation. Interestingly, this fusion of space and time into spacetime is the conclusion of modern physics as well, receiving expression in Einstein's special and general theories of relativity. Within spacetime, the measurement of time's passage is relativized to the reference frame (inertial frame) of the observer and is affected by the state of motion of that inertial frame and the intensity of the gravitational field in which it is embedded. Observers in *different* reference frames may experience the

---

6. Saint Augustine, *The Confessions of St. Augustine*, trans. John K. Ryan (New York: Doubleday, 1960), XI.30:269.

same spacetime event *differently* as past, present, or future. Which is to say, from the standpoint of physics, the passage of time is an *artifact* of one's inertial frame *within* spacetime. But the past, the present, and the future all coexist in spacetime itself. This is the standard interpretation of relativity, and it points toward the *static* nature of spacetime in global (universal) perspective—past, present, and future moments of time are all equally real and time does not flow. In the local (observer's reference frame) perspective, however, time is *dynamic*, the present is the only moment of time that seems real, and time flows into the future as the past ceases to exist.

How is the *global* perspective reconciled with the *local* measurement of time's passage or with the human experience of time's flow and our decision-making freedom within it?[7] Recall that the state of a quantum system is described by an abstract mathematical object called a *wavefunction*. The discipline of *quantum cosmology* applies this mathematical description to the whole universe, merging the description of spacetime in general relativity with the mathematical descriptions of quantum physics to get an unwieldy mathematical monstrosity called the Wheeler-DeWitt equation. The solutions of this equation describe the quantum state of the universe, that is, the *universal wavefunction*.[8] Just like we can consider an ordinary quantum system in two ways—we can look at it as a whole from the *outside*, or we can consider it from the standpoint of something that is *inside* it—we can think about the universal wavefunction this way too. Donald Page and William Wootters have shown how the universal wavefunction can look static from the outside while subsystems within it develop dynamically by an appropriate internal measure of time.[9] Various technical issues with

---

7. I discuss these ideas in much greater and more technical detail in "Idealism and Science: The Quantum-Theoretic and Neuroscientific Foundations of Reality," in Joshua R. Farris and Benedikt P. Göcke, eds. *The Routledge Handbook of Idealism and Immaterialism* (New York: Routledge, forthcoming 2020); and in "Consciousness and Quantum Information," in Brian Krouse and Cristi Cooper, eds. *Minds, Brains, and Consciousness* (Seattle: Discovery Institute Press, forthcoming 2020).

8. The Wheeler-DeWitt equation is the general-relativistic quantum analogue of the Schrödinger equation in ordinary quantum mechanics. Its solutions represent all the information about the geometry and matter content of the universe. See Carlo Rovelli, "The Strange Equation of Quantum Gravity," June 3, 2015, https://arxiv.org/pdf/1506.00927.pdf.

9. Donald Page and William Wootters, "Evolution Without Evolution: Dynamics Described by Stationary Observables," *Physical Review D* 27 (1983): 2885–92.

this proposal have been resolved by Giovannetti, Lloyd, and Maccone.[10] What is more, Moreva et al. have performed an experiment showing how this mechanism works by creating a quantum state in the laboratory that an external observer perceives as static even while mathematically correlated subsystems internally measure each other's development.[11] This reconciliation of global and local perspectives produces two points of view: (1) that of a creator-observer external to the universe (God) and (2) that of internal observers (us). The transcendent creator-observer perceives the whole universe as a static system, but internal observers experience time as flowing from the past into the future. Physics therefore provides a way to reconcile an eternal static perspective with a temporal dynamic one.

What is happening at the level of our psychological experience of freedom, though, especially with respect to its role in grounding moral responsibility? We can avail ourselves of Augustine's genius again. He remarks:

> The past no longer exists, and the future is not yet in being . . . [and the present has no length, for] if it is extended, it is divided into past and future. The present has no space . . . [and yet] O Lord, we perceive intervals of time. . . . If such things were nothing at all, they could not be perceived in any way. Therefore, both future and past times have being. . . . [P]erhaps it might properly be said that there are three times, the present of things past, the present of things present, and the present of things future. These three are in the soul, but elsewhere I do not see them: the present of things past is in memory; the present of things present is in intuition; the present of things future is in

---

10. Vittorio Giovannetti, Seth Lloyd, and Lorenzo Maccone, "Quantum Time," *Physical Review D* 92 (2015): 045033.

11. E. V. Moreva et al., "Time from Quantum Entanglement: an Experimental Illustration," *Physical Review A* 89 (2014): 052122; Ekaterina Moreva et al., "The Time as an Emergent Property of Quantum Mechanics: A Synthetic Description of a First Experimental Approach," *Journal of Physics: Conference Series* 626 (2015): 012019.

expectation. . . . Time [therefore] is nothing more than disten-
tion: but of what thing I know not, and the marvel is, if it is not
of the mind itself.[12]

Every moment of our conscious experience is distended to include
memories of the past and anticipations of the future, all synthesized to
provide a basis for our decisions. If we ask how we can have freedom of
choice and moral responsibility when the future, with every decision we
will make, exists timelessly as a creative act of God, the answer is that
we have freedom *in each moment of consciousness*, and our lives are the
collection of such moments. Each conscious moment gives us freedom of
rational choice within the constraints of our nature, and God eternally
perceives what that choice is. If we would have chosen differently—and
we are created with the freedom to do so—then God, in his timeless
creative act, would have brought a different universe into being. So
from the point in universal history that finite choice first appears, God
includes the chosen actions of all finite moral agents in his timeless
creative act, and, indeed, he can do so transhistorically so that the effect
of a choice at a given point in spacetime history can, if God so wills,
affect *all* of spacetime history.

This is all very interesting, but what's my point? Simply this: from
the standpoint of a timeless universal creative act, there is no distinction
between creation and providence. Every manifestation of providence,
from the regularity of nature to the functionally complex natural structures that surpass it, to specific answers to prayer and any of God's
miraculous actions in history, is included in God's singular timeless
creative act. This subverts the distinction between secondary causation
involving *ceteris paribus* laws fixed in a relatively autonomous natural
order and an occasionalism in which every event in inanimate nature
is the direct result of divine action. Indeed, it favors occasionalism,
because the only *genuine* causal power is possessed by God and by finite
sentient agents whose free actions are incorporated into God's timeless
creative act. The rest of reality is passive; it has no intrinsic causal effi-
cacy. Causal power is exclusively the possession of minds: *all* efficient

---

12. Augustine, *The Confessions of St. Augustine,* XI.15:254; XI.16:255; XI.17:256;
XI.18:258; XI.26:264.

causation is top-down because *all* efficient causation is mental causation. Consciousness isn't what needs explaining; consciousness is what *does* the explaining.[13]

This illumines why the idea of primitive metaphysical necessity grounding secondary causal powers in nature is so weak. Its theistic defenders generally maintain that disallowing it confuses metaphysics with epistemology, that is, the necessary with the analytic or *a priori*. We don't need to see why this causal power flows essentially from that substance's nature, they say, so long as it's clear from God's perspective. But rejecting conceivability as a guide to metaphysical necessity unjustifiably constrains God's power and strips us of the only analytical tool we have, leaving us defenseless against gratuitous assertions. This won't do. Causal effects *not* conceptually manifest in the essential natures of natural kinds only coincide with those kinds because God *freely makes it so*. Different causal effects could have been correlated with them had God so decided. Where does this leave secondary causation? It shows that causal powers are not intrinsic to natural kinds; they do not arise from their natures. So these kinds do not function as secondary causes in their own right. Rather, God continuously acts to produce *that* behavior in *that* kind of thing.[14] Absent intrinsic causal powers, then, the need for continuous divine action is evident, and we move again from secondary causation to occasionalism as the best account of divine providence.

The superiority of occasionalism from the "bottom up" *within* time is also evident. I illustrated this from quantum physics in my main

---

13. The reasons for this, and how it works across the spectrum of the sciences, is discussed at length in my essays "Idealism and Science" and "Consciousness and Quantum Information" (see earlier footnote).

14. Some have tried to argue, on an exegetical basis, that God infuses nature with inherent capacities/powers. Once you start trying to prove modes of divine providence from Scripture, however, you find the knife cuts more than one way, and no side finds the exegesis of any other convincing. As an occasionalist, I would read the following passages as confirming occasionalism: Ps. 104:10, 13–14; Ps. 139:13–16; Matt. 6:28–30; Matt. 10:29–30; Acts 17:25, 28; Col. 1:16–17; Heb. 11:3; etc. But others disagree (see C. John Collins, *The God of Miracles: An Exegetical Examination of God's Action in the World* [Wheaton: Crossway, 2000]). The moral is that biblical exegesis is not the way to resolve this issue. Rather, one must decide what God has done in nature, and how God acts in nature, by examining nature and reflecting on its metaphysical implications. What Scripture tells us is that God acts both creatively and providentially in nature, not the mode of his action. And nature, viewed both from the standpoint of the timeless creative act of God and from within at the most basic level of what we call physical reality, points to the causal impotence of the inanimate world and hence to occasionalism as the superior view.

essay (pp. 150–56), but we can talk about emergence in this context too. Two different mathematical limits show how Newtonian (classical) mechanics can emerge (be recovered) from quantum mechanics.[15] Neither of these continuous limits remove the quantum character of physical systems; they just dampen it. What is happening when the seemingly classical world we experience "emerges" from the quantum world is that the "probability waves" in the quantum wavefunction are interfering with each other, a process that physicists call *environmental decoherence*. You can think of it in terms of two water waves: if the waves have the same height/depth, then when the crest of one wave meets the trough of the other, the waves disappear and the surface of the water is calm. Mathematically described, stable macroscopic reality comes from microscopic reality by a process like that. The destructive interference of quantum probability waves give our macroscopic reality a stable appearance. Even though this mathematical description is useful for scientific and engineering purposes, it does not give us a macroscopic world of material substances. The apparent solidity of the world we experience is a mathematical epiphenomenon of quantum statistics. The underlying phenomena retain their insubstantiality and so fail to give us the material substances needed as possessors of the causal powers secondary causation requires. The causal power producing our reality does not reside within nature. Insofar as emergence is postulated as a *natural explanation* for how the world of our experience arises from quantum phenomena, therefore, it is vacuous. Occasionalism again proves superior.[16]

Finally, we need to discuss whether consciousness can be understood naturalistically as an emergent property of brain function. While Alister

---

15. The two limits in question are the physically unrealistic classical-mechanical limit, in which Planck's constant goes to zero, and the classical-statistical limit, in which temperature increases without bound and density decreases toward zero (also called the ideal-gas limit). See Bruce Gordon, "Maxwell-Boltzmann Statistics and the Metaphysics of Modality," *Synthese* 133, no. 3 (2002): 393–417, especially 402–7, for an extensive examination of the metaphysical significance of these limits.

16. I cannot, in the space I'm allowed here, give a thorough critique of attempts to ground macroscopic reality naturalistically in microphysics using technical formulations of supervenience and emergence in the context of relativistic quantum mechanics and quantum field theory. I've provided just such a critique in my essay "The Incompatibility of Physicalism with Physics," in Joshua Farris and Keith Loftin, eds. *Christian Physicalism: Philosophical Theological Criticisms* (New York: Lexington, 2018), 371–402; and in §4 (Quantum Fields: From Theistic Quantum Idealism to Conscious Realism) of my essay "Idealism and Science."

thinks there is much about being human that science cannot adequately capture, he nonetheless claims that a naturalistic account of humanity can be given within the parameters of science (p. 90). In this context he gives approval to George Ellis's approach (p. 88n35). Ellis maintains, among other assertions of emergence, that consciousness is an emergent property of neural networks in the human brain.[17] Ironically, Michael seems to have greater appreciation of the limits of naturalistic science here, quoting with approval Leibniz's argument that consciousness cannot have a basis in physical processes, no matter how computationally complex (p. 39).

I cannot offer a complete critique of nonreductive naturalist theories of mind here, let alone articulate what I see as the most promising alternative,[18] so I'll focus on a straightforward objection to the idea that consciousness is generated, in whole or in part, by brain function. Saying that consciousness is generated by physical processes and patterns in the brain ignores rather than solves the hard problem of consciousness. It equates cognition (understanding, intentionality, awareness) with material phenomena, when the latter are not intrinsically about anything, nor could they be. Such an approach doesn't offer us a theory of consciousness so much as a theory of how the phenomena of third-person neurobiology might causally and computationally be *correlated* with the components of first-person experience. Now, this in itself is a worthy goal and, I would say, is all we should expect from the neuroscience of consciousness. But it is correlation of the quality of consciousness *with* brain functionality, not causal generation of consciousness *by* brain functionality.

A simple analogy would be to say that neural nets and synaptic traffic in the brain provide information storage and syntactic processing for consciousness to use in the same way that the vocabulary and syntax of natural language provide a tool for meaningful communication. Just as the meaning of natural language is not intrinsic to the aural or visual symbols and syntax used to represent this meaning, the semantic content of thought has no intrinsic relationship to the neurochemical symbols and neurophysiological syntax of the brain. Consciousness is

---

17. See George Ellis, *How Can Physics Underlie the Mind?*, 291–394.
18. See §5 (Neuroscience, Consciousness, and Theistic Quantum Idealism) of my essay "Idealism and Science" for an extensive discussion of these themes.

something fundamentally immaterial that transcends the brain. A useful simile is that consciousness extracts information from the phenomenology of brain-states like a DVD player and screen extract and display information from a DVD. The difference is that consciousness actively interprets the extracted information in the service of *understanding*, whereas the DVD player and screen integrate sight and sound without comprehension, intention, or ability to act. The idea that consciousness emerges from brain activity is therefore simply wrong.

Beyond Milquetoast

Dialogue is nice, but it takes you only so far. Moving beyond milquetoast notions of mutually enriching conversations to a robust metaphysical *integration* of science and philosophical theology is necessary. If a scientifically minded nonbeliever is to recognize the deficiency of their views and move from apathetic complacency to intellectual engagement with Christianity, they need to understand that science *depends on and points to God* and that naturalistic explanations are inadequate not just *outside* science but *within* science as well. This moves well beyond mere acknowledgement of the compatibility of Christianity and science as practiced in the immanent frame and even beyond consideration of the ways reflecting on their relationship might enrich and inform them both. What is needed is a way of successfully doing science that breaks out of the immanent frame and manifests its deficiency, not just as a worldview but as a basis for science itself.

REJOINDER

ALISTER MCGRATH

I am very grateful to Michael and Bruce for such thoughtful engagements with my reflections on a dialogical approach to science and religion. In his wide-ranging response to my piece, Michael raises a range of questions that focus on the question of how we decide—indeed, *if* we can decide—between a theistic and an atheist view of the universe. He illustrates this general issue in relation to the fine-tuning of the universe. How are we to explain this? The answer, of course, is that there are multiple explanations, and we are called upon to make an act of judgment and discernment as to which of these we consider to be the best. It is clear that Michael and I arrive at different conclusions on a series of issues such as the significance of fine-tuning, reflecting the fact that our reasoning rests on nests of embedded working assumptions—for example, about the plausibility of the multiverse hypothesis and its implications for theism, both of which are intensely contested questions. This raises the awkward question of how we can hope to arrive at any secure conclusion on such matters, when the premises on which they are based are epistemically insecure.

My own view is that the complexity of the issues is best accommodated by using the visual images of focus and quality of rendering. What way of thinking seems to bring things into focus and enfold the complexity of our world? My judgment is that a Christian lens—to continue using primarily visual analogies—offers me the most satisfactory rendering of our complex world. Yet we still see through a glass darkly, to use Paul's helpful image (1 Corinthians 13:12 KJV).

Michael suggests that my appeal to some form of natural theology is vulnerable on Darwinian and other grounds. Among those additional concerns, I would note the moral and aesthetic ambiguity of nature, exemplified by the suffering that underlies the evolutionary process; while robust responses may certainly be made from a Christian perspective,[1] there remains a lingering sense of conceptual incongruity at this point. Yet *every* way of reading the "book of nature," whether religious or otherwise, encounters such areas of intellectual tension and perceived incongruity.

Michael rightly points out that I fail to engage the question of how evil is to be accommodated within a natural theology. It is a fair point. I am writing this piece in early May 2020, while the COVID-19 crisis is still causing major public health problems and massive social disruption throughout much of the world. Some have called this virus "evil." Yet what we call "evil" is an interpretation of what is ultimately "natural." Viruses are part of the natural order. They are natural phenomena that we might chose to deem "evil" on account of their impact on us. Yet if the coronavirus were to be allowed to make a rejoinder to this somewhat anthropocentric evaluation of this situation, it might simply point out that it was merely doing what was natural.

So why do we consider certain aspects of the natural order to be evil?[2] Why do so many people see the existence of suffering as morally wrong, not simply existentially irritating? We need an interpretative framework through which we can view the natural order if we are to make such judgments. Yet this framework is not given by the natural order itself. A Christian natural theology, in my view, offers a theological framework that enables us to explain why we see evil and suffering as at least *wrong*, if not *unjust*. It speaks not simply of *nature*, but of *creation*, thus pointing to the need to interpret nature, as we now see it, within the overall context of the "economy of salvation." The world as we now see it is not necessarily the world that was pronounced to be "good" by its Creator (Genesis 1:31).

In responding to Michael's entirely reasonable complaint that I fail

---

1. See, for example, Christopher Southgate, *The Groaning of Creation: God, Evolution, and the Problem of Evil* (Louisville, KY: Westminster John Knox, 2008).

2. For some representative responses to this question, see Willem B. Drees, ed., *Is Nature Ever Evil? Religion, Science, and Value* (London: Routledge, 2003).

to deal with the question of evil, I think it is important to reiterate the importance of the interpretative frameworks with which we approach the natural world. What framework allows us to transpose aspects of the natural order into the moral categories of good and evil? In my view, a purely empirical account of nature cannot make such calls; if we are to use moral categories to refer to nature, we have to appeal—and justify this appeal—to moral philosophy or theology, introducing reflection on what *ought* to be the case. While I do not claim that Christianity has some exclusive capacity to enable such a reflection, I am clear that it does possess such a capacity, and that this is a significant asset in engaging this question. What drew me to Christianity was my growing realization that it offers a way of understanding and inhabiting our world that welcomes the natural sciences, while exposing their limits. To use the language of C. S. Lewis, I found it could "fit in" the natural sciences in a way I found profoundly satisfying.

Bruce likewise raises some important questions and offers some helpful clarifications on the points at which we appear to agree and those on which we differ. While it is always difficult to define strict disciplinary frontiers between science, philosophy, and theology, I sense that Bruce and I have some significant disagreements about the nature of science itself—particularly in terms of how we account for causal processes within the natural world—which inevitably feed into our reflections on the relation of science and faith. My own views on the complex causal networks that we observe in the natural world, including human beings, are similar to those set out in some detail by the cosmologist George Ellis, which I consider to be an excellent account of this issue.[3] Bruce takes a different position on this matter, and that clearly plays into our more theological reflections.

In my article, I raised the question of the role of unobservables in scientific explanation and indicated that this raises some difficulties for certain forms of methodological naturalism. Bruce and I clearly agree that science regularly appeals to what cannot be observed—Newton's concept of gravity being an excellent example—in order to explain what

---

3. George Ellis, *How Can Physics Underlie the Mind? Top-Down Causation in the Human Context* (Heidelberg: Springer, 2016). It is helpful to read Ellis in the light of the points made in Phyllis McKay Illari and Federica Russo, *Causality: Philosophical Theory Meets Scientific Practice* (Oxford: Oxford University Press, 2014).

can. In my published works, I regularly highlight the apologetic importance of this point. I agree with Bruce that we may present God as an
"unobserved theoretical entity postulated to explain observed effects"
(p. 119) and often use this line of approach in offering a defense of the
rationality of theism. My point was rather that the accommodation of
such inferred unobservable entities does raise some theoretical difficulties for methodological naturalism, and perhaps more importantly
for popular forms of atheism in relation to the question of proving
one's belief systems. The point at issue is that, when strictly applied,
methodological naturalism is limited to the world of the observable,
in that the appeal to unobservable entities to explain what is observed
involves *additional judgments* that, in my view, go beyond its stated set
of controlling assumptions.

I share Bruce's suspicions about vague appeals to quantum indeterminacy in naturalistic explanation and often feel that these are of little
genuine value, apart from creating generalized explanatory openings or
windows for divine presence and action. Perhaps more significantly, the
divergences within the leading schools of quantum theory on issues such
as realism and causality are such that I am reluctant to invest too heavily
in an appeal to the quantum world in exploring the relation of science
and faith. Albert Einstein, Werner Heisenberg, and Max Planck are
all excellent dialogue partners for Christian theology and apologetics—
but entering into a dialogue with them does not entail accepting their
outlooks in their totality but rather welcoming the openings they create
and resources they provide for discussion of what Karl Popper helpfully
called "ultimate questions," which so clearly lie beyond the reach of
science to answer.

I was interested in Bruce's extended reflections on the nature of
time and agree that this is an important topic, both scientifically and
theologically. While I am currently working on a paper dealing with
this topic, I do not engage this theme to any significant extent in my
original article. It remains an important area of discussion in dialogue
with philosophy and science, especially the theory of relativity.

Perhaps the most important point at which Bruce and I appear
to have differences lies in the field of metaphysics. "Moving beyond
milquetoast notions of mutually enriching conversations to a robust metaphysical *integration* of science and philosophical theology is necessary"

(p. 127). I am very grateful to Bruce for introducing me to the word *milquetoast*, which was new to me. As I read Bruce at this point, I was delighted to note our intellectual convergence on this matter—at least in relation to the academic issues involved, even if the way we express and enact this differs somewhat. Bruce makes this point as follows: "If a scientifically minded nonbeliever is to recognize the deficiency of their views and move from apathetic complacency to intellectual engagement with Christianity, they need to understand that science *depends on and points to God* and that naturalistic explanations are inadequate not just *outside* science but *within* science as well" (p. 127). I agree with the apologetic point being made. It is important to show that a Christian vision of reality—which can be framed metaphysically—enables, sustains, and informs the natural sciences.[4] Yet I know too many intelligent and reflective nonbelievers to agree with Bruce's suggestion that their stance universally or necessarily amounts to an "apathetic complacency."

Now, perhaps the difference between Bruce and me at this point is ultimately cultural, tinged with influences from my own faith story. Culturally, my British academic heritage means that I don't see "mutually enriching conversations" as feeble, insipid, or bland (the qualities that my dictionary associates with this word *milquetoast*) but as planting the seeds of doubt with their existing ways of thinking and opening doors of reflection. Part of the reason I came to faith was that my atheist misgivings about religious faith were not treated as "apathetic complacency" but as serious concerns that needed to be respected—and answered.

I agree with Bruce that a "robust metaphysical *integration* of science and philosophical theology" (p. 127) is desirable, although I am suspicious of overreaching theories that create suspicion on account of their ambition.[5] I have learned to live with a degree of intellectual messiness and conceptual unclarity, as these seem to me to be the inevitable outcome of the complexity of our world. I now realize that the Enlightenment's attempts to subjugate a complex and messy world to the categories of human reason can never hope to succeed. Christianity offers us a view of the world that is rational, without being restricted to

---

4. See especially Hanby, *No God, No Science?*

5. I warm to Christian Smith's approach in his *Atheist Overreach: What Atheism Can't Deliver* (New York: Oxford University Press, 2019).

that small and existentially dissatisfying world that can be proved by reason alone.

This book has clearly opened up some rich and rewarding questions and is likely to stimulate some excellent discussions on the part of its readers. It is a great pleasure to be able to respond to the important points raised by Michael and Bruce, although it is also frustrating that limits on space mean I can only deal with their points very briefly. As these tentative responses indicate, the relation of science and faith is a fascinating and complex topic, which we have only begun to explore in this volume!

CONSTRAINED INTEGRATION VIEW

*Optimizing Coherence and Seeking Truth in the
Interaction between Science and Christianity*

BRUCE GORDON

Quo Vadimus?

Christianity entails *idealism* in a basic sense: *mind* is foundational to reality, and matter is derivative. The contingent universe we inhabit is not an unexplained material datum but the intelligent product of divine thought, and God is the necessary Being from whom it derives its existence and purpose. Of course, being an idealist in this sense does not require material objects to be mere perceptions. That God is the originator and sustainer of the universe still permits material appearances to be grounded in material substances. Investigating the *nature* of material reality, however, is something to which science, philosophy, and theology must all contribute. Furthermore, their contributions are interwoven: reality is monolithic, and the truth about it must similarly be unified. Science, philosophy, and theology interact and constrain one another in profound ways as we search for an optimally coherent and integrated picture that brings everything we know into proper relationship. There is room for intellectual disagreement, of course, but our responsibility, at all times and to the best of our ability, is to follow the evidence and arguments wherever they lead.

We will begin with the assumptions grounding the very possibility of knowledge about reality before considering special revelation (Scripture) and its relationship to natural revelation (the world around us as investigated through scientific modalities). We will then discuss scientific methodology since the Scientific Revolution and criticize methodological naturalism—the fiat restriction of scientific explanations to natural entities and causes—as a post-Darwinian imposition that, in contrast with a uniformitarianism allowing the detectability of intelligent causation in nature, artificially restricts and impedes scientific inquiry. Philosophical analysis and a foray into quantum physics will then show that: (1) metaphysically naturalistic accounts of physical law fail; and (2) the mode of divine action mandated by quantum physics explains nature's functional integrity while grounding design-theoretic science and the possibility of miracles. Human existence isn't the result of purposeless forces and brute material contingency, nor can it credibly be explained this way; rather, humanity's place in the universe is the intended outcome of events initiated and intelligently directed by God in accordance with his relational nature.

On the Very Possibility of (Scientific) Knowledge

What does is it mean to have knowledge of something? For present purposes, I offer Dallas Willard's rough-and-ready definition:

> *We have knowledge of something when we are representing it (thinking about it, speaking of it, treating it) as it actually is, on an appropriate basis of thought and experience.* Knowledge involves truth or accuracy of representation, but it must also be truth based upon adequate evidence or insight. The evidence or insight comes in various ways, depending on the nature of the subject matter. But it must be there.[1]

What basis assures us, though, that we're representing something as it *actually* is? Two things seem necessary: (1) every contingent state of affairs must have an explanation (a principle of sufficient reason); and (2) our cognitive

---

1. Dallas Willard, *Knowing Christ Today: Why We Can Trust Spiritual Knowledge* (San Francisco: HarperOne, 2009), 15.

faculties aren't the result of blind natural forces with no end in view, but have the goal, when functioning properly, of producing true beliefs.

First, why would knowledge elude us if we were to suppose some contingent states of affairs had no explanation? Briefly, if some states of affairs could lack explanation, the possibility of there being no explanation would become a competing "explanation" for anything that occurred. If something can lack explanation, we are prevented from separating things that have an explanation from those that do not, for there is no basis to conclude that something having an explanation was not, in fact, something occurring for no reason at all. Since no objective probability is assignable when there's no explanation, there being no explanation becomes an inscrutable competitor to every proposed explanation, undermining our ability to decide whether *anything* has an explanation, scientific or otherwise. This means our current state of awareness might also lack explanation, irremediably severing our perceptions from reality. So denying that every contingent state of affairs has an explanation undermines scientific access to truth and opens the door to an irremediable universal skepticism. The principle of sufficient reason is thus a broad logical truth we know *a priori*; it's a precondition for knowledge and the intelligibility of the world.

Whether our universe—or multiverse, if you grant credence to fashionable speculation—had an absolute beginning or is postulated to emerge from some timeless quantum state, the fact that something exists that did not have to exist, is a contingent state of affairs requiring explanation. This explanation cannot be provided by another contingent thing, for it too would require an explanation. Even a beginningless series of contingent universes, each one causing the next in succession (if such were possible), would be something that didn't have to exist and thus beg explanation. Explaining why there is something instead of absolutely nothing must terminate with an entity that exists necessarily and is capable of acting as a cause. This brings us within a hair's breadth of recognizing that a necessary being, God, is required both to ground knowledge and to explain why anything exists to be known.[2]

---

2. See Alexander R. Pruss and Joshua L. Rasmussen, *Necessary Existence* (Oxford: Oxford University Press, 2018), for an extended examination of these themes. The logical consequences of intuitions (positive or negative) regarding necessary being are interactively explorable at www.necessarybeing.com.

Secondly, what follows if our cognitive faculties were produced by blind natural forces? If natural selection sifting chance variations explains their origin, what matters about them is their fitness for ensuring survival and reproduction, not their ability to represent reality as it actually is. Indeed, if natural-selection-driven conscious perception and ratiocination arose accidentally in natural history, the veridicality of our perceptions and the validity of our reasoning processes is, at best, inscrutable. As Alvin Plantinga forcefully argues,[3] undirected evolution provides no ground for supposing our cognitive faculties produce *true* beliefs, and the further removed from immediate survival our beliefs are, the less confidence we should have in their veridicality. This means that evolutionary naturalists have little warrant for believing anything (including evolutionary naturalism) to be true.

While this "evolutionary argument against naturalism" has provoked critical discussion,[4] it is compelling to note that computational evolutionary psychology has drawn the same conclusion. Computational experiments using evolutionary game theory demonstrate that organisms acting in accordance with the true causal structure of their environment will be out-competed and driven to extinction by organisms acting in accordance with arbitrarily-imposed species-specific fitness functions.[5] Ironically, this demonstration can only be trusted if we are *not* organisms with nonveridical fitness functions; otherwise, we have no confidence that conclusions drawn on the basis of experiments we have devised bear any relationship to reality. Without cognitive faculties aimed at true beliefs, all human knowledge, including science, is just a fitness-driven survival mechanism with an inscrutable connection to reality.

However, the probability that properly-functioning cognitive fac-

---

3. The *locus classicus* for Plantinga's argument is chapter 12 of *Warrant and Proper Function* (Oxford: Oxford University Press, 1993).

4. See James Beilby, ed. *Naturalism Defeated? Essays on Plantinga's Evolutionary Argument Against Naturalism* (Ithaca, NY: Cornell University Press, 2002).

5. See Justin T. Mark, Brian B. Marion, and Donald D. Hoffman, "Natural Selection and Veridical Perceptions," *Journal of Theoretical Biology* 266 (2010): 504–15. Note that a "fitness function" is a mathematical expression that characterizes, in terms of the performance of something relative to its alternatives, how close that thing is to achieving a certain goal, for example, survival. What Hoffman et al. showed was that organisms functioning on the basis of accurate (veridical) representations of an objective environment can be outcompeted and driven to extinction by organisms with arbitrary functions tuned to environmental utility (usefulness) rather than veridicality. This means that useful perceptions readily diverge from and replace true perceptions as organisms struggle to survive.

ulties are reliable guides to truth is high *when conditioned on theism*, especially Christian theism, since God not only brings about our existence; he wants us to know and have a relationship with him and intends we understand the world well enough to be its stewards. Christianity gives us access to the world and a basis for thinking that science can lead us to the truth; naturalism takes this away. When the prerequisites of knowledge are considered, therefore, the game seems over for the metaphysical naturalist before it has started; he lacks a basis for thinking any of his beliefs are true.

On Science and Scripture

If God is the creator and sustainer of everything distinct from himself, it is reasonable to think he might communicate with us in a special way beyond the general knowledge of his existence available in nature. That he has done so in the Bible is integral to the Christian worldview, so our discussion will proceed from this assumption. But a clear understanding of the relationship between nature and Scripture must move beyond reactionary defenses of biblical inerrancy to a philosophy of revelation. Speech act theory provides a philosophical framework.

Speech acts are classified as locutionary, illocutionary, or perlocutionary, with locutions being what is said/written, illocutions being what the speaker or writer intends to communicate, and perlocutions being the effect of communication on the hearer/reader. Special revelation is an instance of double-agency discourse: God speaks through human beings, and his inspiration involves either deputization or appropriation.[6] Deputized discourse is direct divine communication through a human speaker/author ("Thus says the Lord"), whereas appropriated discourse involves God saying, "This person is inspired to speak/write for me, so listen to him." In both modes, what God intends to communicate (divine illocution) may transcend what the human authors thought they were communicating (human illocution). Human understanding is bound by temporal and cultural horizons; God's understanding is not. We therefore distinguish between a first and second hermeneutic.[7] The first hermeneutic uses historical-critical methodology (stripped

---

6. Nicholas Wolterstorff, *Divine Discourse: Philosophical Reflections on the Claim that God Speaks* (Cambridge: Cambridge University Press, 1995), 37–57.

7. Wolterstorff, *Divine Discourse*, 183–222.

of naturalistic assumptions) to ascertain the illocutionary force of historically situated human speech. The second hermeneutic seeks to understand the biblical text as divine illocution in the canonical context of Scripture as a whole and subject to God as omniscient, omnipotent, and omnibenevolent, while appropriating its message for our own temporal and cultural horizon.

Grasping the divine-human dynamic between primary and secondary hermeneutics makes us less concerned about the Bible's humanity. Divine inspiration does *not* entail inerrancy in the first hermeneutic because historically situated human understanding may *diverge* from divine illocution in double-agency discourse. Inerrancy, as such, *only applies to the divine illocutionary force of Scripture* insofar as ascertainable in the second hermeneutic, not to biblical locutions *simpliciter*.[8] This does not, however, lead to a hermeneutical free-for-all. Divine illocution is constrained by the lexical and grammatical structures of Scripture, the literary forms and conventions of Scripture, biblical theology and typology in the canonical context of Scripture, and our knowledge of the world. The second hermeneutic must yield interpretations that the human agents of revelation could recognize as the *message* of the text, bracketing limitations of ancient cosmography and sociocultural conventions and given awareness of the full canonical context. It is here that God's transtemporal communication takes place, and where, by divine illumination as we seek God using everything we know, we experience the perlocutionary effects God intends, authoritatively grounded in the historical narratives, anthropological insights, theological truths, and rich perspectival versatility of the divine illocutionary acts in Scripture.

Old Testament scholar Jack Collins helpfully distinguishes between a *world picture* and a *worldview*, separating issues of ancient Near Eastern cosmography from the message of the biblical text.[9] A world

---

8. I'd prefer to avoid epistemically vexed discussions of inerrancy altogether and simply affirm that Scripture, properly interpreted, is trustworthy and authoritative for its primary purpose of making us "wise for salvation through faith in Christ Jesus" (2 Tim. 3:15b). Many evangelical theologians unhelpfully treat *inerrancy in every respect* as if it were a necessary condition for *biblical authority in any respect*. The notions are not related this way (see Michael C. Rea, "Authority and Truth," in *The Enduring Authority of the Christian Scriptures*, ed. D. A. Carson [Grand Rapids: Eerdmans, 2016], 872–98).

9. See C. J. Collins, *Reading Genesis Well: Navigating History, Poetry, Science, and Truth in Genesis 1–11* (Grand Rapids: Zondervan, 2018), 94–95, 243–64.

picture provides a cosmography: the shape of the earth and the things in it, where the land ends and the sea begins, what is under the ground and over the sky, and related matters. A worldview, on the other hand, answers foundational metaphysical and moral questions: whether God exists and what he is like, whether the world is a divine creation or a self-existent entity, whether individual human consciousness survives bodily death, whether there is a universal moral standard, and so on. Let's consider what the biblical cosmography looks like, then, before addressing whether the ancient Hebrews understood it literally and before attempting to discern God's message in the creation account.

In biblical cosmography,[10] the "heavens and the earth" are made from primordial waters brought into being by God (Gen. 1:1–2, 6–10; 2 Pet. 3:5) and partitioned by a solid dome (*raqîa'*) separating the waters above from the waters below (Gen. 1:6–7). This dome, which is supported by the "pillars of the heavens" (Job 26:11), also divides the biblical heavens (*shāmayim*) into the spaces below and above it. Set in the dome are the sun, moon, and stars (Gen. 1:17); over the dome are the "waters . . . above the dome" (Gen. 1:7); and above these waters are the highest heavens, the dwelling place of God (1 Kings 8:27, 30). The dome has "windows" that are opened during Noah's flood to inundate the earth with waters from above it, then closed to bring an end to the flooding (Gen. 7:11; 8:2). Below the dome, birds fly and weather transpires (Gen. 1:20). The waters below the sky-dome are gathered at God's command, causing the dry land to appear (Gen. 1:10–11), and the sky-dome forms a circular horizon on the waters (Job 26:10; Prov. 8:27–28; Isa. 40:21–22). The dry land is flat (Job 38:12–13; Isa. 11:12) and supported over the deep by foundational pillars (1 Sam. 2:8; Job 9:6). The world, so established, cannot be moved (1 Chron. 16:30). Beneath everything are the waters under the earth (Ex. 20:4; Prov. 8:27–31), from which fountains spring forth in Noah's flood and then are closed. Finally, the depths of the earth contain Sheol, the realm of the dead (Deut. 32:22) and the deepest correlate of God's dwelling place in the highest heaven (Ps. 139:8; Isa. 7:11).

It is very doubtful that the ancient Hebrews (or other ancient peoples) understood this world picture with naive literalness.[11] To grasp

---

10. The New Revised Standard Version translates this cosmography clearly.

11. Young-earth creationists—who maintain the Bible teaches a literal six-day creation less than ten thousand years ago and that earth's large-scale geological features are explained

its significance for the biblical worldview, we need to understand what it is being contrasted with and what its imagery represents. First, it is a contrast to the theogonies and cosmogonies of other ancient Near Eastern peoples.[12] The biblical picture of God creating and splitting primordial waters corrects creation myths like the Babylonian Enuma Elish, which antedates Genesis. Enuma Elish divinizes the primeval waters as the god Tiamat, whom the god Marduk slays, splitting her body in two and forming the earth with one half and a solid sky with the other. The biblical corrective rejects deification of the primal waters and battles among nature gods. The one true God created the things these other cultures worship. The primeval waters are subject to his command and he splits them in two, bringing order to chaos and creating a home for living things. The God of the Hebrews does not have an origin and is not composed of visible materials. He has always existed and he created everything else that exists. Biblical monotheism, which rejects the divinization of any part of creation, thus stands in stark contrast to the polytheism surrounding it.

We must also understand the imagery of Genesis 1:1–2:3. The picture of God's dwelling place as resting over a celestial sea, upheld by a solid sky-dome supported by pillars, and forming a shelter enclosing a realm of lights and clouds over a fruitful earth tended by humanity as stewards under God, with the earth itself containing a sanctuary (Eden) and supported by pillars over subterranean waters that surround it, is that of a cosmic temple. It parallels the structure of the Mosaic tabernacle and Solomon's temple and foreshadows the structure of the eschatological temple (the new heavens and the new earth) filled by God's presence (consider Ps. 78:69; Isa. 66:1–2; Heb. 8:1–10:25; Rev. 21:1–22:11).[13] This connection between the cosmos and Israel's

---

by a global Noahic flood—are arbitrarily selective in their literalism. They believe the creation days were literal 24-hour periods, the heavenly lights (the sun, moon, and stars) were created *after* the earth on the fourth day, and Noah's flood was global, but reject a literal reading of the texts referenced above. Their arbitrary selectivity evinces a double standard. Consistency demands *either* naive literalism throughout *or* recognition of a religious cosmography communicating a *worldview* instead of an ancient scientific cosmogony and cosmology.

12. An excellent discussion of Genesis 1–11 in its ancient Near Eastern context is Paul Copan and Douglas Jacoby, *Origins: The Ancient Impact and Modern Implications of Genesis 1–11* (New York: Morgan James, 2019).

13. An excellent biblical-theological treatment is G. K. Beale, *The Temple and the Church's Mission: A Biblical Theology of the Dwelling Place of God* (Downers Grove, IL: IVP Academic, 2004).

tabernacle/temple informed surrounding cultures of Israel's unique connection to the God who made everything: when Israel worshipped, the God of all creation was in their midst. Israel's creation account and associated worship rituals were a theological polemic against pagan theogonies and cosmogonies that appropriated and transformed the symbols and rituals of the surrounding nations to display God's true nature and Israel's unique status.

Dismissing the Genesis creation account as primitive myth or ancient science misunderstands it and the theological message it communicates. While Genesis 1 tells us something historically true—our universe is not self-sufficient and did not always exist, but the one true God, who transcends it, brought it into being—the cosmography it uses is religious, not scientific. Whether the ancient Hebrews understood the creation days literally is also debatable, but even if they did, their misperception would be irrelevant in the second hermeneutic. We can affirm the events of Genesis 1:1–2:3 actually happened in that God acted to bring existence and order to our world, but the concordist game of reading modern science *into* the ancient text, or drawing scientific conclusions *out of* the ancient text, is misconceived and unnecessary. Even so, the image of the cosmic temple remains: God brought the materials and order of the universe into being, it manifests his glory, he is everywhere present in it, and he is to be worshipped there (Ps. 139:7–12; Hab. 2:20).

We must still address Adam and Eve and their fall into sin (Gen. 2:4–3:24). The story gives them a dual role in the biblical narrative of human origins. They function universally as the earliest humans bringing sin and death into the world, but they also function particularly as forerunners and exemplars of Israel, placing Israel's sojourn from origin (exodus) to exile into primordial time.[14] In the first hermeneutic, the human authors and redactors of Scripture likely understood these two roles as united: the Adam who was the ancestor and pattern of Israel was also the ancestor of all humanity. In the second hermeneutic, however, while this fusion serves a theological purpose, the strands can be separated. Fusion is the result of an anachronism, a divine accommodation to an ancient world picture.

---

14. See Peter Enns, *The Evolution of Adam: What the Bible Doesn't Say about Human Origins* (Grand Rapids: Brazos, 2012), 65–70.

Considering Adam as the ancestor of Israel, the depiction of Cain and Abel in Genesis 4 as raising crops and livestock places the story in the Neolithic period no earlier than ten thousand to twelve thousand years ago. Given the abbreviated lineages from Adam to Noah (ten generations) and Noah to Abraham (ten generations), Adam is the historical progenitor of Abraham via truncated lineages giving the line of descent.[15] Understanding the origins of humanity and the significance of the fall in a universal context requires moving to the second hermeneutic, where "Adam" becomes a rigid designator for the first human being to fall into sin. Here, the biblical account is a symbolic story communicating an essential truth about theological anthropology resting on historical events having this significance, the details of which are not provided. The second hermeneutic does not require monogenesis; indeed, Cain's finding a wife and building a city (Genesis 4) counts against it.[16] The Adam of the second hermeneutic is an exemplar of original humanity and the first to sin. This original sin, spread by way of imitation to the Adamic generation of divine image-bearers (Rom. 5:12), is the causal nexus for the innate disposition to sin, our universal spiritual disability (see Ps. 51:5; 1 Cor. 15:21–22; Eph. 2:1–10).

Finally, let me contextualize the significance of death as a consequence of the Fall in the second hermeneutic. In biblical perspective, God purposed to redeem us in Christ logically prior to the world's creation (Eph. 1:4–5). The Old Testament faithful, though not yet

---

15. The ages of individuals in these lineages are not literal but indicative of the ancient custom of ancestral aggrandizement (compare, e.g., the Sumerian King List). For discussion of possible symbolic significance, see Carol A. Hill, "Making Sense of the Numbers of Genesis," *Perspectives on Science and the Christian Faith* 55, no. 4 (2003): 239–51; see also Collins, *Reading Genesis Well*, 182–85.

16. Allowing that God may have created many human beings at first does not require acceptance of common descent. While it is commonly claimed that the first steps to humanity arose in a population of around ten thousand individuals, this population-genetics calculation rests on the assumption that humans and chimpanzees have a common ancestor. An alternative population genetics model is possible that assumes human monogenesis with initial created diversity (four versions of each initial non-sex chromosome), is consistent with the evidence of a block structure in a large percentage of human DNA, and is testable with computer simulations (see Ola Hössjer, Ann Gauger, and Colin Reeves, "Genetic Modeling of Human History Part 1: Comparison of Common Descent and Unique Origin Approaches," *BIO-Complexity* 3 [2016]: 1–15, and "Genetic Modeling of Human History Part 2: A Unique Origin Algorithm," *BIO-Complexity* 4 [2016]: 1–36). While the biblical case for monogenesis is underdetermined, the standard population genetics argument against it begs the question. The issue must be decided on other grounds.

knowing it, were redeemed by union with Christ (Heb. 11:40). Christ's redemptive work has transhistorical effect. Since redemption is predicated on disobedience, the Eden of unbroken relationship with God was always going to be disrupted. So God's eternal purpose was to permit human disobedience and its effects, and these effects were transhistorical too. Exiled from God's presence in our primal disobedience, we encounter a world outside Eden's sanctuary already subject to death and decay (contrast Gen. 2:8–9 with Gen. 3:17–19, 23–24 in light of Rom. 8:19–22),[17] paving the way for the superlative goods of the incarnation and atonement. Creation thus reflects God's glory by displaying all his attributes, including justice and mercy. By displaying God's glory and instantiating his eternal plan, creation thereby manifests its sevenfold (perfect) goodness (Gen. 1:4, 10, 12, 18, 21, 25, 31).[18]

Modern Science, Methodological Naturalism, and Intelligent Design

The Scientific Revolution is often portrayed as replacing Aristotelian conceptions of explanation with methodological naturalism.[19] This is, at best, an exaggeration. For example, even though Robert Boyle (1627–91) and Isaac Newton (1642–1727) were poster boys for the Scientific Revolution, neither embraced methodological naturalism. Boyle thought intelligent direction was inferable from the initial-condition fine-tuning required to produce intended effects from a vast sequence of conspiring causes.[20]

---

17. The joy of existence with unbounded access to God's life-giving presence in Eden (Gen. 2) is contrasted with its alienation and difficulty under death's dominion in exile (Gen. 3). Joining this contrast to the observation in Rom. 8:19ff that God, from the beginning, placed creation in bondage to futility and decay awaiting eschatological redemption, it is reasonable to conclude that futility and decay were always the state of creation *outside* Eden as a transhistorical consequence of Adamic humanity's transgression. Human transgression and alienation as necessary conditions of redemption and restoration were eternally foreknown and play an indispensable role in God's perfect plan for creation.

18. For similar thoughts, see Alvin Plantinga's "Supralapsarianism, or 'O Felix Culpa'," in Peter van Inwagen, ed., *Christian Faith and the Problem of Evil* (Grand Rapids: Eerdmans, 2004), 1–25; and William A. Dembski, *The End of Christianity: Finding a Good God in an Evil World* (Nashville: B&H Academic, 2009).

19. For example, Robert C. Bishop, "God and Methodological Naturalism in the Scientific Revolution and Beyond," *Perspectives on Science and Christian Faith* 65, no. 1 (2013): 10–23. Hans Halvorson, a prominent Christian philosopher-scientist, defends the criterion in "Why Methodological Naturalism?" *The Blackwell Companion to Naturalism*, ed. Kelly James Clark (Chichester, United Kingdom: Wiley & Sons, 2016), 136–49.

20. Robert Boyle, *The Works of the Honourable Robert Boyle* 2 vols. (London: A. Millar, 1744), 1: 447.

Design (formal cause) and purpose (final cause) both governed his conception of efficient material causality. Newton, in the General Scholium to his *Principia*, recognizes initial-condition fine-tuning in the origin and function of our solar system,[21] a judgment confirmed and deepened by contemporary studies of fine-tuning for planetary habitability.[22] The Mechanical Philosophy of Boyle and Newton did not repudiate Aristotle's four causes or embrace methodological naturalism. Their focus on efficient material causality—to which Newton's theory of universal gravitation was a majestic exception—assumed a Christian metaphysics that preserved *formal causes* in the intelligent design of nature's mechanisms, and *final causes* in the purposes they were designed to serve.

The situation in biology from 1600–1900 contradicts the would-be narrative even more dramatically. Design plans (formal causes) identifying species that were placed in the natural order for various purposes (final causes) dominated biological science prior to Darwin.[23] Even Darwin himself agreed that his naturalistic attempt to explain the origin of species amounted to a fundamental reorientation in the science of biology. In the introduction to *The Origin of Species*, he indicates he is going to challenge "the view which most *naturalists* entertain, and which I formerly entertained—namely, each species has been independently created."[24] In short, the historical origin of methodological naturalism as a constraint on scientific explanation is found in Darwin's *The Origin of Species* (1859).

Methodological naturalism's ascent to contemporary orthodoxy starts with Darwin, not the Scientific Revolution. But saying that systematic rational and observational study of nature only became science after Darwin, because only then did methodological naturalism hold sway, begs the question and makes a fiat declaration as unconvincing as

---

21. Isaac Newton (1713), "General Scholium" to the *Principia* (1687), translated from Latin by John Maxwell (1715), https://newtonprojectca.files.wordpress.com/2013/06/newton-general-scholium-in-maxwell-1715-letter-size.pdf.

22. See Guillermo Gonzalez, "Habitable Zones and Fine-Tuning," in *The Nature of Nature: Examining the Role of Naturalism in Science*, eds. Bruce L. Gordon and William A. Dembski (Wilmington, DE: ISI, 2011), 602–38.

23. Consider John Ray (1627–1705), Carl Linnaeus (1707–1778), and Gregor Mendel (1822–1884). On Mendel, see Harry Sootin, *Gregor Mendel: Father of the Science of Genetics* (New York: Vanguard, 1959).

24. Emphasis added. Charles Darwin, *The Origin of Species*, 6, http://darwin-online.org.uk/Variorum/1859/1859–6-dns.html.

it is historically inaccurate. Methodological naturalism's ascendancy is an artifact of a conception of nature that is not intrinsic to the task of scientific explanation. This becomes apparent when we try to analyze and justify it. After all, how does it function as an explanatory constraint? Straightforwardly, it requires that scientific explanations appeal to natural entities and only to natural entities. Insofar as it expresses a mere attitude toward explanations that lacks stable content over time with respect to the entities it postulates to be natural, it is at best a *sociological description* of mainstream scientific culture, not a *normative constraint* on science, and we may safely set it aside. Why? Because if we concern ourselves with a fixed definition for a natural entity giving workable content to the idea that science should restrict itself to such entities for explanatory purposes, we cannot just say that natural entities are whatever science invokes in an explanatory capacity (at any given time) without reasoning in a circle. Even if we were sanguine about this circularity, we would not have defined natural entities in a way that makes methodological naturalism a constraint on scientific research—rather, just the reverse.

In seeking a fixed definition of natural entities, we might define them in terms of spatiotemporality, energy, and mass, taken collectively as indispensable characteristics of physicality. So an entity is natural just in case it is physical or depends on something physical in this fundamental sense. This seems more in the spirit of what is intended, but it has an intractable complication: generic physicalism of this kind, if explanatory completeness is intended, is demonstrably incompatible with what quantum physicists have discovered about nature.[25] We'll see why momentarily, but in the exotic contexts of quantum gravity and quantum cosmology,[26] scientists seek to explain the origin of *space-time itself* as emergent from a more fundamental *non*spatiotemporal reality.[27]

---

25. See the next section.

26. *Quantum gravity* explores how Einstein's general relativity can be reconciled with quantum theory, which is problematic because of the different mathematical structures and ways the two theories treat space and time. *Quantum cosmology* treats the whole universe quantum-mechanically in an effort to remove space-time singularities—the big bang in particular—and explore conceptions of the universal wavefunction implied by quantum entanglement.

27. J. Hartle and S. Hawking, "Wavefunction of the Universe," *Physical Review D* 28 (1983): 2260–75; J. Feldbrugge, J-L Lehners, and N. Turok, "No Smooth Beginning for Spacetime," *Physical Review Letters* 119 (2017): 171301; Brian Swingle and Mark van

These nonspatiotemporal constructs are proclaimed "natural," but they are incompatible with physicality, for they don't occupy space-time and thus cannot be material. They do not fit the fixed definition of a natural entity. Furthermore, if they describe anything, it's something that *did not have to exist*, and therefore, by the principle of sufficient reason, *cannot* be explanatorily fundamental.

Methodological naturalists must therefore embrace at least one of two consequences. Either they must admit that science cannot be the only source of knowledge and there are some things—the existence of the universe, for instance—it cannot explain, or they must broaden their conception of scientific explanation and reject methodological naturalism as a constraint (or both). Embracing both conclusions seems the best path since finding necessary and sufficient criteria distinguishing science from nonscience has proved intractable. Rational explanations range over a spectrum from those that are clearly not scientific to those we would affirm as paradigmatically so. In the latter case, systematic abductive inferences in a uniformitarian framework provide a broader and more adequate approach than methodological naturalism.[28]

Modern uniformitarianism circumscribes scientific explanations by uniformly operating regularities or extrapolations from them. It derives past causes from present effects under the assumption that the causal structure of the world has remained constant and permits reliable inferences. The truth of this notably depends on the principle of sufficient reason. Furthermore, since structures and processes that exhibit a degree of complex-specified information *exceeding* the probability bounds of the observable universe[29] are habitually and uniformly associated with intelligent activity, intelligent causation is part of the causal structure of the world and falls within the purview of scientific investigation. Design-theoretic explanations are a species of uniformitarian analysis.

That the fine-tuning of the initial conditions, laws, and constants of

Raamsdonk, "Universality of Gravity from Entanglement," 2014, https://arxiv.org/pdf/1405 .2933.pdf; and ChunJun Cao, Sean M. Carroll, and Spyridon Michalakis, "Space from Hilbert Space: Recovering Geometry from Bulk Entanglement," *Physical Review D* 95 (2017): 024031.

28. Abductive inferences are inferences to the best explanation, i.e., they consider a range of possible explanations for something and accept the one offering the most likely explanation (see https://plato.stanford.edu/entries/abduction/).

29. Seth Lloyd, "Computational Capacity of the Universe," *Physical Review Letters* 88, no. 23 (2002): 237901.

the universe, and the origin and development of life and consciousness, might best be explained by intelligent causes is eminently reasonable in a theistic context and entirely compatible with the uniformitarian assumptions necessary to science. It is a legitimate scientific enterprise to investigate this question. In Christian perspective, some developments in the history of the universe might require *extraordinary* providence for their proper explanation, while most may be explained by its *ordinary* course. Information is always generated from a reference class of possibilities, so which mode of providence prevails can be discerned from the informational properties of the phenomenon in question. The complex specified information indicative of intelligent design represents a dual reduction of possibilities: a conceptual reduction in accordance with an independently recognizable and improbable pattern *combined* with a physical-phenomenological reduction. Structures or events exhibiting specified complexity must be both complex (highly unlikely under the relevant probability distribution) and specified (conform to an independently recognizable pattern).

Recently, different models of specified complexity involving semiotic,[30] algorithmic,[31] functional,[32] and irreducible[33] complex specified information have been shown to have a common underlying mathematical form that, with additional constraints, allows the construction of generalized (canonical) specified complexity models demonstrating that systems exhibiting a large degree of specified complexity are exceedingly improbable under any relevant probability distribution.[34] These canonical models can be used to create statistical hypothesis tests[35] for specified complexity. Inferring design from a specified-complexity test that assigns large degrees of specified complexity only to features of

30. William A. Dembski, "Specification: The Pattern that Signifies Intelligence," *Philosophia Christi* 7 (2005): 299–343.

31. Winston Jeffrey Ewert, W. A. Dembski, and Robert J. Marks, "On the Improbability of Algorithmic Specified Complexity," *Proceedings of the 2013 45th Southeastern Symposium on System Theory (SSST)*, IEEE, 2013, 68–70.

32. Robert M. Hazen et al., "Functional Information and the Emergence of Biocomplexity," *Proceedings of the National Academy of Sciences (USA)* 104 (2007): 8574–81.

33. Michael J. Behe, *Darwin's Black Box: The Biochemical Challenge to Evolution* (New York: Free Press, 1996).

34. George D. Montañez, "A Unified Model of Complex Specified Information," *BIO-Complexity* 4 (2018): 1–26.

35. For a brief description of statistical hypothesis testing, see https://www.statistics solutions.com/hypothesis-testing/.

designed structures takes the form of a likelihood-ratio test in which the alternative hypothesis is that the structure was most likely produced by intentional design.[36] Under these conditions, rejecting the null hypothesis in favor of the alternative provides good, but defeasible, evidence of particular design (extraordinary providence), and the more evidence of this kind that is gathered, the more certain this conclusion becomes, just as one would expect for any scientific procedure.[37]

Laws of Nature, Quantum Physics, and the Modes of Divine Action

What do we mean by "laws of nature"? Some philosophical naturalists argue they are metaphysical necessities similar to statements like "No mammals are mathematical propositions." This cannot be right. Take Coulomb's law, for example: the fact that two like (or different) charges repel (or attract) each other with a force proportional to the magnitude of the charges and inversely proportional to the square of the distance between them gives no hint of being metaphysically necessary. The world could have been different. Other philosophers have suggested that laws of nature are contingently necessary relationships among universals mirrored among the corresponding particulars. Oxymoronic appearances aside, no coherent account of this claim has been given either. Merely calling something "necessary" doesn't make it so. Finally, other would-be necessitarians propose that physical laws derive from innate causal powers grounded in the essential natures of things and inherent in their material substance. These laws are manifested through forces or fields that necessarily emanate by nature from associated material substances, mediating physical interactions in a necessary way. But it's difficult to see why *this* causal power necessarily flows from *that* material substance.

---

36. A likelihood ratio test compares the goodness of fit of two competing statistical models based on the ratio of their likelihoods (individual goodness of fit to the data). In the present context, one of the hypotheses is the null hypothesis that nothing statistically significant is happening, and the other is the alternative hypothesis that the observed structure is most likely the product of intelligent design. See Montañez, "A Unified Model" for a full technical account.

37. Those familiar with the literature on statistical hypothesis testing and, more particularly, disputes over the mathematics of design inferences, will be aware that advocates of decision-making and hypothesis testing deriving from Bayes's Theorem are critical of hypothesis-testing approaches deriving from the work of Fisher, Neyman, and Pearson. In this regard, it is worth noting that design inferences from Fisherian likelihood ratios can be recast in a Bayesian framework, and they lead to the same conclusions.

Things could have worked differently.[38] On the other hand, if the metaphysical naturalist rejects necessitarian accounts, maintaining that laws of nature are mere regularities, then why is nature regular at all, and what keeps it so? A stable universe of mere regularities is a perpetual miracle.

Even if necessitarian theories weren't *metaphysically* inadequate, however, they fail *empirically* in quantum physics. To understand why, we need some basic quantum theory.[39] Quantum physics sets aside classical conceptions of motion and the interaction of bodies and introduces acts of measurement and probabilities for observational outcomes in an irreducible way not ameliorated by appealing to our limited knowledge. The state of a quantum system is described by an abstract mathematical object called a wave function. As long as the system is unobserved, the wave function develops deterministically, but it only specifies the *probability* that various observables (like position or momentum) will have a particular value when measured. Furthermore, these probabilities can't all equal zero or one and measurement results are *irreducibly* probabilistic. This means no sufficient physical condition exists for one value being observed rather than another permitted by the wave function.

The absence of sufficient material causality in quantum mechanics has a variety of experimentally confirmed consequences that preclude a

---

38. Examples of these necessitarian approaches are: (1) Laws as broad logical necessities: Alexander Bird, "The Dispositional Conception of Law," *Foundations of Science* 10, no. 4 (2005): 353–70; (2) Laws as relationships among universals: D. M. Armstrong, *What Is a Law of Nature?* (Cambridge: Cambridge University Press, 1983); and (3) Laws as causal powers: (a) R. Harré and E. H. Madden, *Causal Powers: A Theory of Natural Necessity* (Oxford: Blackwell, 1975), and (b) J. Bigelow and R. Pargetter, *Science and Necessity* (Cambridge: Cambridge University Press, 1990).

39. Two accessible introductions to quantum physics are Jim Baggott, *Beyond Measure: Modern Physics, Philosophy, and the Meaning of Quantum Theory* (Oxford: Oxford University Press, 2004), and Michael G. Raymer, *Quantum Physics: What Everyone Needs to Know* (Oxford: Oxford University Press, 2017). For extended argumentation regarding the significance of experiments discussed below, see Bruce Gordon, "A Quantum-Theoretic Argument Against Naturalism," in Bruce Gordon and William Dembski, eds., *The Nature of Nature: Examining the Role of Naturalism in Science* (Wilmington, DE: ISI, 2011), 179–214; Bruce Gordon, "The Necessity of Sufficiency: The Argument from the Incompleteness of Nature," in *Two Dozen (or so) Arguments for God: The Plantinga Project*, eds. Jerry L. Walls and Trent Dougherty (Oxford: Oxford University Press, 2018), 417–445; Bruce Gordon, "The Incompatibility of Physicalism with Physics," in R. Keith Loftin and Joshua R. Farris, eds., *Christian Physicalism? Philosophical-Theological Criticisms* (New York: Lexington, 2018), 371–402; and Bruce Gordon, "Idealism and Science: The Quantum-Theoretic and Neuroscientific Foundations of Reality," in J. Farris and B. Göcke, eds., *The Routledge Handbook of Idealism and Immaterialism* (London: Routledge, forthcoming 2020).

world of mind-independent material substances governed by efficient material causation. The most rudimentary is that quantum reality does not exist until it is observed. A straightforward demonstration of this is provided by the delayed-choice quantum eraser experiment.[40] This experiment measures which path a particle took *after* wave function interference inconsistent with particle behavior has already been created. The interference can be turned off or on by choosing whether or not to measure which way the particle went *after* the interference already exists. Choosing to look *erases* wave function interference and gives the system a particle history. This experiment has been performed under Einstein locality conditions guaranteeing that no physical signal could connect the choice to look with the erased interference.[41] The fact that we can make a causally disconnected choice whether wave or particle phenomena manifest in a quantum system demonstrates that no measurement-independent causally-connected substantial material reality exists at the microphysical level.[42]

Consider two more results supporting this conclusion. First, the physically reasonable assumptions that an individual particle cannot serve as an infinite source of energy or be in two places at once entail that particles have zero probability of existing in any bounded spatial region, no matter how large.[43] Closing loopholes extends this result to more general conditions that include nonstandard interpretations of relativity.[44] Unobserved quanta don't exist anywhere in space, and thus have no existence apart from measurement. This consequence has been experimentally confirmed.[45] In short, there is no intelligible notion of

40. M. Scully and K. Drühl, "Quantum Eraser: A Proposed Photon Correlation Experiment Concerning Observation and 'Delayed Choice' in Quantum Mechanics," *Physical Review A* 25 (1982), 2208–13; and Yoon-Ho Kim et al., "Delayed Choice Quantum Eraser," *Physical Review Letters* 84, no. 1 (2000): 1–5.

41. Xiao-Song Ma et al., "Quantum Erasure with Causally Disconnected Choice," *Proceedings of the National Academy of Sciences (USA)* 110, no. 4 (2013), 1221–26.

42. This conclusion also follows from the nonlocality demonstrated by violations of Bell inequalities. See Gordon, "A Quantum-Theoretic Argument Against Naturalism," 183–89.

43. See David B. Malament, "In Defense of Dogma: Why there cannot be a relativistic quantum mechanics of (localizable) particles," in R. Clifton, ed., *Perspectives on Quantum Reality: Non-Relativistic, Relativistic, and Field-Theoretic* (Dordrecht: Kluwer Academic, 1996), 1–9.

44. Hans Halvorson and Rob Clifton, "No Place for Particles in Relativistic Quantum Theories?" *Philosophy of Science* 69 (2002): 1–28.

45. Maria Fuwa et al., "Experimental Proof of Nonlocal Wavefunction Collapse for a Single Particle Using Homodyne Measurement," *Nature Communications* 6 (2015): 6665.

microscopic material objects: particle talk has pragmatic utility in relation to measurement results and macroscopic appearances, but no basis in unobserved (mind-independent) reality.

Secondly, microphysical properties do not require a substrate. The Cheshire cat in *Alice in Wonderland* disappeared leaving only its grin, which prompted Alice to say she'd seen "a cat without a grin, but never a grin without a cat." Quantum physics has its own Cheshire cat in which quantum systems behave like their properties are spatially separated from their positions.[46] For example, an experiment using a neutron interferometer has sent neutrons along one path while their spins follow another.[47] In macroscopic terms, this would be like sending the redness of red balls along one path and their sphericity along another or the spin of tops along one path and their positions along another. Under appropriate experimental conditions, quantum systems are decomposable into disembodied properties—a collection of Cheshire cat grins.

But what about the macroscopic world of our experience? How should we understand the transition between the microscopic and macroscopic worlds? Every quantum wave function is expressible as a superposition of different possibilities (states) in which the thing it describes fails to possess the properties those possibilities specify. No quantum system ever has simultaneously determinate values for all its associated properties.[48] This applies to macroscopic as well microscopic systems, since, under special laboratory conditions, we can create macroscopic superpositions. Large organic molecules have been put into superposition,[49] and Superconducting Quantum Interference Devices (SQUIDs) have superposed a billion electrons moving clockwise around a superconducting ring with another billion electrons moving anticlockwise, so that *two incompatible macroscopic currents are in superposition*.[50]

46. Yakir Aharonov et al., "Quantum Cheshire Cats," *New Journal of Physics* 15 (2013): 113018.

47. Tobias Denkmayr et al., "Observation of a Quantum Cheshire Cat in a Matter-Wave Interferometer Experiment," *Nature Communications* 5 (2014): 4492.

48. Radek Lapkiewicz et al., "Experimental Non-Classicality of an Indivisible Quantum System," *Nature* 474 (2011): 490–93.

49. Sandra Eibenberger et al., "Matter-Wave Interference of Particles Selected from a Molecular Library with Masses Exceeding 10,000 Amu," *Physical Chemistry and Chemical Physics* 15 (2013): 14696–700.

50. Jonathan R. Friedman et al., "Quantum Superposition of Distinct Macroscopic States," *Letters to Nature* 406 (2000): 43–46.

Contrary to some philosophers of physics who argue this provides evidence of dynamically interacting parallel realities,[51] I would contend that none of the mathematical-structural components of these quantum states are materially real and note, in the case of laboratory-created macroscopic superpositions, that our conscious self is not in the superposition but rather observing it. What superpositions demonstrate is that quantum reality is not materially substantial; it is merely phenomenological. Quantum reality goes no deeper than multimodal percepts superimposed in conscious awareness. The macroscopic stability we observe is the product of what physicists call environmental decoherence—the destructive interference of probability waves as quantum systems interact. But what does this imply about the world of our experience?

We are on the cusp of a theistic idealism more profound than we countenanced at the start of this essay. Even if necessitarian theories of physical law weren't philosophically intractable, enduring materially substantial particulars still wouldn't exist to possess the intrinsic properties needed by necessitarian accounts. Necessitarian theories of natural law cannot gain a purchase point in fundamental physical theory and must be set aside, leaving us with a regularist account in which there are universal regularities, but no physical necessities. What this means is that nature behaves in ways we expect and can mathematically describe, but it does so for no discernible physical reason. The absence of a physical reason for the regularity of nature, by way of the principle of sufficient reason, shows there is an immaterial metaphysical ground for natural regularities. So not only does our manifestly contingent universe lack any explanation for its existence apart from a necessarily existent causal ground, it doesn't even function autonomously after it exists. Christians are not surprised: God doesn't just create the world; he also sustains it.

How are the regularities of nature related to divine action? Interestingly, *not* by secondary causation. Secondary causation requires God to create material substances exercising intrinsic causal powers

---

51. This is the so-called many worlds interpretation of quantum physics. It had its genesis in the work of Hugh Everett but has since been elaborated to grapple with its technical problems. David Wallace's book *The Emergent Multiverse: Quantum Theory According to the Everett Interpretation* (Oxford: Oxford University Press, 2012) ably represents the state-of-the-art. An excellent compendium of critical discussions is Simon Saunders et al., eds., *Many Worlds? Everett, Quantum Theory, & Reality* (Oxford: Oxford University Press), 2010.

while he (ordinarily) only acts as the primary cause sustaining these substances. But quantum physics precludes the existence of enduring material substances with causal powers, so secondary causation lacks a purchase point. While God *might* have created a world in which secondary material causality functions, he evidently did not do so. Everything that happens in the world involves an occasion of direct divine action. The appropriate model of divine providence is therefore occasionalism: God is the sole efficient cause of every state of affairs in the universe not subject to the influence of creatures with libertarian freedom.[52]

In the absence of causally effective material substances and the presence of quantum-mechanical probabilities for observables, a "physical law" becomes a regularity of divine action. We may gloss this as follows: if collective conditions C were observed, all other things being equal, with quantum-mechanical probability p, God would cause state of affairs S to be observable. For example, if the temperature of fresh water at sea level were observed to be raised to 100 degrees centigrade, all other things being equal, with high quantum-mechanical probability, God would cause the boiling of that water to be observable. The mathematically describable regularities of nature are thus *active* expressions of God's perpetual faithfulness (Pss. 33:4; 119:90; 2 Tim. 2:13). God is the one in whom we live and move and have our being (Acts 17:28), the one who is before all things, and in whom all things hold together (Col. 1:17).

A realistic understanding of quantum physics therefore pulls us toward a theistic idealism akin to that of the philosopher-theologians George Berkeley (1685–1753) and Jonathan Edwards (1703–58). Whether we endorse occasionalist idealism or settle for an occasionalism involving God's continual creation of material substances—as represented variously by Gabriel Biel (1420–95), Nicolas Malebranche (1638–1715), Abraham Kuyper (1837–1920), Gerrit Berkouwer (1903–96), and Alvin Plantinga (1932–), among others[53]—we recognize that while every event in created reality is an occasion of direct divine action, divine activity

---

52. Cf. Alfred J. Freddoso, "Medieval Aristotelianism and the Case Against Secondary Causation in Nature," in Thomas V. Morris, ed., *Divine and Human Action: Essays in the Metaphysics of Theism* (Ithaca, NY: Cornell University Press, 1988), 74–118.

53. Those surprised to find Plantinga's name here should read *Where the Conflict Really Lies: Science, Religion, and Naturalism* (Oxford: Oxford University Press, 2011), 113–21 and "Law, Cause, and Occasionalism," in Michael Bergmann and Jeffrey E. Brouwer, eds., *Reason and Faith: Themes from Richard Swinburne* (Oxford: Oxford University Press, 2016), 126–44.

subdivides into ordinary versus extraordinary modes. As summarized in Berkouwer's discussion of Kuyper, God's extraordinary or miraculous providence is not against the backdrop of a mechanistic nature in which he intervenes; rather, a miracle "means nothing more than that God at a given moment wills a certain thing to occur differently than it had up to that moment been willed by Him to occur. . . . Miracles are not occasional interferences by God in a fixed order of nature, [but rather] extraordinary ways of God's rule over all things."[54] As such, and subject to the will of God, departures from the ordinary course of nature—whether by developments in natural history that the ordinary course of nature cannot explain, or by extraordinary manifestations of divine grace in human history revealing God's purposes or in response to prayer—are not only possible, but in many instances, evidentially detectable.[55]

The Universe, Life, and Everything: A Test Case

Can a scientific account alone, making reference only to natural laws and material entities, explain the appearance and nature of *Homo sapiens* without reference to divine action? No. If not, can divine action be incorporated into a scientific explanation? Under reasonable interpretation, yes. As we have seen, natural laws and material entities are insufficient to explain the origin and function of the universe, so they are not, as we will see, adequate to explain the origin and development of life. Theism metaphysically grounds reality and the truth-conduciveness of the scientific enterprise, and, as argued, methodological naturalism should be replaced by a uniformitarianism that includes design inferences in the toolbox of scientific explanations. Intelligent causation in natural history, especially in cosmology, is most plausibly understood as transcendent, coming from outside of nature, and is reasonably interpreted as extraordinary divine action. The causal insufficiency of nature manifested in quantum physics

---

See also Gordon, "The Necessity of Sufficiency: The Argument from the Incompleteness of Nature."

54. G. C. Berkouwer, *Studies in Dogmatics: The Providence of God* (Grand Rapids: Eerdmans, 1952), 196–97.

55. See our earlier critique of methodological naturalism; also Montañez, "A Unified Model." Regarding miracles and Humean animadversions, see Timothy McGrew, "Miracles," *The Stanford Encyclopedia of Philosophy, 2019* (https://plato.stanford. edu/ archives/spr2019 /entries/miracles/) and Craig S. Keener, *Miracles: The Credibility of the New Testament Accounts*, 2 vols. (Grand Rapids: Baker Academic, 2011). Keener's discussion includes extensive evaluation of miracle claims throughout history up to the present.

shows natural regularities to be *ordinary* divine action, leaving ample room for *extraordinary* providence that is, at times, detectable. And when design is clearly detected, only a specious appeal to methodological naturalism would prevent its inclusion in a scientific explanation.

This much said, let's briefly discuss evidence for intelligent causation (extraordinary providence) in the origin and properties of the universe and the origin and development of life. The principle of sufficient reason requires the existence of a contingent universe to be explained by a necessary being. The fine-tuning of the universe's initial conditions, laws, and constants, and the demands of scientific rationality confirm this by pointing to the intelligent action of this being—such cosmological precision is not an informational free lunch.[56] Furthermore, this fine-tuning cannot be explained by appealing to a multiverse that is contingent, has metalaws that also need explaining, inevitably presumes quantum-mechanical relations, and whose mechanisms destroy scientific rationality.[57] An inference to design as the best explanation is conspicuously warranted. Some will call this "natural theology" and exclude it from science by fiat invocation of a deficient methodological naturalism, but what you decide to call it doesn't make the argument less compelling; it just affects who pays attention (which is why the classification matters).

Intelligent design is also very much evident in the origin and development of life. It is important to distinguish the issue of universal

---

56. See especially Luke A. Barnes, "The Fine-Tuning of the Universe for Intelligent Life," *Proceedings of the Astronomical Society of Australia* 29 (2012): 529–64 and "Fine-Tuning in the Context of Bayesian Theory Testing," *European Journal for the Philosophy of Science* 8, no. 2 (2018): 253–69. Also Robin Collins, "Evidence for Fine-Tuning," in *God and Design: The Teleological Argument and Modern Science*, ed. Neil A. Manson (New York: Routledge, 2003), 178–99; "The Teleological Argument: An Exploration of the Fine-Tuning of the Universe," in *The Blackwell Companion to Natural Theology*, ed. William Lane Craig and J. P. Moreland (Oxford: Blackwell, 2009), 202–81; and "The Fine-Tuning Evidence is Convincing," in *Debating Christian Theism*, eds. J. P. Moreland, Chad Meister, and Khaldoun A. Sweis (New York: Oxford University Press, 2013), 35–46.

57. See Bruce Gordon, "Balloons on a String: A Critique of Multiverse Cosmology," in Bruce Gordon and William Dembski, eds., *The Nature of Nature*, 558–601; also Robin Collins, "Design and the Many Worlds Hypothesis," in William Lane Craig, ed. *Philosophy of Religion: A Reader and Guide* (New Brunswick: Rutgers University Press, 2002), 130–48; Robin Collins, "The Multiverse Hypothesis: A Theistic Perspective," in Bernard Carr, ed., *Universe or Multiverse?* (Cambridge: Cambridge University Press, 2007), 459–80; and R. Marks, "Diversity Inadequacies of Parallel Universes: When the Multiverse Becomes Insufficient to Account for Conflicting Contradistinctions," *Perspectives on Science and the Christian Faith* 71, no. 3 (2019): 1–7.

common descent from whether the development of life is directed. Both could be true. But even if universal common ancestry (monophyletic origin) is false, polyphyletic origin theories,[58] which certainly require intelligent causation to explain the independent origin of different phyla, still allow for more limited chains of branching descent that, in light of the intractability of the waiting-time problem, still require intelligent direction. But let's not get ahead of ourselves.

How did life on earth get started? The origin of the biological information for the simplest self-replicating cells must be explained. Consider the coding information for protein synthesis in the simplest cells. The protein-coding segments of DNA must produce amino acid sequences that fold into biologically functional proteins in three dimensions. However, the sequence of nucleotides along the sugar-phosphate backbone of DNA is not determined by biochemical laws or self-organizational properties. It is like the chemistry of ink bonding to paper, which provides a necessary but insufficient condition for the content of a book. The biochemical independence of nucleotide sequences from the backbone is necessary for the vast information-carrying capacity of DNA. Biochemical dependence would constrain the permissible order and severely limit the possible sequences. So the relevant question is how frequently functional protein folds occur in amino acid sequence space because this functionally specified information[59] is precisely what the physically undetermined sequences of nucleotides represent, and highly improbable functionally-specified information requires design.

Careful laboratory testing of substitution tolerances has shown that a *single* protein folding domain (i.e., *one* stand-alone functional protein fold[60]) has an average probability in sequence space of about 1 in 10^{74}.[61] Now take one of the simplest (albeit non-self-sustaining) self-replicating

---

58. Polyphyletic theories postulate *separate* origins for many phyla.

59. As defined by Hazen et al. (2007, 8574), functional information "represents the probability that an arbitrary configuration of a system will achieve a specific function to a specified degree."

60. A protein fold is the compact three-dimensional structure into which a linear sequence of amino acids constituting a stand-alone protein will coil due to various chemical affinities (hydrogen bonding, covalent bonding, disulfide bridges, hydrophobic or hydrophilic properties, etc.) among the amino acids that compose it.

61. Douglas D. Axe, "The Case Against a Darwinian Origin of Protein Folds," *BIO-Complexity* 1 (2010): 1–12; also Douglas D. Axe, *Undeniable: How Biology Confirms Our Intuition That Life Is Designed* (San Francisco: HarperOne, 2016).

cells, *Mycoplasma genitalium*. It utilizes proteins from 268 independent folding domains. The probability of getting all these domains—and this is just *collecting* the protein parts *without constructing* the organism itself—is roughly 1 in $10^{(74 \times 268)}$ = 1 in $10^{18,632}$. The computational capacity of the observable universe allows, at best, for the undirected generation of 10^{120} bits of functionally-specified information,[62] so functionally-specified structures with probability less than 1 in 10^{120} are best explained by an intelligent cause, not a blind natural process.[63] In the entire history of the universe, we therefore should expect the undirected production of no more than two protein folds (having a joint probability of 1 in 10^{148}), yet one of our simplest known organisms requires 268 folds, and life on earth as a whole requires over a thousand of them (thus having no more than a 1 in $10^{74,000}$ chance of existence).[64] The origin of the first cell as a functionally-integrated self-replicating system that assembles and uses such proteins is so unattainable by undirected means, and various research proposals for its undirected evolution so obviously inadequate, that one prominent origin-of-life researcher has appealed to the idea of a multiverse (in which anything that can happen does happen) to circumvent a design inference.[65]

In the last thirty years or so, it has also been discovered that the protein-coding regions of DNA are *not* the only ones containing functionally-specified information and that DNA molecules contain nested instructions and codes that overlap each other in sophisticated ways.[66] Intelligent design is the only realistic explanation for the origin of this information. For example, the information for constructing *individual* proteins is sometimes drawn from *multiple* locations along a DNA strand, and in addition to providing the template for constructing the messenger RNA

62. Lloyd, "Computational Capacity of the Universe."

63. For technical accounts of design-theoretic mathematics, see: William A. Dembski, *The Design Inference: Eliminating Chance through Small Probabilities* (Cambridge: Cambridge University Press, 1998); Robert J. Marks II, William J. Dembski, and Winston Ewert, *Introduction to Evolutionary Informatics* (Singapore: World Scientific, 2017); and Montañez, "A Unified Model."

64. For those thinking that this problem can be resolved by evolving new proteins from old ones, the intractability of protein evolution will be addressed momentarily.

65. Eugene V. Koonin, "The Cosmological Model of Eternal Inflation and the Transition from Chance to Biological Evolution in the History of Life," *Biology Direct* 2 (2007): 15.

66. An excellent overview is Jonathan Wells, *The Myth of Junk DNA* (Seattle: Discovery Institute Press, 2011).

facilitating this task, is also the template for other RNAs not involved in protein synthesis but part of a regulatory system crucial to embryonic development and specification of organismal body plans.[67]

Furthermore, it has been discovered that regulatory RNAs are constructed from both strands of DNA, and those constructed from the "anti-sense" strand are a major part of the transcriptome (the entirety of an organism's RNA).[68] As researchers noted, the frequency of overlapping coding regions with highly specified functionality "is nearly impossible by chance."[69] Overlapping codes also profoundly reduce the probability of beneficial mutation.[70] In the last few years it has become clear that highly specified epigenetic information (information not involving changes in DNA code, but affecting construction of RNAs and proteins and larger-scale organismal development) also plays a significant role in animal body plan formation.[71]

But suppose you already had the first cell with its suite of proteins. Could you expect new proteins with new functions to arise by undirected evolution? No, and here's why.[72] Suppose we have a species of ancient bacteria with an effective population size of ten billion passing through ten thousand generations each year.[73] Also suppose a generous mutation rate of one per cell (300 times higher than observed rates)[74] over five

---

67. Philipp Kapranov et al., "Genome-Wide Transcription and the Implications for Genomic Organization," *Nature Reviews Genetics* 8 (2007): 413–23; John S. Mattick and Igor V. Makunin, "Non-Coding RNA," *Human Molecular Genetics* 15 (2006): R17–R29; Eugene V. Makeyev and Tom Maniatis, "Multilevel Regulation of Gene Expression by MicroRNAs," *Science* 319 (2008): 1789–90; and Gennadi V. Glinsky, "Phenotype-Defining Functions of Multiple Non-Coding RNA Pathways," *Cell Cycle* 7 (2008): 1630–39.

68. S. Katayama et al., "Antisense Transcription in the Mammalian Transcriptome," *Science* 309 (2005): 1564–66; and Kevin V. Morris et al., "Bidirectional Transcription Directs Both Transcriptional Gene Activation and Suppression in Human Cells," *PLoS Genetics* 4, no. 11 (2008): e1000258.

69. Wen-Yu Chung et al., "A First Look at Arfome: Dual-Coding Genes in Mammalian Genomes," *PLoS Computational Biology* 3, no. 5 (2007): e91.

70. G. Montañez et al., "Multiple Overlapping Genetic Codes Profoundly Reduce the Probability of Beneficial Mutation," in Robert J. Marks II et al., *Biological Information: New Perspectives* (Singapore: World Scientific, 2013), 139–67.

71. Jonathan Wells, "Membrane Patterns Carry Ontogenetic Information that Is Specified Independently of DNA," *BIO-Complexity* 2 (2014): 1–28 (extensive footnotes give an overview of epigenetic research).

72. Axe, "The Case Against a Darwinian Origin of Protein Folds," 5.

73. Michael Lynch and John S. Conery, "The Origins of Genome Complexity," *Science* 302 (2003): 1401–4.

74. John W. Drake et al., "Rates of Spontaneous Mutation," *Genetics* 148 (1998): 1667–86.

billion years. Then there would be at most $5 \times 10^9 \times 10^4 \times 10^{10} = 5 \times 10^{23}$ opportunities for undirected mutation and natural selection to produce a new functional protein. A relatively short protein of only 153 amino-acid residues has just one chance in anywhere from 10^{53} to 10^{77} of being functional,[75] while a more standard protein of 300 residues rescales to a functional probability of one in 10^{104} to 10^{151}.[76] Given 10^{14} chances per year and taking an average probability of one in 10^{65} for shorter proteins and one in 10^{127} for proteins of standard length, undirected generation of another functional protein respectively would not happen for 10^{51} to 10^{113} years.

A co-option solution (conversion of function among structurally similar proteins or enzymes) also faces severe waiting-time barriers. Using two enzymes structurally very similar to a third enzyme, researchers tested 70 percent of double-mutation combinations (roughly eight million for each enzyme) with no indication of converted function.[77] They concluded that *at least* three mutations would be required for conversion by the standard recruitment mechanism and this meant a waiting time of 10^{15} years. These waiting-time problems carry over into standard evolutionary scenarios. For example, the proposed Pakicetus-to-whale transition has at best nine million years to happen and requires more than *fifteen* body-plan adaptations, but merely *two* favorable genetic mutations need at least forty-three million years.[78] The proposed divergence of chimpanzees and humans from a common ancestor, which had six to thirteen million years to happen, faces a similar problem, with estimates for fixing two favorable mutations in creatures with long generation times and small populations ranging from eighty-four million to five hundred million years.[79] The history of life on earth is replete

75. Douglas D. Axe, "Estimating the Prevalence of Protein Sequences Adopting Functional Enzyme Folds," *Journal of Molecular Biology* 341 (2004): 1310.

76. Axe, "The Case Against a Darwinian Origin of Protein Folds," 6.

77. M. Reeves, A. Gauger, and D. Axe, "Enzyme Families—Shared Evolutionary History or Shared Design? A Study of the GABA-Aminotransferase Family," *BIO-Complexity* 4 (2014): 1–16.

78. James C. LeMaster, "Evolution's Waiting-Time Problem and Suggested Ways to Overcome It—A Critical Survey," *BIO-Complexity* 2 (2018): 3; also J. Wells, "Walking Whales," in *Zombie Science: More Icons of Evolution* (Seattle: Discovery Institute, 2017), 99–114.

79. Michael Lynch and Adam Abegg, "The Rate of Establishment of Complex Adaptations," *Molecular Biology and Evolution* 27, no. 6 (2010): 1404–14; Rick Durrett and Deena Schmidt, "Waiting for Two Mutations: with Applications to Regulatory Sequence

with instances of new species appearing much faster than undirected evolutionary mechanisms can explain,[80] often on large scales, as in the Cambrian explosion, the marine Mesozoic revolution, the angiosperm "big bloom," the mammalian radiation, and so on.[81]

The difficulties for standard evolutionary biology and universal common descent do not stop here. Partaking of the tree of knowledge bars access to the Darwinian tree of life: the picture of life's history as a sequence of branching lineages from a single-celled origin to today's diversity is riddled with missing evidence, evidential interpretations *assuming* universal common descent for justification, and contradictory evidence undermining the thesis altogether.[82] First, the paleontological record is staggeringly incomplete and mostly missing plausible transitional forms. As evolutionary biologist James Valentine has remarked, "Organisms with the characteristic body plans that we identity as living phyla appear abruptly in the fossil record, many within a narrow window of geological time . . . [and] none of them can be traced through fossil intermediates to an ancestral group."[83] The Cambrian explosion is, of course, a prime example, but there are many others.

Furthermore, when we do have fossils, structural similarity (anatomical homology) is only evidence of their relatedness on the *assumption* of universal common descent. If one requires that extinct organisms must have arisen through undirected processes, then common descent plausibly explains their anatomical similarity despite separation in time and place, but anatomical homology only counts as evidence for common ancestry *on the assumption that common ancestry explains the similarities*. The relationship between evidence and theory here is incestuous, which doesn't bode well for its progeny. As British paleontologist and senior

Evolution and the Limits of Darwinian Evolution," *Genetics* 180, no. 3 (2008): 1501–9; and John Sanford et al., "The Waiting Time Problem in a Model Hominin Population," *Theoretical Biology and Medical Modelling* 12, no. 8 (2015): 1–29.

80. Douglas D. Axe, "The Limits of Complex Adaptation: An Analysis Based on a Simple Model of Structured Bacterial Populations," *BIO-Complexity* 4 (2010): 1–10.

81. Stephen C. Meyer, *Darwin's Doubt: The Explosive Origin of Animal Life and the Case for Intelligent Design* (San Francisco: HarperOne, 2013) comprehensively discusses these difficulties.

82. A more complete account of these deficiencies with extensive citations of the scientific literature can be found in J. Wells, "The Tree of Life," in *Zombie Science: More Icons of Evolution* (Seattle: Discovery Institute, 2017), 25–48.

83. James W. Valentine, *On the Origin of Phyla* (Chicago: University of Chicago Press, 2004), 37.

editor of *Nature*, Henry Gee, reflected, "To take a line of fossils and claim that they represent a lineage is not a scientific hypothesis that can be tested, but an assertion that carries the same validity as a bedtime story, [it is perhaps] instructive, but not scientific."[84]

Neither does genetic evidence from molecular homology (comparing sequence similarities in DNA, RNA, and proteins across species) supply what is missing. Two obvious difficulties arise in comparing sequence similarity after alignment. The first is that, with rare exception, such sequences are only available for *living* organisms. Inferences about their evolutionary past are hypothetical and derived on the assumption of common descent. The second is that before comparison is possible, sequences have to be aligned, and sequences in living things contain repeated or deleted segments, often making it unclear where alignment should start. Long sequences can be aligned more than one way, so phylogenetic analysis (the estimation of an evolutionary relationship among species) depends on which alignment is chosen. Computer programs doing the analysis depend on parameters programmed into them, and outputs are often biologically implausible. A 2009 survey found that "more than half of evolutionary biologists intervene manually in their sequence alignments and more than three-quarters of phylogeneticists do so."[85] More tellingly, "a proliferation of alignment methods . . . produce detectably different multiple sequence alignments in almost all realistic cases."[86]

Unsurprisingly, sequence comparisons often produce conflicting evolutionary trees. In 2008, an international team of eighteen biologists constructed a phylogeny of animal groups using 150 different genes that was contradicted the following year by another international team of twenty biologists using 128 genes.[87] The current status of molecular phylogeny is well expressed by another group of biologists: "Incongruences

84. Henry Gee, *In Search of Deep Time: Beyond the Fossil Record to a New History of Life* (New York: The Free Press, 1999), 32; see also pp. 113–17.

85. David A. Morrison, "Why Would Phylogeneticists Ignore Computerized Sequence Alignment?" *Systematic Biology* 58 (2009): 150–58.

86. David A. Morrison, "Is Sequence Alignment an Art or a Science?" *Systematic Botany* 40 (2015): 14–26.

87. Compare Casey W. Dunn et al., "Broad Phylogenomic Sampling Improves Resolution of the Animal Tree of Life," *Nature* 452 (2008): 745–49, with Hervé Philippe et al., "Phylogenomics Revives Traditional Views on Deep Animal Relationships," *Current Biology* 19 (2009): 706–12.

between phylogenies derived from morphological versus molecular analyses, and between trees based on different subsets of molecular sequences, has become pervasive."[88] Paleontological "bedtime stories" are not improved, therefore, by molecular evidence, but the increasing implausibility of the motivating picture is instructive. Combine these pervasive inconsistencies with the discovery that many DNA sequences are unique to specific taxonomic groups (taxa),[89] then consider the waiting-time problem, the intractability of evolvability from the standpoint of embryogenesis, and the pervasiveness of specified-functional information amenable to design-theoretic analysis, and the Darwinian tree of life looks increasingly like an inspirational symbol in a metaphysical naturalist's fairy tale.

A different approach is needed. The idea that materialist science, making reference only to natural laws and material entities, could account for the existence and properties of the universe as well as the appearance and nature of human beings in the course of its history, is untenable on so many levels that those who persist in maintaining it can only be seen as ideological captives of metaphysical naturalism. While it is important to study what can be accomplished in the *ordinary* course of nature, once it is known that intelligent causation provides the best explanation for certain phenomena, this scientific question has been answered and a wide range of *new* questions come into view that draw on resources across the spectrum of the engineering disciplines: biomolecular engineering, genetic engineering, systems engineering, process engineering, computer engineering, nano-engineering, and so on. Such research investigates the means by which functionally specified information in nature is implemented, degraded, reconstructible/reverse-engineerable, optimized/optimizable, integrated, and for human purposes, imitable (biomimetics). Answering one scientific question opens the door for another to be asked. Intelligent design is *not* a science-stopper. When its

---

88. Liliana M. Dávalos et al., "Understanding Phylogenetic Incongruence: Lessons from Phyllostomid Bats," *Biological Reviews of the Cambridge Philosophical Society* 87 (2012): 991–1024.

89. Protein-coding regions of DNA are called "open reading frames" (ORFs), so taxa-specific ORFs, in relation to universal common descent, are called "ORFans" (orphans). ORFan genes are found in bacteria, yeast, fruit flies, mice, squids, octopi, humans, and a variety of other taxonomic categories.

insights are found applicable, it redirects scientific research from dead ends to fruitful paths.

Concluding Unscientific Postscript

Our journey has taken us from the metaphysical and epistemic foundations of science, through questions of its history and methodology, to an understanding of the way that natural regularities are dependent on transcendent causation and how such causation is detectable in the origin and fine-tuning of the universe as well as the origin and development of life. Einstein famously remarked that "I want to know how God created this world. I am not interested in this or that phenomenon, in the spectrum of this or that element. I want to know His thoughts; the rest are details."[90] But *everything* we experience in this world, including the details in which Einstein had little interest, involves God. In his speech at the Areopagus, the apostle Paul appropriates Epimenides' reflection that "in him [God] we live and move and have our being" (Acts 17:28a). As it turns out, this is quite true. We have the privilege of exploring the endless variety, beauty, and subtlety of God's reality-defining thoughts and actions, a scientific adventure made all the more meaningful when God's role is recognized and the personal and relational character of the universe embraced.

---

90. Esther Salaman, "A Talk with Einstein," *The Listener* 54 (1955): 370–71.

MICHAEL RUSE

I think that there is a difference between Alister McGrath's essay and Bruce Gordon's essay. The former tries to formulate a particular way of addressing the science-religion relationship, one not necessarily accepted by all, and hence requiring careful exposition. I responded in the same spirit, trying to get Alister's whole position out front before commenting. The latter defends a well-known conservative reading of religion and, given this reading, a well-trodden approach to science. For this reason, I am going to comment on Bruce's essay more or less as it comes.

God?

I start right on line 1. "Christianity entails *idealism* in a basic sense: *mind* is foundational to reality, and matter is derivative." At once, Bruce pushes on us philosophies that most would not accept. Here he presupposes Cartesian monism, where we can separate out mind and matter—*res cogitans* and *res extensa*—and makes the latter dependent on the former. "Mind is foundational." The implication is that we could have mind without matter, even if we could not have matter without mind. But most of us—most philosophers of all ilks—would not accept this. Apart from those like Daniel Dennett, who think that matter can do everything (so mind could not be foundational), we want matter to have a full place at the table. Some, emergentists, would start with matter and have mind emerge. Others, and I have shown in my response to Alister that I would count myself in here, opt for some kind of monism, where mind and matter are one. Panpsychism is the popular version today.

Right off I am going to reject Bruce's God. "The contingent universe we inhabit is not an unexplained material datum but the intelligent product of divine thought, and God is the necessary Being from whom it derives its existence and purpose" (p. 155). Now, you know that I am not going to accept this sort of stuff. I am a nonbeliever, but this is not quite my point here. My point is that were I a believer, I would reject Bruce's God. And with this goes a lot, I think, that Bruce wants to get out of or from this God. I am uncomfortable with the idea of God existing and then at some point rolling up his sleeves and getting into the creation business, like a baker grabs some yeast and flour and water and gets into the bread business. (Except, for Bruce, God is going to make the ingredients also.) I am not about to have slipped across at me, surreptitiously, the kind of creator God that we get in the early chapters of Genesis. I don't know whether God could exist without his creation, for instance. Perhaps origins in the way Bruce thinks of them are just not plausible. You might say that this argument is not very satisfactory. But it is very much part of my apophatic theology. I have faith that God exists and that he is in some sense a loving creator who cares for his children. After that, I just don't know. It is a mystery hidden from me—from Bruce Gordon too. I don't know, I am not expected to know, and I couldn't know, given the limited creature I am. It is for me to fall down and worship with thanks, in awe.

Plantinga

Nonsense, says Bruce, briskly. (I am not saying he reminds me of my headmaster. He does remind me of my mother.) We know a lot about God, about us, and about our relationship to God. For a start, we know that God is not a deceiver. He created this world, and he made us in his image, hence we are going to be able to make out the true nature of this world. But only because of God. "Explaining why there is something instead of absolutely nothing must terminate with an entity that exists *necessarily* and is capable of acting as a cause. This brings us within a hair's breadth of recognizing that a necessary being, God, is required both to ground knowledge and to explain why anything exists to be known" (p. 137).

Well, what about someone like me who is a Darwinian naturalist? I think we are animals produced by natural selection; it is to our adaptive advantage to know what is going on in the world: What is that big hairy beast that seems to have me in its sights? And so we have features that report back on the surroundings in which we find ourselves—ears, noses, and so forth—together with onboard computers (aka brains) to process this information.[1] It is at this point that (dare I say, expectedly) Bruce trots out Alvin Plantinga. Our various organs feeding us information and helping us process it are not interested in objective truth. They care only about getting us through life and doing better than the chap next to us—where "doing better" means being more successful reproductively.

> As Alvin Plantinga forcefully argues [The locus classicus for Plantinga's argument is chapter 12 of *Warrant and Proper Function* (Oxford: Oxford University Press, 1993).], undirected evolution provides no ground for supposing our cognitive faculties produce true beliefs, and the further removed from immediate survival our beliefs are, the less confidence we should have in their veridicality. This means that evolutionary naturalists have little warrant for believing anything (including evolutionary naturalism) to be true (p. 138).

Let's take a moment to dig into this argument a little more deeply. Plantinga floats the example of thinking one is dining in college with Richard Dawkins and A. J. Ayer, when truly one is fighting off crocodiles in Africa. "Under this possibility . . . beliefs wouldn't have (or needn't have) any purpose or function; they would be more like unintended by-products, and the likelihood that they are mostly true would be low."[2] I agree. But what Darwinian evolutionist ever rested their case on such a ludicrous example? If evolution is going to deceive us, it will be for a very good reason. Edward O. Wilson believes the success of religions stems from the fact that they promote group solidarity.[3] The adaptive virtues of working together outweigh the costs, if such there be, of believing in totally fictitious figures. Boozing it up with Freddie

---

1. I have discussed my Darwinian position in many places. Begin, as I began, with my *Taking Darwin Seriously: A Naturalistic Approach to Philosophy* (Oxford: Blackwell, 1986).

2. Alvin Plantinga, "Is Belief in God Properly Basic?" *Noûs* 15 (1981): 34.

3. Edward O. Wilson, *On Human Nature* (Cambridge, MA: Harvard University Press, 1978).

Ayer is not a good thought to have when someone or something is trying to tear your guts out.

Plantinga asks: What if we are systematically deceived? Looking at an assembly line in a factory, we think the produced widgets are red. Once we remove our rose-tinted protective glasses, we see our mistake. Perhaps in real life, we are stuck with the glasses. Just as the widgets in the factory are not really red, so the results of the deceptions of evolution yield no true knowledge. Two responses are in order. First, the critique certainly points us toward a coherence theory of truth rather than a correspondence theory. But so what? As a pragmatist I am happy to say that what you get is all you are going to get, and if it works well, and the information fed to us by our Darwinian adaptations does seem to work well, so what? Be happy with what you have. Second, what is the Plantinga alternative? He as a Calvinist opts for a *sensus divinitatis*, a kind of Skyping ability that has God at the other end. Remember, "a necessary being, God, is required both to ground knowledge and to explain why anything exists to be known" (p. 137). But what then do you say about alternative religious positions, each equally convinced it has the truth? Are you going to say that you uniquely have the proper apparatus and the other Christians—Catholics, Orthodox, and more— not to mention Jews, Muslims, Buddhists, Hindus, and many more are just wrong, that they have flawed Skyping equipment? If you have any modicum of modesty and decency about you, you are going to go for some kind of religious pluralism, as promoted by John Hick.[4] In the words of Rudyard Kipling,

> There are nine-and-sixty ways of constructing tribal lays,
> And every single one of them is right![5]

Back to my apophatic theology. God is unknown and unknowable. Everyone tries to approach him in his or her own way. They are all appropriate. Darwinian pragmatism doesn't look too bad under a scenario like this.

---

4. John Hick, *God and the Universe of Faiths* (New York: St. Martin's, 1973).
5. Rudyard Kipling, "In the Neolithic Age," in *Rudyard Kipling: Selected Poems*, ed. Peter Keating (London: Penguin Classics, 2000), 46.

Crabby Interlude

Before I move on, I cannot forbear making two comments about the analytic philosophical tradition that Plantinga represents. First, I am so sick of smart-alecky examples like the crocodile one. Analytic philosophers pride themselves so much on these, and yet the illustrations really are not worthy of us. Darwinian evolutionary biology is a powerful science. Perhaps it does have its limitations. It would be odd if it didn't. But try to understand it before you start criticizing. Second, I am equally sick of the flagrant ahistoricism of analytic philosophy. Bruce—as do many others—holds up Plantinga's argument against Darwinian naturalism as the greatest discovery since the categorical imperative. Why not acknowledge that this was an argument around for a hundred years before Plantinga? Arthur J. Balfour—philosopher, future prime minister of Great Britain, and whose signature is on the Balfour Declaration of 1917, giving support for a Jewish homeland—had a full and careful exposition of the point that Plantinga would make. Darwinism cares naught for truth, only for reproduction. If the needs of reproduction ride roughshod over the search for truth, so be it.

> To suppose that a course of development carried out, not with the object of extending knowledge or satisfying curiosity, but solely with that of promoting life, on an area so insignificant as the surface of the earth, between limits of temperature and pressure so narrow, and under general conditions so exceptional, should have ended in supplying us with senses even approximately adequate to the apprehension of Nature in all her complexities, is to believe in a coincidence more astounding than the most audacious novelist has ever employed to cut the knot of some entangled tale . . . .
>
> Not only does Nature take no interest in our general education, not only is she quite indifferent to the growth of enlightenment, unless the enlightenment improve our chances in the struggle for existence, but she positively objects to the very existence of faculties by which these ends might, perhaps, be attained. She regards them as mere hindrances in the only race which she desires to see run.[6]

---

6. Arthur J. Balfour, *The Foundations of Belief* (New York: Longmans, Green, 1895), 70.

Couldn't have said it better myself, even if my name were Alvin Plantinga.

Methodological Naturalism: Old or New?

Incidentally, while we are on these sorts of things, naturalism in particular, let me take things out of order and object to Bruce's reading of history, especially with respect to methodological naturalism——refusing to let God play any role in your science. Bruce tells us that this philosophy is of recent standing, a new innovation after Darwin. The implication being that it has not had time to truly establish its worth.

> Methodological naturalism's ascent to contemporary orthodoxy starts with Darwin, not the Scientific Revolution. But saying that systematic rational and observational study of nature only became science after Darwin, because only then did methodological naturalism hold sway, begs the question and makes a fiat declaration as unconvincing as it is historically inaccurate. Methodological naturalism's ascendancy is an artifact of a conception of nature that is not intrinsic to the task of scientific explanation (p. 146–47).

With respect, this really isn't so. By the time the Scientific Revolution was coming to an end, the late seventeenth century, three things were true. Methodological naturalism was the way of science. Everyone thought God was behind creation. Organisms were a problem. Robert Boyle is a paradigm. First, he wanted to keep God out of his science. He distinguishes himself from those who would bring God into the story—miracles and intentions and such things.

> And methinks the difference between their opinion of God's agency in the world, and that which I would propose, may be somewhat adumbrated by saying that they seem to imagine the world to be after the nature of a puppet, whose contrivance indeed may be very artificial, but yet is such that almost every particular motion the artificer is fain (by drawing sometimes one wire or string, sometimes another) to guide, and oftentimes overrule, the actions of the engine; whereas, according to us,

it is like a rare clock, such as may be that at Strasbourg, where all things are so skillfully contrived that the engine being once set a-moving, all things proceed according to the artificer's first design, and the motions of the little statues that as such hours perform these or those motions do not require (like those of puppets) the peculiar interposing of the artificer or any intelligent agent employed by him, but perform their functions on particular occasions by virtue of the general and primitive contrivance of the whole engine.[7]

Second, for Boyle, God is behind it all.

When I consider how many things that seem anomalies to us do frequently enough happen in the world, I think it is more consonant to the respect we owe to divine providence to conceive that, as God is a most free as well as a most wise agent, and may in many things have ends unknown to us, he very well foresaw and thought it fit that such seeming anomalies should come to pass, since he made them (as is evident in the eclipses of the sun and moon) the genuine consequences of the order he was pleased to settle in the world, by whose laws the grand agents in the universe were empowered and determined to act according to the respective natures he had given them; and the course of things was allowed to run on, though that would infer the happening of seeming anomalies and things really repugnant to the good or welfare of divers particular portions of the universe.[8]

Third, organisms are a problem because they do seem to call for intention, for design, for final causes. Boyle admitted this. His gambit was to say that this was religion, not science!

---

7. Robert Boyle, *A Free Enquiry into the Vulgarly Received Notion of Nature* (Cambridge: Cambridge University Press, 1996), 12–13. The Strasbourg Clock, the second of three, completed in 1574, was a remarkable mechanical contrivance set on a globe, with planets and eclipses, panels of the creation, the resurrection of the dead, and the last judgment, not to mention moving figures and a six-tune carillon and a cock that crowed every day at noon from the cathedral's cupola. It also told the time!

8. Boyle, *A Free Enquiry*, 13.

There are some things in nature so curiously contrived, and so exquisitely fitted for certain operations and uses, that it seems little less than blindness in him, that acknowledges, with the Cartesians, a most wise Author of things, not to conclude, that, though they may have been designed for other (and perhaps higher) uses, yet they were designed for this use.[9]

Boyle continued, supposing that "a man's eyes were made by chance, argues, that they need have no relation to a designing agent; and the use, that a man makes of them, may be either casual too, or at least may be an effect of his knowledge, not of nature's." But this reasoning not only takes us away from the urge to dissect and to understand—how the eye "is as exquisitely fitted to be an organ of sight, as the best artificer in the world could have framed a little engine, purposely and mainly designed for the use of seeing"—but also takes us away from the designing intelligence behind it.

A compromise, perhaps not a happy compromise, although a lot of good biological science was done under this umbrella. At the end of the eighteenth century, we find Kant, who wanted desperately to keep God out of science, suggesting that the design of biology was merely heuristic.[10] Although this did condemn biology to being a second-rate science. "There will never be a Newton of the blade of grass." It took Darwin to cut the Gordian Knot—no pun intended—by showing how natural selection could give a methodological naturalistic explanation of the designlike nature of organisms. His was the breakthrough, but it extended the reach of methodological naturalism; it didn't create something new. Note, incidentally, that—although by the time of the *Descent* (1871), he had become an agnostic—in the *Origin* (1859), Darwin is a deist. God is behind everything as much as he is for Robert Boyle.

Authors of the highest eminence seem to be fully satisfied with the view that each species has been independently created. To my mind it accords better with what we know of the laws impressed on matter by the Creator, that the production and extinction of

9. Robert Boyle, *A Disquisition about the Final Causes of Natural Things* (Hildesheim: Georg Olms, 1966), 297–98.

10. Immanuel Kant (1790), *Critique of Judgement* (*Third Critique*). For a full discussion, see my *On Purpose* (Oxford: Oxford University Press, 2017).

the past and present inhabitants of the world should have been due to secondary causes, like those determining the birth and death of the individual. When I view all beings not as special creations, but as the lineal descendants of some few beings which lived long before the first bed of the Silurian system was deposited, they seem to me to become ennobled.[11]

Reading Scripture

Like Alister, Bruce decries a simplistic literal reading of the text, but, in the end, he is a lot more literal than Alister. As I read him, he does not believe in evolution; he believes God created about ten thousand or so humans about ten thousand years ago, one specific human—call him Adam—sinned and the rest copied him, and we are off and running down to Jesus and the need for substitutionary atonement. A certain amount of reconstruction of a discussion is needed here that, frankly, I find somewhat opaque, but I am trying hard not to distort and think I have the true picture. Certainly I am right about a lot of it, starting with the fact that Bruce states that "the biblical account is a symbolic story communicating an essential truth about theological anthropology resting on historical events having this significance, the details of which are not provided" (p. 144).

What can I say, except that I don't believe a word of it and that sixty years after the publication of the creationist classic *The Genesis Flood* by John Whitcomb and Henry Morris, the antievolution arguments are no more well taken than they ever were. In fact, they are weaker. Bruce tells us that the paleontological record is staggeringly incomplete and mostly missing plausible transitional forms. Has he never heard of *Archaeopteryx*? Does he know nothing of *Tiktaalik*, a fossil found in Canada at the beginning of this century? Dated from about 375 million years ago, it is a stunning example of a fish already on the way to being a tetrapod, four-legged, and thus fitted to live out of the water on land. And what of Lucy, *Australopithecus afarensis*, about three million plus years old, with a chimpanzee-size brain and yet bipedal? She was not just bipedal but shows signs that, like her immediate ancestors, she would have been much better at climbing trees than we modern humans. In fact, to say

---

11. Charles Darwin, *On the Origin of Species* (London: John Murray, 1859), 488–89.

of the human line that there is inadequate evidence is just wrong. More and more is being turned up, and while sometimes it is surprising, it all fits: the Denisovans, for instance, another now-extinct group like the Neanderthals; or, famously, the hobbit—*Homo floresiensis*—found in Indonesia, which was just over a meter high and lived until about fifty thousand years ago. In addition to the fossils, although Bruce somewhat downplays it, massive genetic evidence backs the picture of evolution generally and human evolution in particular. Everybody knows now—except, apparently, Bruce—about ancient DNA. We can get DNA out of fossils and see what it all means. The most staggering story of them all is that Europeans apparently had ancestors that cohabited with the Neanderthals. About 5 percent of our DNA comes from our ape-man ancestors.[12]

I will not spend more time on this because I have been arguing it for forty years and more, as have Bruce and his predecessors on his side.[13] There are other parts to the argument than fossils. For instance, Bruce brings up the old chestnut about the randomness of mutation making impossible the advances we supposedly see in evolution.

> For example, the proposed Pakicetus-to-whale transition has at best nine million years to happen and requires more than *fifteen* body-plan adaptations, but merely *two* favorable genetic mutations need at least forty-three million years. The proposed divergence of chimpanzees and humans from a common ancestor, which had six to thirteen million years to happen, faces a similar problem, with estimates for fixing two favorable mutations in creatures with long generation times and small populations ranging from eighty-four million to five hundred million years. The history of life on earth is replete with instances of new species appearing much faster than undirected evolutionary mechanisms can explain, often on large scales, as in the Cambrian explosion,

---

12. Start with David Reich, *Who We Are and How We Got Here* (New York: Pantheon, 2018).

13. I am not one to back off from a good fight, but I am writing a response, not a whole new book in its own right. I will therefore simply direct readers to my own account of the creationism controversy, in Michael Ruse with Robert Pennock, *But Is It Science? The Philosophical Question in the Evolution/Creation Controversy*, 2nd ed. (Buffalo: Prometheus, 2008). My defense of Darwinian evolutionary theory is given in Michael Ruse, *Darwinism and Its Discontents* (Cambridge: Cambridge University Press, 2006).

the marine Mesozoic revolution, the angiosperm "big bloom," the mammalian radiation, and so on (p. 161–62).[14]

There is never any discussion of the standard Darwinian response, going back to Theodosius Dobzhansky and his balanced heterozygote theory of populations, something his student Richard Lewontin confirmed using molecular techniques, which suggests that all natural populations carry a huge amount of variation. So when new needs and challenges arise, there is no need to wait for favorable variations.[15] There is always something there you can use. A new predator turns up. Then there is a gene for camouflage or a gene for distastefulness or a gene for hiding or a gene for getting the hell out of that part of the world or . . . It's all a bit like having an essay to write—say, on dictators—and having a library to draw on (if you cannot find something on Hitler, then look under Stalin), but then having to wait for something suitable to arrive from the book-of-the-month club.

Worlds Apart

Bruce, like Alister, is into fine tuning. "That the fine-tuning of the initial conditions, laws, and constants of the universe, and the origin and development of life and consciousness, might best be explained by intelligent causes is eminently reasonable in a theistic context and entirely compatible with the uniformitarian assumptions necessary to science" (p. 149). To which all I can do is quote Steven Weinberg again.

[I] am not terribly impressed by the examples of fine-tuning of constants of nature that have been presented. To be a little bit more precise about the case of carbon, the energy levels of carbon, which is the most notorious example that's always cited, there is an energy level that is 7.65 MeV above the ground state of carbon. If it was .06 of an MeV higher, then carbon production would be greatly diminished and there would be much less chance of life forming. That looks like a 1% fine-tuning of the constants of nature. . . . However, as has been realized subsequently after

---

14. For brevity, I have dropped the references, which can be found in Bruce's original text.

15. Richard Lewontin, *The Genetic Basis of Evolutionary Change* (New York: Columbia University Press, 1974). I take up this issue in Michael Ruse, *Darwinism Defended: A Guide to the Evolution Controversies* (Reading, MA: Benjamin-Cummings, 1982).

this 'fine-tuning' was pointed out, you should really measure the energy level not above the ground state of carbon but above the state of the nucleus Beryllium 8 (8Be) plus a helium nucleus. . . . In other words, the fine-tuning is not 1% but it's something like 25%. So, it's not very impressive fine-tuning at all.[16]

Let me end, if not more constructively, where I do think there is more of a meeting of minds. We both agree that modern science, methodologically naturalistic science, cannot answer all the genuine questions about reality. Why is there something rather than nothing, for example. Bruce spends some effort on quantum mechanics showing how a materialistic picture of the world is negated by theories and evidence from that area of science. There has to be something more, and this points to the Christian God.

> [N]ature behaves in ways we expect and can mathematically describe, but it does so for no discernible *physical* reason. The absence of a physical reason for the regularity of nature, by way of the principle of sufficient reason, shows there is an *immaterial metaphysical ground* for natural regularities. So not only does our manifestly contingent universe lack any explanation for its *existence* apart from a necessarily existent causal ground, it doesn't even *function* autonomously after it exists. Christians are not surprised: God doesn't just create the world; he also *sustains* it (p. 154).

Well, perhaps there really isn't a meeting of minds after all. I have agreed that the world is queerer than we think or could think. I have agreed that our minds are limited and there is no reason to think we can peer into all the mysteries of the universe. I just don't see why this brings in the Christian God. I am an agnostic. I don't deny God. I don't see the need to invoke him. Perhaps things just are. Albert Camus talked of existence as being absurd. At the metaphysical level, he could be right.[17] Leave it at that.

---

16. Steven Weinberg, "Not So Fine Tuned after All." This article is based on a talk given in April 1999 at the Conference on Cosmic Design of the American Association for the Advancement of Science in Washington, DC, http://www.focus.org.uk/weinberg.pdf.

17. "At the metaphysical level." In my *A Meaning to Life* (Oxford: Oxford University Press, 2019), I argue that, at the lived level, life is anything but absurd. What Alister and Bruce and I are doing now is far from absurd, in Camus's sense. That is still consistent with me being the only one of us who is right!

RESPONSE TO BRUCE GORDON

ALISTER MCGRATH

I am delighted to respond to Bruce's "Constrained Integration View" of the relation of the natural sciences and Christianity. This is the first time I have encountered this term, although I was already familiar with the idea of "constrained integration" in a mathematical context. My first concern was to try to work out what Bruce means by this phrase and how this approach is distinguished from those that Michael and I offer in this volume. I wondered if it might have been helpful for Bruce to open his piece with a brief account of the overall shape of this view, distinguishing it from its alternatives, so that I could orient myself to the specific nature and distinctive features of his approach.

Ian Barbour's influential 1960s taxonomy of potential relationships between science and religious belief identifies four such possibilities: conflict, independence, dialogue, and integration.[1] The first is exemplified by Richard Dawkins (not a contributor to this volume!), the second by Michael, and the third by me. So does Bruce adopt the fourth approach, as identified by Barbour? It seems unlikely, as Barbour's notion of integration seems to entail the dissolution or minimalization of distinctiveness on the part of what is being integrated. My hunch was that Bruce's use of the qualifying term *constrained* indicates that the integration that was being proposed was more limited in its scope than Barbour's version of this approach.

Bruce opens with a bold and striking theological statement: our

---

1. For a critical account of Barbour's taxonomy, see Geoffrey Cantor and Chris Kenny, "Barbour's Fourfold Way: Problems with His Taxonomy of Science-Religion Relationships," *Zygon* 36 (2001): 765–81.

universe is the "intelligent product of divine thought." As a theologian, I can agree with this. I would, however, prefer to follow the long-standing theological tradition, which goes back to fourth-century writers such as Athanasius of Alexandria, in drawing on the biblical language of *logos* (such as John 1:14), which helps us think of our universe as the *logikos* ("rational" or "intelligible"—but surely not "intelligent") product of the divine mind.

The Possibility of Knowledge

I warmed immediately to Bruce's reference to constructing an "optimally coherent and integrated picture," a theme that is integral to my own understanding of the relation of science and religious belief. Christianity affirms an ordered world that is intelligible to a God-given mind. This has been a fundamental theme of Christian theology down the ages.

Bruce prefaces his discussion of his approach by offering us a philosophical framework that enables us to affirm the possibility of reliable knowledge. I found myself a little perplexed by this opening reflection. Scientists don't depend on philosophical prolegomena in investigating our world. They use an empirical method and see where it leads them. As Einstein pointed out, "the scientific method can teach us nothing else beyond how facts are related to, and conditioned by, each other."[2] A scientific methodology does not make any philosophical or metaphysical presuppositions about the nature of reality; it aims to explore this by empirical investigation.

As a Christian, I find myself already embedded within a rich conceptual world that is grounded in core theological ideas that naturally point toward a realist view of a regular and ordered world and a human mind that seems adapted to discern and represent these structures. The natural sciences, however, do not start out from a set of preconceived philosophical assumptions; this is one of the main problems with metaphysical naturalism, which rests on philosophical presuppositions that are essentially independent of the scientific method. While I personally take the view that a realist epistemology makes more sense of the successes of the natural sciences than its instrumentalist or nonrealistic alternatives, I cannot *prove* I am right on scientific or other grounds.[3]

---

2. Albert Einstein, *Ideas and Opinions* (New York: Crown, 1954), 41–2.

3. On the empirical relation of realism and instrumentalism, see Theo A. F. Kuipers, *From Instrumentalism to Constructive Realism: On Some Relations between Confirmation, Empirical Progress, and Truth Approximation* (Dordrecht: Kluwer Academic, 2000).

Some theologians, particularly in the post-Enlightenment era, saw laying a philosophical or methodological foundation for their works of dogmatic theology as essential. Yet this habit has generally been abandoned, in that it risks making theology dependent on controlling and historically conditioned cultural paradigms. Thomas F. Torrance, a Scottish Reformed theologian who was particularly significant in framing the science-religion discussion in explicitly theological terms, rightly criticized this trend. Theology begins with the *actuality* of divine self-disclosure and then reflects on its implications. As Torrance pointed out, neither science nor theology need defend how knowledge of nature or of God are possible; their *possibility* is confirmed by their *actuality*.[4] To put this another way, the issue is not to show that theology can be rationally justified; it is rather to show that theology can provide a framework for understanding the dilemmas of human rationality.[5]

I was interested in Bruce's philosophical defense of the possibility of knowledge. I agree with him (and suspect that most evolutionary biologists would concur) that evolution seems to select for survival value rather than a capacity to find our way to the truth. I constantly find myself amazed that we possess the capacity to discern the deep mathematical structures of our universe, when this seems to confer no obvious evolutionary advantages. I also agree with Bruce that we need to develop intellectual strategies to distinguish *doxa* from *epistēmē*, mere opinion from knowledge—while recognizing that, in both philosophy and science, this proves to be somewhat more complex than we might hope.

I can see what Bruce is getting at when he insists that "every contingent state of affairs has an explanation' (p. 137). Yet in science, explanations often take statistical or probabilistic forms. Imagine that I am observing a single atom of tritium, a radioactive isotope of hydrogen. I can predict that in twelve and a half years, half the tritium atoms in a sample will decay, yielding an isotope of helium. But I cannot predict when any given single atom will decay; nor can I explain why it decayed *at that moment*. There is no known causal explanation. This doesn't worry scientists, but it is a problem if you frame the issue as Bruce does.

---

4. For his classic statements of these themes, see Thomas F. Torrance, *Theological Science* (London: Oxford University Press, 1969).

5. Lydia Schumacher, "The Logic of Faith: Prolegomena to a Theological Theory of Knowledge," *New Blackfriars* 92, no. 1042 (2011): 664–77.

As Alvin Plantinga and C. S. Lewis both observe, evolutionary naturalists have little warrant for believing anything (including their own evolutionary naturalism) to be *true*; they are, in effect, sawing off the epistemic branch on which they are perched. Yet the situation is more complex than Bruce concedes. The issue here is *pragmatic*: methodological naturalism seems to *work*, irrespective of whatever explanation is offered for the origins and emergence of human cognitive capacities. There is an important parallel here with David Hume's inductive skepticism.[6] As Bertrand Russell pointed out, Hume's arguments mean that science ends up being dependent on something that cannot be shown to be true. "Our inductive principle is at any rate not capable of being *disproved* by an appeal to experience. The inductive principle, however, is equally incapable of being *proved* by an appeal to experience."[7] Most natural scientists I know are aware that Hume's critique of inductivism undermines ideas such as the "laws of nature." Yet their response is pragmatic: we know about this theoretical problem, but in practice it doesn't seem to make any difference. So we keep on using this approach, which seems to work well.

Bruce is quite right to suggest that a Christian way of thinking causes us to comprehend human rationality in certain specific ways. Traditionally, Christian theology frames such discussions in terms of humanity bearing the "image of God," which is understood to have implications for an understanding of human reasoning and relationality. For Augustine of Hippo, human beings possess the rational capacity to recognize the existence of God and to appreciate that God might be the ultimate goal of their longing and aspirations. I assume that some such point lies behind Bruce's statement that "the probability that properly-functioning cognitive faculties are reliable guides to truth is high *when conditioned on theism*, especially Christian theism, since God not only brings about our existence; he wants us to know and have a relationship with him and intends we understand the world well enough to be its stewards" (p. 139).

---

6. David Papineau, "Reliabilism, Induction and Scepticism," *Philosophical Quarterly* 42, no. 166 (1992): 1–20.

7. Bertrand Russell, *The Problems of Philosophy* (London: Oxford University Press, 1912), 99.

On Science and Scripture

I was intrigued by Bruce's opening statement in this section: "If God is the creator and sustainer of everything distinct from himself, it is reasonable to think he might communicate with us in a special way beyond the general knowledge of his existence available in nature" (p. 139). What, I wondered, does Bruce mean by "reasonable"? Which concept of rationality is he appealing to? As the rise of deism in England and North America indicates, the transition from a "God who creates" to a "God who also reveals" is not quite as straightforward as Bruce suggests. I fully concede that it makes sense within a specifically Christian rational framework, which affirms that God creates, reveals, and reconciles. Bruce's assumption is thus "reasonable" from a Christian perspective—but not from the perspectives of other worldviews, which inevitably shape human perceptions of rationality. (One important approach to apologetics is to invite someone to stand within a Christian rational framework and then invite them to reimagine and reconceive the world in its light—and hence grasp its intrinsic coherence.)

Bruce then sets out an account of how the Bible is to be interpreted, which highlights the importance of the "divine-human dynamic between primary and secondary hermeneutics" (p. 140). I found this section difficult to read, partly because of its verbal and conceptual density, which at times made it rather opaque. I also had difficulty in seeing how this discussion led to its intended conclusion. Like others, I have read and benefitted from Jack Collins's distinction between a "world picture" and "worldview," although I am also aware that a case can be made for suggesting that ancient Israel did not have a single "world picture" but rather retained several images of the universe that diverge and at times conflict with one another, without reconciling or integrating them.[8] I think Bruce is right in arguing that the cosmography of the Old Testament is "religious, not scientific." Yet how does this help us in our reflections?

I greatly appreciated reading Collins's interpretation of Genesis but cannot help but notice its marked divergence from older conservative

---

8. See, for example, Cornelis Houtman, *Der Himmel im Alten Testament: Israels Weltbild und Weltanschauung* (Leiden: Brill, 1993), 283–317.

Protestant interpretations of the same text. The main problem, as I see it, is this: it is an observable fact that Christian interpretation of many Old Testament texts has shifted significantly over time, and there is no "metaauthority" by which Protestants can determine which of those readings is to be regarded as right. Bruce is right to suggest that North American debates about the inerrancy of Scripture are "epistemically vexed." My point is that the affirmation of inerrancy does nothing to help us ascertain what is the *right* or the *best* interpretation of Scripture. Yet any attempt to relate Christianity and science on the basis of the Bible has to confront the question of which biblical interpretation relevant to the framing of this relationship is *right*?

From a Protestant perspective, there is no authority *beyond* the Bible itself by which any interpretation of the Bible may be judged. Pragmatically, most Protestants have learned to deal with this issue. Bruce is surely right to suggest that "reading modern science *into* the ancient text, or drawing scientific conclusions *out of* the ancient text" (p. 143) is not acceptable. We have to develop rational and imaginative frameworks of interpretation that avoid such unhelpful outcomes.

Methodological Naturalism and Intelligent Design

I found Bruce's discussion of methodological naturalism and intelligent design to be the most stimulating part of his essay, opening up some important issues for exploration and discussion. He rightly notes the tendency to retroject modern thinking about scientific methodology onto earlier periods in scientific history, without appreciating that early modern science was much more open to, for example, the idea of divine action than is the case today. Australian intellectual historian Peter Harrison brought this point out clearly in a detailed historical study of attitudes toward God and the laws of nature in the late seventeenth and early eighteenth centuries.[9] Richard Bentley, for example, interpreted Newton's idea of gravity as "the immediate fiat and finger of God." Many Newtonians held that many of the miracles recorded in the Old Testament were not merely consistent with the new science but were actually the most likely scientific explanations of certain features of

---

9. Peter Harrison, "Newtonian Science, Miracles, and the Laws of Nature," *Journal of the History of Ideas* 56, no. 4 (1995): 531–53.

the world. God had indeed created the laws of nature, but this did not prevent direct divine action when this was appropriate.

Darwin himself was not a philosophical naturalist but rather anticipated the approach now known as "inference to the best explanation."[10] His achievement was to propose a mechanism that lay behind the phenomenon of evolution—a mechanism Darwin unhelpfully (in that it suggested nature itself actively selected) termed "natural selection."[11] Darwin was unable to prove that this explanation was correct; he therefore sought to demonstrate that it was better than the two main current accounts of the origins and character of the biosphere: the religious idea of the special creation of individual species, found especially in the writings of William Paley, and Lamarck's "transformist" theory of evolution.[12]

In demonstrating that his own theory of the mechanism of evolution was better than those already in circulation, Darwin was obliged to criticize Paley's religious account of the origin of species. This could, I fully concede, easily be seen as a criticism of religion in general or Christianity in particular. Darwin, however, was careful to avoid any such implication, dealing with Paley's specific theories rather than a generalized Christian approach. It is important to note that Darwin welcomed the theological contribution of Charles Kingsley, who held—whether rightly or not—that Darwin's theory clarified the mechanism of creation. "We knew of old that God was so wise that he could make all things; but, behold, he is so much wiser than even that, that he can make all things make themselves."[13] Darwin had no objection to this Christian interpretation of his theory, which emphasized the role of divine providence in guiding the evolutionary process.

Bruce sets out some concerns about methodological naturalism, including its potentially imperialist aspirations. Most natural scientists take the view that science offers a specific intellectual tool kit, which

---

10. Francisco J. Ayala, "Darwin and the Scientific Method," *PNAS* 106 (2009): Supplement 1 10033–39.

11. Mark A. Largent, "Darwin's Analogy between Artificial and Natural Selection in the Origin of Species," in *The Cambridge Companion to the "Origin of Species"*, eds. Michael Ruse and Robert J. Richards (Cambridge: Cambridge University Press, 2009), 12–29.

12. Pietro Corsi, "Before Darwin: Transformist Concepts in European Natural History," *Journal of the History of Biology* 38, no. 1 (2005): 67–83.

13. Charles Kingsley, *Westminster Sermons* (London: Macmillan, 1874), xxv.

determines what kind of knowledge is "scientific"—but do not draw from this the conclusion that science is the only source of knowledge or that it provides a uniquely privileged form of knowledge. I concede that there are some high-profile science popularizers who hold that science has some kind of monopoly on reliable knowledge. These are best challenged about the legitimacy of their views on scientific grounds. Bruce is quite right to point out that there is an important debate about what constitutes "natural."[14] This has been given increased intellectual traction by "new materialists" such as Bruno Latour, who have pointed out that "nature" is not an empirical notion but is rather partly the outcome of a process of social construction.

Bruce states that "the fine-tuning of the initial conditions, laws, and constants of the universe" might best be explained by "intelligent causes." He suggests that this is "eminently reasonable in a theistic context" and "entirely compatible with the uniformitarian assumptions necessary to science" (p. 149). I don't agree, however, with Bruce's suggestion that this makes the evaluation of intelligent design a *scientific* topic of research, even though I am sympathetic to Bruce's intentions. If science is characterized by methodological naturalism, this is not a *scientific* question. It is a *theological* question, in which the intellectual framework of the Christian faith is shown to provide an epistemically explanatory device that could posit the harmony of theistic belief and cosmic fine-tuning. I've argued that, and so have lots of others.[15] But it's not science, and it's not a problem that it's not science. I cannot see any good reason for suggesting it is scientific, unless the concern is to benefit from the epistemic privilege that some—but only some—believe this association with science conveys.

I share Bruce's belief that fine-tuning is "eminently reasonable in a theistic context," in that I find that belief in the Christian God provides a robust explanatory framework for this otherwise puzzling phenomenon. Yet this is essentially a theological question about how well the scientific enterprise fits into a theistic context. Most scientists

---

14. See, for example, Scott Tanona, "The Pursuit of the Natural," *Philosophical Studies* 148, no. 1 (2010): 79–87.

15. See my 2009 Gifford Lectures at the University of Aberdeen: Alister E. McGrath, *A Fine-Tuned Universe: The Quest for God in Science and Theology* (Louisville: Westminster John Knox Press, 2009).

hold that science has a very limited capacity to investigate or illuminate the question of what lies behind and beyond the big bang. I'm sympathetic to Bruce's concerns but wonder whether these might be better explored using John Polkinghorne's notion of "metaquestions"—that is, identifying those questions that are raised by the natural sciences but that nevertheless lie beyond their scope to answer.[16] For example: Why is there something rather than nothing? Why is the physical universe so rationally transparent to us, so that we can discern its pattern and structure, even in the quantum world, which bears little relation to our everyday experience? Why is it that some of the most beautiful patterns proposed by pure mathematicians are actually found to occur in the structure of the physical world?

A second strategy might be to focus on the acknowledged limitations of scientific explanation. In an important recent discussion of the scope of the explanatory capacities of the natural sciences, Steven Weinberg remarks that it seems clear that "we will never be able to explain our most fundamental scientific principles."[17] We can, he suggests, hope to develop a "set of simple universal laws of nature;" we cannot, however, explain *why* these specific laws of nature pertain. They exist; they have explanatory capacity, on the basis of accepted models of scientific explanation; yet they themselves cannot be explained. An explanatory regress is thus terminated at a certain point. Yet this is precisely the form of objection that Richard Dawkins raises against belief in God—that it represents an arbitrary foreclosure of an explanatory regress. Weinberg's analysis clearly suggests that explanatory regresses are a problem for science, and not merely theology.

Intelligent Design and the Origins of Life

Bruce brings his essay to an end by reflecting on what he considers to be some difficulties in the current state of evolutionary theory, citing critiques associated with the Discovery Institute or the intelligent design movement. There are indeed some problems with the evolutionary

---

16. John Polkinghorne, "The New Natural Theology," *Studies in World Christianity* 1, no. 1 (1995): 41–50.

17. Steven Weinberg, "Can Science Explain Everything? Can Science Explain Anything?" In *Explanations: Styles of Explanation in Science,* ed. John Cornwell (Oxford: Oxford University Press, 2004), 36.

synthesis, which have been noted by biologists, theologians, and philosophers.[18] Although some biologists unwisely offer a philosophical absolutization of the evolutionary synthesis, leading to the emergence of a worldview they term "universal Darwinism," most scientists regard it as a scientific theory that is open to modification, correction, and development in the light of empirical evidence, having no necessary impact on religious belief. I, like many others, have been strongly critical of such metaphysically inflated accounts of evolutionary theory[19] and their application to wider cultural issues, including the rationality of belief in God.

Yet I remain unclear how Bruce's approach offers an advantage over others, particularly the dialogic model I represent. Bruce sees intelligent design as a way of critiquing unjustified scientific explanatory moves and of affirming the rationality of belief in a creator God. I agree with Bruce in pursuing those two goals yet see them as arising naturally and properly from a critical yet constructive dialogue between theologians and biologists, without having to take the problematic position that intelligent design is a *scientific* concept. A dialogic position allows these points to be made in conversations between theologians and scientists without proposing any modification of existing understandings of scientific methodology.

This does not in any way make me, or others who do not agree with Bruce's approach, "ideological captives of metaphysical naturalism"; it rather offers us a theologically informed standpoint to explore the limits of methodological naturalism. Theologian Thomas F. Torrance made this point in a series of lectures during the 1930s: "Science only informs us what light is thrown upon reality by the empirical observation of the facts of external nature. When science claims that this is all that can be said, it is no longer science but the species of philosophical theory called naturalism."[20]

---

18. See, for example, Massimo Pigliucci and Leonard Finkelman, "The Extended (Evolutionary) Synthesis Debate: Where Science Meets Philosophy," *BioScience* 64, no. 6 (2014): 511–16; Kevin N. Laland et al., "The Extended Evolutionary Synthesis: Its Structure, Assumptions and Predictions," *Proceedings of the Royal Society* 282, no. 1813 (August 2015): https://doi.org/10.1098/rspb.2015.1019.

19. Alister E. McGrath, *Dawkins' God: From the Selfish Gene to the God Delusion*, 2nd ed. (Oxford: Wiley-Blackwell, 2015), 120–43.

20. Cited in Alister E. McGrath, *Thomas F. Torrance: An Intellectual Biography* (Edinburgh: T. & T. Clark, 1999), 201.

I do not accept that *methodological* naturalism entails *metaphysical* naturalism. I have no doubt that some do make this connection; my point is that they are not justified in doing so and that theologians and philosophers are well placed to make this point.[21]

Bruce and I share a delight at the wonder and beauty of the creation, which we see as pointing to the wisdom and rationality of God as its creator. We also share a deep belief in the rationality of the Christian faith and are hostile to metaphysically inflated extensions of science, evident in metaphysical naturalism or Dawkins's "universal Darwinism." Our difference seems to lie mainly in Bruce's emphasis on the *scientific* plausibility of the notion of an intelligent designer, and hence the legitimacy of seeing the hypothesis of the intelligent design of the universe as a subject for scientific investigation. I see this as unnecessary. Science throws up questions that its own methods cannot answer, thus creating space for theologians and philosophers to suggest there is more to life than the scientific method is able to discover on its own. Christianity offers us a way of conceiving and representing our world that is admirably adapted to explaining the successes of the natural sciences while at the same time identifying their limits.

---

21. Like Bruce, I regard Alvin Plantinga as a good critic of metaphysical naturalism: Alvin Plantinga, *Where the Conflict Really Lies: Science, Religion, and Naturalism* (New York: Oxford University Press, 2011).

BRUCE GORDON

I'm grateful for the opportunity I've had to interact with Michael and Alister. I've enjoyed it, and I've learned a few things. It's important to start on this positive and conciliatory note because, as presenting and defending contrasting views requires, I'm about to be quite critical regarding the remarks of my interlocutors, especially in Michael's case. I've smiled at Michael's shoot-from-the-hip style and laughed at his friendly insults; I hope he takes my occasional dig in the same spirit. Alister has been overwhelmingly pleasant, which is very disarming, so it pains me to disagree with him on anything, but I do, and I've tried to be straightforward about it. I respect you both. I also have an oxygen tank for Michael, if he needs it.

To Michael

Since I've triggered Michael's mother issues (p. 167), I feel obliged to help him clean his room. We can't straighten everything, but let's put a few things right. First, Michael objects to saying Christianity is idealist when it affirms mind as foundational and matter as derivative. He says this presupposes a Cartesian dualism rejected by philosophers of all ilks (p. 166). It doesn't. It merely affirms God's immateriality and creation of all matter. It's basic theism. All theistic philosophers accept it while having many different views of the human mind. Secondly, Michael's attitudes toward God are incoherent. He says he's an agnostic, skeptic, and nonbeliever but then affirms an "apophatic theology" with "faith that God exists and is in some sense a loving creator who cares for his children," allowing him "to fall down and worship with thanks, in awe" (p. 167). After this, he's a panpsychist who thinks that mind and matter are dual aspects of one substance (p. 166)[1] and then a "Darwinian naturalist" (p. 167) who says "I don't have faith . . . I want to live my life now . . . rather than for the hope of true happiness in the hereafter" (p. 115). Forsaking rationality, he lets bodily desires chart his course, despite God's availability and knowability to those who seek him.[2]

Darwinian naturalism and irrationalism go together. Michael implicitly admits this, *agreeing* with Plantinga that our beliefs are unintended by-products of adaptive traits and "the likelihood they are mostly true would be low" (p. 168). But he calls Plantinga's amusing illustrations "ludicrous" (p. 168) and, in a "crabby interlude," informs us that "Darwinian evolutionary biology is powerful science," but "if the needs of reproduction run roughshod over the search for truth, so be it" (p. 170). Besides, he gripes, Plantinga's observations aren't new; Arthur Balfour made similar points in 1895 (p. 170).[3] Indeed. Michael's irrelevancies miss the point. If our minds don't aim at truth as correspondence with reality, and if our conception of "coherence" is an accidental by-product of evolution expressing how our minds just *happen* to work, then we have no basis for thinking *anything* we believe (including Darwinian naturalism) is true. So Plantinga's amusing examples cannot be dismissed as false. Checkmate.

Michael's attempt to deny that methodological naturalism became entrenched *after* Darwin rather than *with* the Scientific Revolution ignores that Boyle inferred fine-tuning as part of his *natural* philosophy: the front-loaded intelligent design of initial conditions accounts for the clockwork unfolding of reality. Boyle denies God's quotidian involvement, but design *is* evident in nature. Furthermore, Boyle didn't dismiss inferences to design in biology as "religious." This is Michael's misleading gloss on the text, as the reader can discern.

---

1. Ironically, since mind is an irreducible mode in panpsychism, it qualifies as a kind of idealism. It also could motivate design inferences in nature. Oops.

2. I pray Michael will yet take the advice offered in my earlier response.

3. Forget Balfour; Darwin himself said, "With me, the horrid doubt always arises whether the convictions of man's mind, which has been developed from the mind of the lower animals, are of any value or at all trustworthy" (Charles Darwin to William Graham, July 3, 1881). Similar thoughts relating the origin of our faculties to their reliability can be found in Thomas Reid and Blaise Pascal and maybe even earlier. It's the point that matters, not who made it.

In evaluating my discussion of science and Scripture, Michael misses the versatility of the first and second hermeneutic, foisting on me an interpretation of the historical Adam I don't hold. I refer readers to my original discussion (pp. 139–45). While I affirm an "Adamic" personage originating the spread of sin, the roles of Adam as the historical ancestor of Israel versus the universal originator of sin, assimilated in the first hermeneutic, are separable in the second, which sees the fusion of these roles as an anachronism reflecting divine accommodation to an ancient world picture and recognizes the story's symbolism. The actual origin of divine image bearers and events constituting the fall occur much earlier in natural history.

Next, Michael (1) lambasts my understanding of paleontology, wondering if I've heard of *Archaeopteryx* or *Tiktaalik* or *Australopithecus*, (2) asserts that massive genetic evidence, including ancient DNA, supports common ancestry, and (3) complains I never discuss the standard Darwinian response to waiting-time issues, going back to Dobzhansky and Lewontin, that the huge amount of variation in natural populations obviates the problem (p. 176). Michael is blowing smoke and living up to his surname here. He ignores that *similarity is not evidence for transformation* and transformation is the target of evolutionary explanation, appealing to outdated science. Recall paleontologist Henry Gee's remark (p. 163): stringing fossils together and saying they're a lineage is telling stories, not doing science. Michael assumes the transformation problem is solved by pointing at extinct forms, then chooses poor examples. Archaeopteryx, for instance, long touted as the ancestor of all modern birds, isn't. Its status is still in flux. Specialists resolved temporal paradoxes with its fossil ancestors occurring *after it* by postulating ad hoc ghost lineages of earlier origin. Subsequent discovery of earlier feathered forms, *Anchiornis* and *Aurornis*, partially obviated the embarrassment but created a serious waiting-time problem for the appearance of pennaceous bird feathers from filamentous dino fuzz in two to three million years.[4] Similarly, *Tiktaalik* was touted as the ancestor of tetrapods. It's not. Fossil evidence out of Poland demonstrates the existence of tetrapods preceding it by millions of years.[5] Lastly, where hominin transitions are

---

4. L. M. Witmer, "Feathered Dinosaurs in a Tangle," *Nature* 461 (2009): 601–602. I correct Michael's obfuscation of the waiting-time problem below.

5. G. Niedźwiedzki et al., (2010) "Tetrapod Trackways from the Early Middle Devonian Period of Poland," *Nature* 463, no. 7 (2010): 43–48; M. Qvarnström et al., "Non-Marine

concerned, it doesn't all fit. The genetic data is deeply problematic,[6] and the character distribution of primitive and derived traits is very incongruent and doesn't support a consistent transitional series. For example, some forms have primitive leg-skeleton but derived skull characteristics, and others have derived leg-skeleton but primitive skull characteristics. This implies a lot of homoplasy (convergence), and rampant homoplasy radically underdetermines all phylogenetic trees.[7]

Regarding ancient DNA evidence and the waiting-time problem, several points must be made. First, little credence should be given to genetic similarity estimates from *extant* species, let alone from fragmentary *ancient* DNA. It's often unclear whether the analysis comes from protein-coding regions only, or these plus flanking sequences and introns, or whole "genomes," including the repetitive sequences that make alignment difficult. Humans differ markedly from chimps, yet our protein-coding DNA is 98 percent similar. The differences arise from regulatory metaprograms using their respective protein-coding sequences in radically different ways. Second, DNA from recent fossil remains of the genus *Homo* only shows interbreeding, raising questions about whether we're dealing with different species. Third, natural genetic variation in populations doesn't solve the waiting-time problem. Adaptations need mutations to *arise* and *spread* in a population, leading to waiting times based on mutation rates, population sizes, and generation length. Getting workable numbers often requires falsely assuming infinite population sizes. Smaller populations and longer generations—common for mammals—require longer waiting times, especially for coordinated mutations. This is widely known. So where does Michael err? Let's start with Dobzhansky. In 1937 Dobzhansky acknowledged "we are compelled at the present level of knowledge reluctantly to put a sign of equality between the mechanisms of macro- and microevolution, and proceeding on this assumption, to push our investigations as far

Palaeoenvironment Associated to the Earliest Tetrapod Tracks," *Scientific Reports* 8 (2018), article 1074.

6. J. Hawks et al., "Population Bottlenecks and Pleistocene Human Evolution," *Molecular Biology and Evolution* 17, no. 1 (2000): 2–22.

7. See discussions of human evolution in J. P. Moreland et al., *Theistic Evolution: A Scientific, Philosophical, and Theological Critique* (Wheaton: Crossway, 2017) Part 2, especially essays by G. Bechly and S. C. Meyer, C. Luskin, and A. K. Gauger, O Hössjer, and C. R. Reeves.

ahead as this working hypothesis will permit."[8] This hardly solves the waiting-time problem for major phenotypic changes, let alone for the Cambrian explosion.[9] But what of Lewontin's innovations?[10] The relevant part of Lewontin's theory was developed and explored by Günter Wagner and Peter Stadler. Here's their assessment:

> Transition between different "types" is only possible if the transitional forms have all the characters that the ancestral and the derived types have, and are thus compatible with the factorization of both types. Transitional forms thus have to go over a "complexity hump" where they have more quasi-independent characters than either the ancestral as well as the derived type. The only logical, but biologically unlikely, alternative is a "hopeful monster" that transforms in a single step from the ancestral type to the derived type. . . . [Phenotypes] have a statistical tendency of retaining evolutionary trajectories within their interior and thus add to the evolutionary persistence of types.[11]

In short, Michael says that quantitative neo-Darwinian population-genetic theory, which has *no room* for the emergence of phenotypic innovations, has shown these innovations are derivable on its basis. He knows not whereof he speaks. Neo-Darwinism is dead in the water. Let's not pretend its bloated corpse will float evolutionary theory, let alone the ruse of naturalism.[12]

Finally, in dealing with fine-tuning, Michael cites Steven Weinberg's

8. Theodosius Dobzhansky, *Genetics and the Origin of Species* (New York: Columbia University Press, 1937), 12.

9. See Stephen C. Meyer, *Darwin's Doubt: The Explosive Origin of Animal Life and the Case for Intelligent Design* (San Francisco: HarperOne, 2013), Part 2.

10. See Richard C. Lewontin, *The Genetic Basis of Evolutionary Change* (New York: Columbia University Press, 1974); and R. C. Lewontin, "Adaptation," *Scientific American* 239 (1978): 156–69.

11. Günter P. Wagner and Peter F. Stadler, "Quasi-Independence, Homology and the Unity of Type: A Topological Theory of Characters," *Journal of Theoretical Biology* 220 (2003): 505–27; see also Jürgen Jost, "Relations and Dependencies between Morphological Characters," *Theory in Biosciences* 136 (2017): 69–83.

12. I'm a philosopher of physics, but good biologist friends over the last quarter-century, in conversations and writings, have given me a basic understanding of some important things. I'm responsible for any mistakes, but thanks Paul Nelson, Steve Meyer, Doug Axe, Jonathan Wells, Mike Behe, Rick Sternberg, Ann Gauger, and Günter Bechly for your friendship and for sharing your knowledge.

response to the Hoyle resonance in carbon and considers himself done (pp. 176–77). Aside from Weinberg overlooking factors to reduce the fine-tuning to an unimpressive 25 percent—the fine-structure constant, for instance, can only vary 0.00001 percent for the resonance to exist—there are many other startling instances of cosmological fine-tuning: initial-condition entropic fine-tuning is hyperexponential at one part in $10^{10\exp(123)}$; the cosmological constant is fine-tuned to one part in 10^{120}; the strength of gravity in relation to the strong, weak, and electromagnetic forces is fine-tuned to one part in 10^{36}; and so on.[13] These fine-tunings need an explanation, and theism is the best available—a multiverse just relocates the fine-tuning and leaves the fundamental question of why there is something rather than nothing unanswered. Michael suggests it doesn't need an answer: "Perhaps things just are. Albert Camus talked about existence as being absurd. At the metaphysical level, he could be right. Leave it at that" (p. 178). This sentiment suits Michael's irrationalism, but we can't live that way, and the truth is, it's not metaphysically possible. As I argued responding to Michael's main essay, if it's *possible* a contingent state of affairs has an explanation, then it *necessarily* has an explanation, so every contingent state of affairs *has* an explanation. Denying this requires the impossible task of showing it's impossible for some contingent things to have an explanation. Opening this self-defeating Pandora's box also destroys all knowledge. But then again, Michael is an irrationalist, so pray he comes to his senses!

To Alister

Alister and I aren't that far apart, but Alister thinks I misunderstand science by rejecting methodological naturalism (MN), whereas I maintain he's mistaken in thinking that science has a fixed essence. What science *is* depends largely on how human beings understand *the nature of nature itself*. This should be open to investigation and malleable. Alister partly gets this, recognizing that different scientific disciplines have different methodologies (p. 79), but he's not willing to include design

---

13. See Luke A. Barnes, "The Fine-Tuning of the Universe for Intelligent Life," *Publications of the Astronomical Society of Australia* 29 (2012): 529–64; and Bruce L. Gordon, "Divine Action and the World of Science: What Cosmology and Quantum Physics Teach Us about the Role of Providence in Nature," *Journal of Biblical and Theological Studies* 2 (2) (2017): 247–98.

methodologies because, applied to nature, they seem to violate MN (pp. 88, 98–101). Whether MN is reasonable, however, depends on nature's nature: if nature *isn't* a causally closed system and is subject to detectable nonmaterial influences, then adhering to MN precludes science from getting a grip on *all* the aspects of reality it's equipped to investigate. Natural science has its name not because of methodological restrictions on *how* nature is studied but because it's the natural world that is the *object* of study. And here's the thing: nature's nature is itself an empirical question, not one decided *a priori*, let alone on the basis of social pressure from philosophically naive scientists or theologians wanting to protect their territory. If our goal is an *integrated and adequate scientific understanding of reality* rather than a compartmentalized and deficient one, we need to hold our methodologies loosely and follow the evidence where it leads. So while Alister complains that scientists don't indulge in philosophical prolegomena—a point I will address next—but focus on empirical methods to see where they lead (p. 79), it remains true that empirical methods, if pursued without presumptive naturalistic constraints, show that naturalism should not function to limit scientific explanations. Why? Because it's empirically discernible that intelligent causes played a role in the origin and development of nature and play an active role in its function. Switching to a theological perspective, then, this is why I say the universe is an *intelligent* product of divine thought, not just an *intelligible* product of divine thought (p. 135), though the latter grounds recognition of the former. I am not advocating cosmopsychism, if this is Alister's puzzlement. The universe is not an intelligent entity, even though it would still be something contingent, created by God, if it were.[14]

There's a deeper consideration that, despite his animadversions on philosophical prolegomena, Alister acknowledges. He affirms that the metaphysical and epistemological basis for science is undermined by irreducibly probabilistic explanations in a naturalistic context (p. 100), and he acknowledges that Darwinian naturalism undermines the methodological and epistemological foundations of science (p. 91). He says this doesn't matter to scientists because they aren't concerned about

---

14. See my response to Philip Goff's agentive cosmopsychism in my essay "Mind Over Matter: Idealism Ascendant," in Brian Krouse and Cristi Cooper, eds., *Minds, Brains, and Consciousness* (Seattle: Discovery Institute , 2020).

presuppositions, they're pragmatic and want results: MN works and that's all they care about (p. 91). This is myopic. First, unless the question is begged by excluding empirical design inferences on grounds of MN, it's not the case MN works when design inferences imply violations of it. Absent question begging, then, Alister's assertion is false. Secondly, if we focus on what *works* and not on what's *true*, we're instrumental-ists, a position Alister rejects but thinks irrefutable (p. 80–81). Under instrumentalism, however, MN isn't violated because scientific practice has no ontological import. So design-theoretic science is instrumentally unobjectionable if it works. Thirdly, by acknowledging my points about irreducible probabilities and the self-defeating character of evolutionary naturalism, Alister shares my judgment that theism is better for science than naturalism. Why, then, would he acquiesce to a methodology that requires him to proceed *as if* metaphysical naturalism were true[15] when it isn't, and a broader scientific methodology that includes intelligent causation avoids this charade? Fourth, when Alister says "a scientific methodology doesn't make any . . . metaphysical assumptions about the nature of reality" (p. 188), he undermines his case for MN in science. As already argued, the metaphysics of nature should not be presupposed where scientific methodology is concerned, so empirical detection of nonmaterial causes and evidence that reality transcends materiality should be fair game. Finally, Alister says the "natural sciences . . . do not start out from a set of preconceived philosophical assumptions" (p. 180). Fairness requires emphasizing the word *preconceived*, for *a completely presuppositionless science is impossible*. Beyond presupposing the existence of an investigator, a world to investigate, and the ordered intelligibility of the world investigated, as Thomas Kuhn and others have taught us, nothing counts as data in science until you have a theory in mind, and data is always, to some extent, theory-laden.[16] If more scientists knew such things, criticism of design-theoretic methodology would be more self-aware and less self-certain.

---

15. This is what theists who advocate MN do. They're right that methodological natu-ralism doesn't entail metaphysical naturalism (p. 189) but prescind from anything that might go beyond immanent natural causes while doing science, thereby acting as if metaphysical naturalism were true for the purposes of scientific explanation.

16. Thomas S. Kuhn, *The Structure of Scientific Revolutions* (Chicago: University of Chicago Press, 1962 [1996]); see also seminal works by Norwood Russell Hanson, Stephen E. Toulmin, and by Paul K. Feyerabend in this regard.

Alister is right that "our difference seems to lie mainly in Bruce's emphasis on the *scientific* plausibility . . . [and] legitimacy of seeing the hypothesis of the intelligent design of the universe as a subject for scientific investigation" (p. 189). Our worldviews largely coincide, but we see science differently. Still, when Alister says the limits of scientific methodology "create space for theologians and philosophers to suggest there is more to life" than science can discover (p. 189), I wince. I'm not interested in leftovers. Science is impossible foundationally and incomplete methodologically within the immanent frame. No position short of this will do.

CONCLUSION

PAUL COPAN

Most of the volumes in Zondervan's Counterpoints series involve specifically Christian scholars who take different perspectives on a specific doctrine or topic such as the Trinity or hell. Occasionally those outside the creedal Christian tradition will participate. For example, the late pluralist philosopher of religion John Hick participated in the book on salvation.[1] In this particular work, Michael presents his perspective as an agnostic philosopher of science, which adds an important element of engagement to what might otherwise be an in-house discussion between believers.

In this book on the relationship of Christianity and science, the participants reject the conflict view. Michael adopts the independence view, Alister the dialogue view, and Bruce the constrained integration view. As noted earlier, these four views have been part of a frequently used "religion-science" categorization articulated by Ian Barbour, though Bruce adds "constrained" to describe his own style of integration. These contributors articulate their respective positions and engage with one another in their own particular style. (We'll leave *that* specific labeling to the readers.)

This closing portion of the book briefly summarizes each presenter's position and offers reflections on certain themes.

---

1. Dennis L. Okholm and W. Gary Phillips, eds., *Four Views on Salvation in a Pluralistic World* (Grand Rapids: Zondervan, 1996).

Summary of Three Views

Independence View (Michael Ruse)

Michael summarizes his position: "Science and religion cannot clash because I don't think they are in the same ballpark" (p. 114). However, Michael is a more sympathetic participant than, say, a strident atheist such as Richard Dawkins or Daniel Dennett would be. For one thing, Michael agrees with the other contributors that the "warfare model" between science and the Christian faith is rooted in a flawed, now-debunked historiography (pp. 22–23). And though an agnostic ("I truly don't know") and a "skeptic," he affirms that he does "care very much" about the topic of God's existence (p. 19).

Michael affirms that Scripture was never intended to be treated as "a work of science" (p. 21). The danger exists of matching up the latest scientific theories with Scripture—theories which may be, and often have been, eventually displaced. The author of Genesis had in mind something other than science. But if one insists on the idea that all humanity came from an original pair or that humans are born with original sin, this would run contrary to acceptable science and the evolutionary synthesis.

Also, science requires not metaphysical naturalism but methodological naturalism, which a believing scientist could happily adopt. Any appeal to "nonnatural causes" cannot be scientific (p. 36). Beyond this, Ruse is unpersuaded by attempts at natural theology that argue for the existence and nature of God without appeal to special revelation such as Scripture. Michael allows that people may believe in design because they believe in God, but to infer God's existence from, say, the universe's design is misguided. Michael himself is unimpressed with such efforts.

When it comes to miracles, Michael asks, "Would I allow a miracle in the sense of a break or intervention in the natural chain?" (p. 35). He sides with David Hume: it would take a lot to persuade him that a miracle could happen. While some might consider the remarkable rescue at Dunkirk a miracle, this doesn't break the "natural chain." Those who spend time trying to "prove" a miracle happened are wasting their time.

Michael brings up the problem of evil. He rejects the seemingly "smug" free will explanation as inadequate to deal with the Hitlers and Himmlers of the world (p. 33). Michael repudiates the idea that God will make all things right in the end. Indeed, he says, "I don't want the Christian God to exist" (p. 33). Michael's alternative proposal is that natural selection goes a long way in explaining the evils that exist.

The Dialogue View (Alister McGrath)

The Renaissance metaphor Alister uses to frame his dialogue view is that of God's "two books"—namely, nature and Scripture. This metaphor provides "an imaginative and conceptual framework for considering the relation of Scripture and science" (p. 96). Each contributes distinctive but complementary insights to the conversation and can be viewed as different "maps" of reality that, when brought together, offer "a deeper rendering of our world" (p. 100). For example, Christ's death can be understood from different angles—historically, legally, and theologically—without any inherent conflict (p. 100).

McGrath notes the significant role the Christian faith has played in giving rise to and shaping modern science. He agrees with Michael that Scripture isn't a scientific textbook. This is all the more reason for him to bring his Christian faith into conversation with science. Though distinctive, each contributes something valuable to this dialogue.

The Scriptures can accommodate evolution as the mechanism God used to create—as was propounded by Princeton's B. B. Warfield—but any evolutionary theory that smuggles in a naturalistic metaphysic must obviously be rejected. Though Alister acknowledges problems with the "evolutionary synthesis," he considers it a theory "open to modification, correction, and development in the light of empirical evidence, having no necessary impact on religious belief" (p. 188). McGrath is emphatic that a purely physical account of human beings via science is inadequate; including theology is essential to make sense of human identity and our inbuilt interest in meaning and purpose.

Like Michael, Alister affirms a methodological naturalism. Science is metaphysically agnostic, presupposing no metaphysical beliefs such as materialism. But since knowledge comes from a wide range of sources and disciplines such as philosophy or theology, listening only to the voice of science will leave us with a rather impoverished, reductionistic view of reality: "I am not sure whether . . . we can (or should) achieve a unification of human knowledge. But creating conceptual space for a productive conversation seems to be a good start—even if much more needs to be done!" (p. 57). Again, Alister's adherence to methodological naturalism in science is not the same as metaphysical naturalism. Science does not exclude the possibility of miracles, and Alister firmly believes in the miraculous. Yet both the universe's orderliness and miracles are representative of God's general and special action in the world. We need not pit one against the other.

As for natural theology, some have charged that this project may equally lend support to a mere deism; theism isn't more the obvious view. And trying to "prove" God's existence or "create faith" by natural theology is too heavy a burden for it to bear (p. 52). That said, natural theology has a place within the conversation of the "two books": it displays the broader rationality of belief in God. And Alister acknowledges that people have come to faith by observing, say, the remarkable intricacies within the universe. He disagrees with Bruce, though, that design is a *scientific* concept.

The Constrained Integration View (Bruce Gordon)

Bruce's position is this: "Science, philosophy, and theology interact and constrain one another in profound ways as we search for an optimally coherent and integrated picture that brings everything we know into proper relationship" (p. 135). Thus, he considers Alister's perspective too loose-fitting, claiming instead to offer a robust, more compelling view than "mere" dialogue; this alternative, he believes, can challenge the scientifically minded nonbeliever to see the inadequacy of their worldview and their very basis for doing science itself. (Of course, Alister maintains that dialogue includes critical thinking and full-bodied integration insofar as we are able; a certain "messiness" is inevitable given the complexities of the world.)

Bruce claims that the Christian faith begins not with matter but with mind: "*mind* is foundational to reality, and matter is derivative" (p. 135). This weaker form of idealism is uncontroversial; the stronger form—that the only reality that exists is ideas and the minds that hold them—is one many Christians would reject. Furthermore, it is rational minds that are required in order to study the material world.

Behind Bruce's assertion is the idea that "science *depends on and points to God* and that naturalistic explanations are inadequate not just *outside* science but *within* science as well" (p. 127). Thus, Bruce maintains that, given naturalism, knowledge is elusive and unstable at best—and impossible at worst. As Darwin himself wondered, why trust the convictions of a monkey's mind—or even our own? By contrast, (Christian) theism raises the probability of knowledge over against naturalism: as divine image-bearers, we have been created with cognitive faculties that, when functioning properly, are designed to lead us to truth, both in the sciences and other disciplines. By contrast, naturalistic evolution isn't interested in true beliefs but rather in survival and reproduction, and false beliefs could enhance survival and reproduction equally well.

When it comes to science and Scripture, Bruce likewise rejects the "Scripture as science textbook" approach. He similarly repudiates "concordism"—reading into ancient Scriptures the findings of modern science (p. 156), which may come to be displaced at some future time.

According to him, methodological naturalism is circular and turns out to be an actual constraint on scientific research (pp. 156–58). Affirming nature's general patterns and causal regularities (uniformitarianism) is sufficient for science to operate—not methodological naturalism. If science is truly metaphysically agnostic, it would be wrong-headed to assume a closed universe that leaves no room for divine activity within it.

Moreover, the contingent universe did not have to exist, and its laws could have been otherwise. And the universe's finely tuned structures and processes display "a degree of complex-specified information *exceeding* the probability bounds of the observable universe"; it is precisely such structures and patterns that are "habitually and uniformly associated with intelligent activity"; indeed, "intelligent causation is part of the causal structure of the world and falls within the purview of scientific investigation" (p. 149).[2]

When it comes to "the appearance and nature" of human beings, science alone cannot account for it (p. 164). The simplest self-replicating

---

2. Bruce holds to occasionalism: "God is the sole efficient cause of every state of affairs in the universe not subject to the influence of creatures with libertarian freedom" (p. 155). Usually, the occasionalism held by some Christian philosophers and theologians is more stark than this, seemingly undermining human moral responsibility and implying that God is the author of evil. For example, see William Lane Craig, "Response to Jeff Koperski," Reasonable Faith, https://www.reasonablefaith.org/writings/scholarly-writings/christian-doctrines/response-to-jeff-koperski/ (accessed June 8, 2020). Also, other Christians would debate that "there is no distinction between creation and providence" and that each "manifestation of providence . . . is included in God's singular timeless creative act" (p. 123).

cell—informationally rich and functionally specified—is best explained by an intelligent cause rather than the result of undirected means. Bruce raises other considerations, such as the immense lengths of time required for cellular changes, the sudden emergence of variegated and complex life-forms in the Cambrian explosion, the gaps in the fossil record, and so on. Bruce's perspective seeks to expose metaphysical naturalism's untenability at many levels and to show that a Creator and Designer is necessary to make sense of the universe, its properties, and unique human beings (p. 164).

Reflections
Science and Scientism

For our purposes, we should distinguish between science and scientism. Roughly, science is *the attempted objective study of the natural world whose theories rationally connect to specific empirical phenomena and whose concepts and explanations do not (normally) depart from the natural realm.*[3] The word *normally* is critical—and debated. It raises the question about whether one will leave open the possibility of design and divine (nonnatural) action in the world to explain certain physical phenomena. While Alister and Michael would exclude the word *normally* when it comes to defining science, Bruce would include it. But let that pass.

All three discussants reject the dominant notion of scientism—that all knowledge must be scientifically verifiable.[4] They recognize that scientism is both *arbitrary* (why think science alone is the source of knowledge?) and *self-refuting* (how can one scientifically prove that all knowledge is scientifically provable?).

How does scientism fit into the broader metaphysical picture? This brings us to the philosophy of naturalism. In its *strict* version,[5] naturalism holds to three fundamental tenets; these pertain to reality, causality, and knowledge: a metaphysic of materialism, an etiology of determinism, and

---

3. This is adapted from the work of Del Ratzsch, *Science and Its Limits: Natural Sciences in Christian Perspective* (Downers Grove, IL: InterVarsity, 2000); see also his *Nature, Design, and Science: The Status of Design in Natural Science* (Albany: SUNY, 2001),

4. This is the *strong* version of scientism. There is also a *weak* version: science is the best way to achieve knowledge, even if other ways of knowing are possible.

5. For further discussion on naturalism (both strict and broad) and theism, see Paul Copan and Charles Taliaferro, eds., *The Naturalness of Belief: New Essays on Theism's Rationality* (Lanham, MD: Lexington /Rowman & Littlefield, 2018).

an epistemology of scientism. Many naturalists in the academy accept the epistemological assumption that any knowledge claim requires scientific proof. But this is not science, which is simply one pathway for knowledge. Other knowledge pathways exist. As Alister observes, even within science, different levels of explanation are available to us. As we look at issues such as meaning, purpose, morality, and human identity, science offers no guidance here—yet these questions press deeply upon us as humans. So we must look elsewhere—theology or philosophy, for example—to shed light on these concerns that are so fundamental to our very humanity.

Miracles and Methodological Naturalism

Miracles are typically defined by theists as events that are the result of God's direct action in the world that cannot be predicted based on natural causes and effects. If nature's processes ran their course without such divine action, no miracle would take place.

Miracles are not the only manifestation of divine engagement with the world. They are distinct from God's *ordinary* providence of rain, sunshine, seasons, and an abundant earth: God "has shown kindness by giving you rain from heaven and crops in their seasons; he provides you with plenty of food and fills your hearts with joy" (Acts 14:17). They are also distinct from God's *extraordinary* providence, in which God's ordering of natural (nonmiraculous) events is propitiously coordinated, say, in answer to someone's prayer at just the right time. Such a remarkably timed natural event points to divine involvement. (Perhaps the rescue at Dunkirk could be included in *this* category, though not technically a "miracle.")

David Hume claimed that miracles were "violations" of nature's laws. Critics have accused Hume of arguing in a circle and rigging his worldview in such a way that miracle claims could never be taken seriously. He insisted that since these laws could not be violated, miracles could not take place. Of course, Hume's "problem of induction" implies that we can't close the door on the possibility of miracles; even if we are wise to make choices according to the regularities of nature, it's possible that the sun might not rise tomorrow. We would just have to wait and see.

Michael says that he can go along with someone's claim that real water was turned into real wine; that's all fine, "so long as they don't try to make me believe on evidence" (p. 35). That said, we do wonder—with Bruce—about what Michael means, exactly. After all, he dismisses those who "spend their time trying to prove that the resurrection really is a historically attested fact, reasonable to believe on empirical grounds" because they "are doing bad science, bad history, and bad philosophy" (p. 40). But if, unlike most other traditional religions, the Christian faith is rooted in historical events, then these events would be empirically verifiable at least in principle. But apparently, no amount of evidence would be sufficient to persuade Michael that a resurrection like Jesus's or a resuscitation like Lazarus's took place (pp. 35–40).

Biblical Faith and Empirical Evidence

Faith and *religion* can be misleading labels. Many different definitions for *religion* exist, and there is no agreement at present—nor is there likely to be. (The term *worldview* might be a more satisfactory, neutral categorization.) Some religions may see the physical world as illusory, and a number of religions may care nothing about any objective evidence—philosophical, historical, or otherwise—in support of their truth claims. By contrast, the Christian faith does take evidence seriously. It emphasizes public "signs and wonders," "witnesses," and indicators of miracles, such as an empty tomb. If one is concerned about evidence, there are places one can look for it.

Michael points to Thomas the Doubter as a seeker of evidence who does not rest on what appears to be a blind, leap-in-the-dark "faith." After all, the resurrected Jesus commends those who have not yet seen but still believe (John 20:29). In response (as Bruce has noted), Thomas should have believed his fellow disciples, who exclaimed, "We have seen the Lord!" (20:25). In addition, the very next verses following Jesus's declaration to Thomas indicate that faith and evidence are not opposed: in fact, the signs that Jesus performed and are recounted in John's gospel can serve as the basis for belief or faith (vv. 30–31). We see the same kind of appeal in 1 Corinthians 15:3–10, where Paul lists the eyewitness evidence for Jesus's bodily resurrection.

The Christian faith is a knowledge tradition, and its Scriptures affirm the relevance of giving a defense, of eyewitnesses, and of public signs and wonders. Faith is a matter of *personal trust* and *commitment*, and one can trust in God in light of evidences such as miracles. True, the Christian faith allows for mystery and acknowledges the limitations of our understanding. In their final rejoinders, both Michael and Alister appeal to 1 Corinthians 13:12—that we see in a glass darkly (pp. 72, 128)—whether this be theological or scientific. But this does not mean signs and pointers to God are unavailable to us.

What's more, no reputable Christian theologian would adopt Michael's view that faith is immune to evidence, even if faith trusts in God beyond the available evidence. As Bruce writes, "We trust God because of what we *know* when facing what we do not know" (p. 61).

True, "faith" in many other religious traditions may have a fideistic quality to it such that nothing in principle could ever falsify the adherent's belief. But Scripture offers criteria of falsifiability—especially concerning the resurrection. If the body of Jesus was not raised from the dead and the tomb was not empty, the Christian faith crumbles (1 Corinthians 15:13–20).

The Problem of Evil and Morality

Michael raises the problem of evil—"a great barrier to religious belief" (p. 32)—and no thinking Christian would disagree. But evil is a problem for *any* worldview, but some worldviews will dismiss it as illusory or nonexistent. Perhaps the more fundamental question is: Which worldview does the most adequate job of making sense of evil and, if possible, offers resources to assist us intellectually and emotionally? Michael claims natural selection can offer insight where theism does not. The existence of Hitler, Himmler, and their company leads Michael to conclude that "the world of the theists" is not for him (p. 33).

This leaves us wondering: if Michael is right that morality is a "corporate illusion" that has been "fobbed off on us by our genes to get us to cooperate,"[6] then isn't belief in the immorality of Hitler and Himmler part of that illusion that enhances survival and reproduction and has no being beyond that adaptive value? How do we get from the "is" of natural processes to the "ought" of moral obligations ("you ought not act like Hitler")?

---

6. ichael Ruse and E. O. Wilson, "The Evolution of Ethics," in *Religion and the Natural Sciences*, ed. J. E. Huchingson (Orlando: Harcourt Brace, 1993), 310–11. For discussion on this, see Matthew H. Nitecki and Doris V. Nitecki, *Evolutionary Ethics* (Albany: State University of New York Press, 1993), 8.

Questions

This book has wrestled with questions of how we are to understand the relationship between the Christian faith and science. These include some of the following topics:

Design and Natural Theology

Do the origin, causal structures, and patterns of the universe exhibit design that serve as a pointer to a powerful, intelligent Creator? Should we incorporate notions of design into science? Would the inclusion of design be helpful in differentiating natural processes—like the buildup of tree rings or of seasonal layers of sediment deposits (varves)—from the creation of human artifacts? Should the Search for Extraterrestrial Intelligence, which seems design-oriented, be considered a scientific enterprise, or is this of a different order?

Methodological Naturalism

Does true science necessarily adhere to a methodological naturalism? Does methodological naturalism largely or even exclusively reflect the presuppositions of a metaphysical or philosophical naturalism? What would it take for a methodological naturalist—whether theist or not—to affirm that a genuine miracle took place in the physical world? If miracles involve material like water (turned into wine) or thoroughly dead bodies (raised to life), then would there not be physical traces and indicators that are detectable in principle? On what basis would a believing methodological naturalist have to conclude that a demonic being might be afflicting a disturbed human being's mind rather than a deep mental disorder (though we're not denying there can be overlap)?

Demarcating Science from Nonscience

What exactly differentiates science from nonscience? Can we truly establish a "line of demarcation" distinguishing between science and nonscience—falsifiability, repeatability, and so on? How should we think about the reality that demarcation problems have not really been resolved, as the noted philosopher Larry Laudan has pointed out?[7]

---

7. Larry Laudan, "The Demise of the Demarcation Problem," in R. S. Cohen and L.

Human Origins

While Bruce has raised methodological and evidential considerations concerning evolution's feasibility, which can be debated in their own right, is there any inherent conflict in God's appropriating the evolutionary process to bring about his purposes? Is Alvin Plantinga correct that the most basic issue for the believer is not evolution per se but *unguided* evolution?[8] If God did indeed use the evolutionary process to bring about his purposes, could this not mean that God directly bestowed certain moral, volitional, and spiritual capacities on a pair of hominins from which all of us humans today have descended? And when it comes to original sin, what if God graciously curtailed the influences of our animalistic past when bestowing upon us the divine image, but then withdrew that gracious influence when humans rebelled?

These topics and questions are the subject of much interesting debate and discussion. This book's three stellar representatives have given us much to ponder, and we trust that this volume will lead to deeper, meaningful, fruitful engagement about the relationship of the Christian faith and science.

Laudan, eds., *Physics, Philosophy and Psychoanalysis: Essays in Honor of Adolf Grünbaum*, Boston Studies in the Philosophy of Science, 76 (Dordrecht: D. Reidel, 1983), 111–27. See the interesting discussion at the Panda's Thumb website: "Laudan, Demarcation and the Vacuity of Intelligent Design," https://pandasthumb.org/archives/2006/06/laudan-demarcat.html (accessed June 6, 2020).

8. Alvin Plantinga, *Where the Conflict Really Lies: Science, Religion, and Naturalism* (Oxford: Oxford University Press, 2011).

GENERAL INDEX

Adam
  as forerunner of Israel, 141–42, 189
  and original sin, 20–21, 111, 141, 142,
    172, 189
Anselm of Canterbury, 26, 27, 62, 63
Aquinas, Thomas, 24, 27, 65, 81
arms races, evolutionary, 42, 45, 46, 66
aseity, 27, 63
Athanasius of Alexandria, 91, 96, 177
atonement theory, 74
Augustine of Hippo
  and evil, 67
  and existence of God, 91, 119, 179
  and God's involvement in evolution, 102
  and human ability to understand the
    universe, 91, 179
  and lack of understanding of science as
    harming Christian witness, 9–10
  and original sin, 48
  and time, 119, 121–22
balanced heterozygote theory of
    populations, 174
Balfour, Arthur J., 168, 188
Barbour, Ian, 13–17, 106, 176, 197
Barth, Karl, 93, 113
Belgic Confession, the, 83–84
Bentley, Peter, 181
Berkeley, George, 153
Berkouwer, Gerrit, 153, 154
Beza, Theodore, 92
Bhaskar, Roy, 54
Biel, Gabriel, 153
Blomberg, Craig, 67–68
Boyle, Robert, 143–44, 169–71, 188
Brandon, Robert, 43
Brooke, John Hedley, 77
Browne, Thomas, 83
Brunner, Emil, 95
Calvin, John, 83, 84, 92, 97
Camus, Albert, 73
causation
  bottom-up, 88, 123
  and explanation, 90–91

  intelligent, 68, 117, 118, 134, 146, 154–56,
    162, 201
  material, 149–50
  secondary, 122, 123, 124, 152–53
  top-down, 88, 115, 116–17, 118, 122–23
  transcendent, 163
Christianity
  as a form of science, 81, 89, 107
  as concerned with questions of
    meaning, 88, 90, 107
  definition of, 12
  as framework for determining good and
    evil, 128–29
  as idealist, 133, 152, 153, 164, 187, 200
  as multilayered, 87, 88–89
  as offering different perspective of
    reality than science, 86–89, 129
  and Scripture as basis of understanding
    of the world, 81–82, 107–8, 137,
    180–81
coherence, 62, 86, 167, 180, 188
Collins, Jack, 138, 180
conflict view of Christianity and science,
    14–15, 78, 80, 82, 83, 176, 197
consciousness
  and the brain, 115, 124–26
  and freedom, 122
  and the image of God, 40
  origin of, 119, 147, 174
  understanding, 39, 45, 109, 115, 123
constrained integration view of
    Christianity and science
  explained, 133–63
  rejoinder, 187–95
  response to, 164–75, 176–86
  summary of, 200–202
contrivance, 93
convergence, evolutionary, 43, 45, 66, 66n8,
    190
cosmography, biblical, 138, 139, 141, 180
Cotes, Roger, 99
Coulson, Charles A., 86, 87
Craig, Bill, 67

creation
    as both event and process, 102
    date of, 56
    doctrine of, 11, 56, 91, 102, 110, 116,
        119
    ex nihilo, 11, 119
    God as author of, 9
    of individual species as separate, 182
    ontic and epistemic elements of
        doctrine of, 91, 116
    as proof of existence of God, 62, 75,
        91, 92–94, 102, 107, 110–11, 143,
        186, 206
    and providence, 122, 201n2
cultural mandate, the, 9
Darwin, Charles
    and Christianity, 29–30, 56, 105, 112,
        171–72, 182
    and evil, 31–32, 33
    and intelligent design, 75, 182
    and methodological naturalism, 144,
        169, 171, 188
    and morality, 38–39
    and natural selection, 28–30, 41–42, 182
    and reliability of the human mind,
        188n3, 201
Dawkins, Richard
    atheism of, 56, 95, 198
    and conflict view of Christianity and
        science, 176
    and existence of God, 27, 52, 101, 184
    and intelligent design, 32, 81
    and natural selection, 32, 34, 42
deism, 27, 51, 98, 180, 200
Dennett, Daniel, 39, 164, 198
De Sebonde, Raimundo, 92
dialogue, definition of, 78–79
dialogue view of Christianity and science
    definition of, 16
    explained, 77–103
    rejoinder, 127–32
    response to, 104–14, 115–26
    summary of, 199–200
discourse, 137, 138
Dobzhansky, Theodosius, 174, 189, 190–91
Edwards, Jonathan, 153
Einstein, Albert, 119, 130, 163, 177
Elizabethan Settlement, the, 25

Ellis, George, 88, 118–19, 125, 129
emergence
    of humanity, 102, 109, 110, 115, 118–25
    of the natural sciences, 50, 83, 97, 202
encephalization quotient (EQ), 42
environmental decoherence, 124, 152
Evans, Craig, 67
evil
    existence of as argument against God's
        existence, 31–34, 66, 112–13, 198–99
    and natural selection, 34, 198, 205
    as part of natural order, 128–29
    as turning away from God, 67
evolution
    Darwin and, 33, 41–42, 56, 182
    genetic evidence for, 173
    as mechanism used by God, 33, 97, 102,
        199, 207
    and survival vs. truth, 178, 201
    undirected, 65, 136, 157, 158, 160, 166,
        173, 207
    waiting-time problem in, 159
explanation, 90–91, 134, 135, 178, 192
explanatory understanding, 91
faith, 23, 34, 58–62, 113, 199, 204–5
fine-tuning, 65, 143–44, 146–47, 155, 163,
    174–75, 183, 188, 191–92
Frazer, James George, 81
free will, 33, 66, 120–22, 198
Gee, Henry, 161
God
    acting in the world, 98–101
    as author of both Scripture and the
        natural world, 13, 15, 83, 84, 85, 96,
        97
    causal argument for existence of, 27,
        64–65
    creation as proof of existence of, 62, 75,
        91, 92–94, 102, 107, 110–11, 143,
        186, 206
    evil as argument against existence of,
        31–34, 66, 112–13, 198–99
    extraordinary providence of, 147, 148,
        155, 203
    and laws of nature, 98–99
    maximal greatness of, 63, 65
    natural theology and proof of existence of,
        23–34, 50–52. 62–67

ontological argument for existence of, 26–27, 62–63
ordinary providence of, 203
quantum mechanics as argument for, 149–54, 175
and regularities of nature, 152–53, 155, 163
as requirement for knowledge, 137, 165, 167
teleological argument for existence of, 28–31, 65
and time, 119–22
as unknowable, 165, 167
God's image, humans made in
and human reasoning, 21, 40, 91, 103, 111, 165, 179, 201
and free will, 33
as source of human extraordinariness, 105
Hardy, Thomas, 31
Harris, Sam, 95
Harrison, Peter, 48, 77–78, 105, 181
Heisenberg, Werner, 130
Hick, John, 167
Hodge, Charles, 97
humans
origins of, 41–46, 55–57, 101–3, 142, 154–63, 207
God as involved in evolution of, 33, 97, 102, 199, 207
intelligent design of. See intelligent design
monogenesis of, 142n16
as stewards of nature, 9, 95, 103, 137, 140, 179
Hume, David, 28, 65, 90, 98, 179, 198, 203
imitatio Christi, 60–61
incarnation theory, 74
independence view of Christianity and science
definition of, 15–16
explained, 19–46
rejoinder, 70–76
response to, 46–57, 58–69
summary of, 198–99
inference
abductive, 146, 146n28
design, 50, 118, 148n37, 154, 155, 157, 188, 194
to the best explanation, 68, 146n28, 182

inspiration, 137–38
integration view of Christianity and science. See constrained integration view of Christianity and science
intelligence, development of, 41–46
intelligent design
complexity of life as argument for, 110, 134, 146–48, 154–63, 174, 183, 201–2
Darwin and, 30–31, 75
existence of God as proof of, 25–26, 40, 94
fine-tuning as evidence of, 65, 143–44, 146–47, 155, 163, 174–75, 183, 188, 191–92
incompleteness of paleontological record as argument for, 160–61, 172–74
as proof of God's existence, 93–94
uniformitarianism and, 146–48, 201
as unscientific, 36
waiting-time problem and, 156, 159, 162
James, William, 73
John Paul II, 16, 24
Kant, Immanuel, 36, 171
Kauffman, Stuart, 44
Keats, John, 51–52
Kingsley, Charles, 102, 118, 182
knowledge
assumptions grounding possibility of, 134–37, 177–80
definition of, 134
faith and, 36, 59, 61, 62
of God, 13, 84, 94, 165, 167
human, spectrum of, 53, 54, 57, 84, 95, 199
necessity of cognitive faculties aimed at true beliefs for, 136
principle of sufficient reason as precondition for, 134–35
scientific, 48, 52, 53, 183, 202, 203
spiritual, 59, 60, 61
Krauss, Lawrence, 36–37, 38, 53
K-selection, 34
Kuhn, Thomas, 37–38
Kuyper, Abraham, 153, 154
Latour, Bruno, 183
laws of nature, 98–99, 148–49, 152, 154, 179, 182, 184

Leibniz, Gottfried Wilhelm, 39, 62–63, 124
levels of explanation, 88
Lewis, C. S., 179
Lewontin, Richard, 174, 189, 191
Malebranche, Nicolas, 153
materialism, 54–55, 80
McShea, Daniel, 43
metaphors
  of science, 37–38
  two books, 13, 50, 54, 82–85
  war between Christianity and science, 83, 105
metaphysical naturalism, 80, 106, 162, 177, 185, 186, 200, 202
metaquestions, 184
methodological naturalism
  definition of, 13, 79, 100, 134
  as impeding scientific inquiry, 134, 145–46, 182–83, 193, 201
  and miracles, 67–69, 203–4, 206
  necessity of for science, 36–40, 52–55, 68, 79–80, 117–18, 198, 199
  necessity of observability for, 80, 100, 117–18, 129–30
  origin of, 143–47, 169, 171, 188
  religion as, 107
  as valid even if not explainable, 179
miracles
  as extraordinary providence, 147, 148, 154, 155, 203
  and laws of nature, 68, 98, 154, 181–82, 198
  methodological naturalism and, 67–69, 200, 203–4, 206
  and science, 40, 80, 106
Mitchell, Basil, 90
molecular homology, inability of to explain human evolution, 65, 161–62
monism, 109, 164
Moore, Aubrey, 30
morality, 38–39, 40, 66–67, 205
Morris, Simon Conway, 43
naturalism, 202–3
natural philosophy, 52
natural selection
  Darwin and, 28–30, 41–42, 182
  and evil, 34, 198, 205

and intelligent design, 65–66, 171
and our cognitive faculties, 136, 165–66
and survival vs. truth, 136, 178, 201
natural theology
  definition of, 23, 50, 83, 92
  and design, 155, 200, 206
  and evil, 128
  and existence of God, 200
  from God to nature, 93, 108
  from nature to God, 92–93
  and proof of existence of God, 93–94, 103, 107
  role of, 23–34, 50 52, 62–67, 116
  and the two books metaphor, 92–95
nature
  defining, 183
  humans as stewards of, 9, 95, 103, 137, 140, 179
  spirituality of, 94–85, 108
New Atheism, 14, 95
Newman, John Henry, 25, 28, 75, 93–94, 108
Newton, Isaac, 143, 144
nones, 10
Numbers, Ronald, 105
occasionalism, 122, 123, 123n14, 124, 152, 201n2
"Old Princeton" school of theology, 97
ontological naturalism, 54
original sin, 20–21, 48, 111–12, 141–42, 172, 189, 198, 207
paleontological record, incompleteness of
  as argument for intelligent design, 160–61, 172–74, 202
Paley, William, 25, 51, 93, 102, 182
Pascal, Blaise, 60, 188n3
perception, 39, 50, 59–60
philosophical naturalism, 15, 15n17
physicotheology, 92
Planck, Max, 55, 130
Plantinga, Alvin
  and existence of God, 63, 80
  and maximal greatness of God, 63
  and occasionalism, 153
  and original sin, 70
  and unguided evolution, 136, 166–67, 207
  and validity of human reasoning, 136, 166–67, 179, 188

Polkinghorne, John, 184
Popper, Karl, 22, 49, 95, 130
protein coding, complexity of as argument
    for intelligent design, 156–60
providence
    and creation, 122, 201n2
    and evolution, 102, 118, 182
    extraordinary, 147, 148, 154, 155, 203
    occasionalism and, 123, 153, 201n2
quantum cosmology, 120–21, 145, 145n26
quantum mechanics, as argument for God,
    149–54, 175
reality, assumptions grounding knowledge
    about, 134–37
regularities
    as background for rational expectations,
        66, 146, 149, 203
    as expression of divine faithfulness, 68,
        99, 152–53, 155, 163, 175
    and laws of nature, 149, 201
    universal, 152
Reid, Thomas, 59, 188n3
religions, evaluating different, 61n5
relativity, 119, 120, 130, 145n26
resurrection, Jesus, 35, 40, 58, 62, 67, 68–69
Robinson, Marilynne, 81
Rose, Steven, 79, 82
r-selection, 34
Russell, Bertrand, 179
saltations, 34
Scholl, Sophie, 33, 41, 73
science
    Christianity as form of, 81, 89, 107
    as concerned with questions of how the
        world works, 88, 90
    definition of, 9, 12–13, 106, 202
    as form of religion, 89
    lack of understanding of as harmful to
        Christian witness, 9–11
    and miracles, 40, 80, 106
    necessity of methodological naturalism
        for, 36–40, 52–55, 68, 79, 198
    vs. nonscience, 206
    as nontheistic, 80, 106
    as offering different perspective of
        reality than Christianity, 86–89
    provisionality of, 49, 53
    root metaphors of, 37–38

vs. scientism, 202–3
Scripture shaping, 20–21, 48–49, 84,
    96–97, 111–12, 141, 181, 198, 199,
    201
    shaping interpretation of Scripture, 22,
        49, 97, 141, 181, 201
Scientific Revolution, the, 84, 134, 143,
    144, 169, 188
scientism, 36, 37, 51, 95, 116, 202–3, 202n4
Scott, Eugenie, 80, 106
Scripture
    and evolution, 199
    human interpretations of as fallible, 13
    inerrancy of, 137, 138, 138n8, 181
    science shaping interpretation of, 22, 49,
        97, 141, 181, 201
    shaping science, 20–21, 48–49, 84, 96–97,
        111–12, 141, 181, 198, 199, 201
    as source of God's special revelation, 13
spacetime, 119–20
speech act theory, 137–38
spirituality of nature, 94–95
Stadler, Peter, 191
sufficient reason, principle of, 134, 135,
    146, 152, 155, 175
Swinburne, Richard, 67
technology, 90
theism, 60, 137, 187, 192, 194, 200, 201
theodicies, 66
Thirty-Nine Articles, the, 20
Thomas the Doubter, 24, 58, 61–62, 204
time, 119–21
    creation of, 119
    God and, 119
    passage of, 119–21
Torrance, Thomas F., 178, 185
two-books metaphor, 13, 50, 54, 82–85,
    92–97, 103, 105–6, 116, 199
uniformitarianism, 117, 118, 134, 146,
    154, 201
universal common descent, 155–56, 160,
    161, 189
universal Darwinism, 185, 186
Valentine, James, 160
Wagner, Gunter, 191
waiting-time problem, 65, 156, 159, 162,
    189, 190–91, 202
Warfield, Benjamin B., 49, 97–98, 199

Weinberg, Steven, 110–11, 174, 184, 191–92
Wesley, John, 49
Whewell, William, 36, 53
Williams, Rowan, 78
Wilson, Edward O., 166
Wittgenstein, Ludwig, 37, 38, 90

world picture, biblical 138–41, 180
worldview, biblical 138, 139, 140, 180, 204
Wright, N. T., 67
young earth creationists (YEC), 20, 58, 139–40n11
zero-force evolutionary law, 43–44, 45–46, 66

Four Views on Creation, Evolution, and Intelligent Design

Ken Ham, Hugh Ross, Deborah Haarsma, Stephen C. Meyer
J. B. Stump, general editor
Stanley N. Gundry, series editor

Four Views on Creation, Evolution, and Intelligent Design presents the current "state of the conversation" about origins among evangelicals representing four key positions:

- Young Earth Creationism-Ken Ham (Answers in Genesis)
- Old Earth (Progressive) Creationism-Hugh Ross (Reasons to Believe)
- Evolutionary Creation-Deborah B. Haarsma (BioLogos)
- Intelligent Design-Stephen C. Meyer (The Discovery Institute)

The contributors offer their best defense of their position addressing questions such as: What is your position on origins-understood broadly to include the physical universe, life, and human beings in particular? What do you take to be the most persuasive arguments in defense of your position? How do you demarcate and correlate evidence about origins from current science and from divine revelation? What hinges on answering these questions correctly?

Available in stores and online!

Genesis: History, Fiction, or Neither?

Three Views on the Bible's Earliest Chapters

James K. Hoffmeier, Gordon John Wenham, Kenton Sparks
Charles Halton, general editor
Stanley N. Gundry, series editor

There is little doubt that in recent years the nature of the Genesis narrative has sparked much debate among Christians. This Counterpoints volume introduces three predominant interpretive genres and their implications for biblical understanding. Each contributor identifies their position on the genre of Genesis 1–11, addressing why it is appropriate to the text, and contributes examples of its application to a variety of passages.

The contributors and views include:

- James K. Hoffmeier: Theological History
- Gordon J. Wenham: Proto-History
- Kenton L. Sparks: Ancient Historiography

General editor and Old Testament scholar Charles Halton explains the importance of genre and provides historical insight in the introduction and helpful summaries of each position in the conclusion. In the reader-friendly Counterpoints format, this book helps readers to reflect on the strengths and weaknesses of each view and draw informed conclusions in this much-debated topic.

Available in stores and online!

Four Views on the Historical Adam

C. John Collins, William D. Barrick,
Gregory A. Boyd, Philip G. Ryken, Denis
Lamoureux, John H. Walton
Matthew Barrett, general editor
Ardel Caneday, general editor
Stanley N. Gundry, series editor

As a part of the Counterpoints series, *Four Views on the Historical Adam* clearly outlines four primary views on Adam held by evangelicals, featuring top-notch proponents of each view presenting their positions in their own words and critiquing the positions with which they disagree. You will come away with a better understanding of the key biblical and theological issues at stake and of the implications of Adam for contemporary Christian witness and church life.

Contributors include Denis O. Lamoureux, John H. Walton, C. John Collins, and William Barrick. Each focuses his essay on answering the following questions:

- What is the biblical case for your viewpoint, and how do you reconcile it both with modern science and with passages and potential interpretations that seem to counter it?
- In what ways is your view more theologically consistent and coherent than other views?
- What are the implications of your view for the spiritual life and public witness of the church and individual believers, and how is your view a healthier alternative for both?

Concluding reflections by pastor-scholars Gregory A. Boyd and Philip Graham Ryken highlight the significance of the topic in the faith of everyday believers.

Available in stores and online!